SECRETS OF LOVE

SECRETS OF LOVE

LO&VE

PARTNERSHIP

The Astrological Guide for
Finding Your "One and Only"

HAJO BANZHAF • BRIGITTE THELER

SAMUEL WEISER, INC.
York Beach, Maine

First published in 1998 by
SAMUEL WEISER, INC.
P. O. Box 612
York Beach, ME 03910-0612

Library of Congress Cataloging-in-Publication Data

Banzhaf, Hajo.
    [Du bist alles was mir fehlt. English]
    Secrets of love and partnership : the astrological guide
for finding your "one and only" / Hajo Banzhaf, Brigitte
Theler.
          p. cm.
    Includes bibliographical references (p.   ) and index.
    ISBN 1-57863-040-1 (alk. paper)
    1. Astrology. 2. Love--Miscellanea. 3. Mate selection--
Miscellanea. I. Theler, Brigitte. II. Title.
    BF1729.L6B3613 1998
    133.5'864677----dc21   98-19023
                                                      CIP

MG

Translated by Christine M. Grimm
Typeset in 10.5 Garamond
Printed in the United States of America

06 05 04 03 02 01 00 99 98
10 9 8 7 6 5 4 3 2 1

The paper used in this publication meets all the minimum requirements of the
American National Standard for Permanence of Paper for
Printed Library Materials Z39.48-1984.

Contents

List of Tables

We give our thanks to all those who, through their friendship, in relationships and partnerships, have loved the best parts of us, have had conflicts with us, and have confronted us time and again with our unloved parts. It is often easier to appreciate the latter afterward! In addition, we thank all our friends, acquaintances, and relatives who appeared in front of our inner eye during the development of the individual character-type descriptions. They were our models and, without their knowledge, have made an essential contribution to the creation of this book.

We would like to especially thank our friend Sonja Hermann for the warm atmosphere in which we were able to write major portions of this book, for her extensive support, constructive criticism, and, above all, for checking the manuscript for realism and applicability.

—BRIGITTE THELER
HAJO BANZHAF

Introduction

If we take a look at human longings in the mirror of the music industry, love and partnership seem to be be the most desirable possessions of our age. If we believe our lyrics, then this goal must actually be quite easy to achieve. The intensity of this love, which bears all the signs of a mother-child relationship ("I can't live without you," "You and only you alone"), has clear traits of mass hypnosis. In accordance with this concept, most people—in our Western culture—seem to (at least secretly) hope that some day the right person will appear and everything will finally be okay—whatever they imagine "okay" to be.

If we compared this wishful thinking with reality, we would be amazed at so much optimism. Perhaps our fantasies are a result of the gentle but suggestive steady stream of background music provided by the media. Most people think that the phase of falling in love is an expression of "true love"; on the other hand, the disappointment that the natural fading of this feeling of infatuation brings with it is constantly seen as proof that a person has made a mistake and that the partner wasn't the right one after all. And so we always hope the next time will be better.

But if we look around us with our eyes open, we find that relationships without intense crises tend to be the exception to the rule. Lively and intact relationships must frequently go through deep crises before they become truly mature. There appears to be more to our love life than meeting the Dream Woman and Prince Charming and enjoying carefree bliss in an eternal embrace from that moment on. It even appears that friction in a relationship is necessary so that each person can bring out the best in him- or herself.

If we consider striving for wholeness an important part of the life process, then we also know that conflict with the opposite sex (in an active partnership) is an essential catalyst for important developmental steps on this path. As we will see, this is not a matter of just developing the conscious personality but also of developing the wholeness of our initially unconscious, inner opposite sexuality, which C. G. Jung named *anima* and *animus*. As long as we experience things harmoniously, we will not become particularly conscious of our own nature. Only when we are involved in conflict do we wake up. As long as Adam and Eve knew nothing about the tree of knowledge, they lived in paradisiacal harmony.

xii SECRETS OF LOVE AND PARTNERSHIP

The state before we attain knowledge is often paradisiacal, and nothing within us urges us on to more knowledge during these phases. Only when there is trouble in paradise, when things are suddenly not as wonderful as they were, do we ask ourselves what has gone wrong. Perception always results from the conflict that tears us out of the slumber of paradisiacal simplicity. This is why the original knowledge, the awakening of humanity to consciousness, is often connected with guilt, sin, and original sin, because someone must bear the blame that this lovely time of naive innocence is over. This is why Adam very bluntly put the blame on God: "It wasn't me but the woman *you* gave me!" Eve was a bit less impudent and just passed her blame on to the serpent, which in turn couldn't shift it on to anyone else and since that time writhes as the epitome of evil slyness. In the same manner, many psychotherapies today are parent-blaming sessions in which the patients pin the reason for all their disappointments and problems on their parents, instead of comprehending that the natural price for maturity, perception, and becoming an adult inevitably includes being disappointed in our childlike and naive expectations of happiness. If we consider falling in love as the paradisiacal time in our adult life, then it's no wonder that we indignantly blame God and the world when we notice that the person we are involved with is no longer our Prince Charming or our Dream Woman, but increasingly turns out to be deceptive packaging.

But shouldn't this make us ask questions? We constantly hear about the transfiguration caused by the symbiotic state of infatuation from the hit parade, and the media reports all the fairy-tale weddings, while the divorce rate climbs to record highs from year to year, our relationships become increasingly noncommittal and short-lived, and all that's left of the original life-partner is a companion who stays around for a phase.

The 20th century will probably go down in the annals of history as the period when values declined. Whatever can't be expressed in terms of cash value is considered worthless. Now that even time has turned into money, it's not surprising that people have little time for leisure, contemplation, and other "worthless" activities. The Western world set out during antiquity to glorify the mind, and placed increasingly less value on everything physical and material during the course of the last 2,000 years—ultimately condemning it in the truest sense. However, in the meantime, the massively repressed antithesis has apparently caught up with this tendency and is now virtually smothering us with the very materialism that had once been despised.

The consequence is that human beings have lost the meaning that can't be squeezed out of money, even with the best of will. But since every human being is driven by a deep need for the fulfillment of meaning in life, and the answers given by religion are increasingly less convincing, many people today look for meaning in areas that are actually overtaxed by this demand. The areas of work, love, and a sensuality reduced to the three letters in "sex" are the preferred sources from which people hope for fulfillment and meaning in life. It's obvious that each of these segments is hopelessly overtaxed because meaning can only be experienced holistically. However, the disappointments that we face time and again are accordingly great when a new task or a new love loses its initial power of fascination. Since this had completely fulfilled us at one time, we sadly discover that the unanswered questions related to meaning knock at our door in an increasingly urgent way.

Even if love and partnership alone cannot convey to us the meaning of life, there are some important and extremely *meaning*ful experiences to be had in this area. These are not to be found in the soppy, sweet platitudes that are sung thousandfold; instead, they reveal themselves only to those individuals who are willing to go deeper and experience transformation. "The meeting of two personalities," according to C. G. Jung, "is like the contact of two chemical substances: if there is any reaction, both are transformed." The transformation of a person through a relationship is one of the essential meanings of a relationship. How and why this occurs will be illustrated by this book.

PART I

The TWO CENTERS
of CONFLICT

We Seek What We Lack

According to ancient teachings, God first created the four elements and wove the entire Creation from them. This is why all creatures—and this includes every human being—is made of fire, earth, air, and water in varying mixtures. This original teaching of the four basic temperaments forms not only the basis of the twelve astrological signs but also has its counterparts in the classical, as well as the modern, typologies. Well-known characterologies are also models of four, which correspond with each other as shown in Table 1.

The mutual structure of four in these typologies has a deeper significance in so far as the whole is traditionally described in the form of four aspects. C. G. Jung spoke of this as an archetype, since, according to his perceptions, the psyche always describes the whole in four aspects.

In contrast to common concepts, this characterology should not be understood in the sense that a person "has" or lives just one of the four elements and the others are therefore no longer significant. To the contrary: all

Table 1. Parallels between Four Basic Characters in Typologies				
TYPOLOGY				
Elements	Fire	Earth	Air	Water
Temperaments	Choleric	Melancholic	Sanguine	Phlegmatic
Fritz Riemann[*]	Hysteric	Compulsive	Schizoid	Depressive
C.G. Jung[†]	Emotion	Sensation	Thought	Intuition[††]

[*]Fritz Riemann, Grundformen der Angst [*Basic Forms of Fear*] (Munich: Reinhardt, 1961/82).
[†]C. G. Jung, *Psychological Types,* vol. 6 in *The Collected Works of C. G. Jung,* translated by H. G. Baynes and F. R. C. Hull, Bollingen Series XX (Princeton: Princeton Universtiy Press, 1971).
[††]Even among the experts, there is no agreement upon a clear classification of the emotion and intuition types.

four elements are inherent to each individual as four structures of consciousness, as four ways of perceiving reality. However, they are not developed to the same extent. But as long as even one element remains more or less unconscious and is lacking in our consciousness, we perceive reality in a distorted and incomplete manner. This can be compared with how a color print requires four printing processes, of which only the fourth reproduces the complete coloration of the picture. We cannot perceive life in its true abundance if we haven't developed one of these aspects of reality within us. Consequently, on the path to becoming whole it is initially important to find out which elements are inherent to us and can be easily developed and where we have our weak points that particularly require attention.

As C. G. Jung was able to prove through his experience as a physician and therapist, as well as by employing the symbolic language of myths and fairy tales, and the fundamentals of alchemy, each person initially develops three of these basic qualities to a greater or lesser degree, while the fourth is neglected and therefore remains largely unconscious. This phenomenon corresponds to the frequently encountered fairy-tale motif of a soul that has been sold, or a ball—as in the Frog Prince—that falls into the well at the beginning of the story. Since the ball is a typical symbol of wholeness, its loss, as well as the selling of the soul, means that the fairy-tale hero loses the wholeness that is a part of his disposition, yet unconscious at the beginning of the story; he only achieves it and consciously experiences it again when he succeeds in getting the ball back out of the depths, or the soul back from the underworld—the unconscious.

As Jung also demonstrated, an individual's path of maturation is initially concerned with the structures of consciousness, which means developing the elements that are strongly inherent to us. However, during the course of life, the missing element increasingly becomes an important topic, since we not only lack it in terms of our wholeness, but also because it is frequently the source of our errors. Myths and fairy tales depict the search for the missing element as the search for a possession that is difficult to attain, for the treasure that must be dug up.

The power that guides us in this search is the soul's deep longing for wholeness. We are all familiar with the inner urge during playful experiences as the desire to complete a solitaire game or puzzle, or as the passion of a collector who can't rest until the collection is complete. On the path to our inner "completeness," this internal drive constantly guides us or involves us in new situations, which helps us regain our suppressed and lost element. Whether our consciousness truly understands these clues, or just becomes indignant and annoyed about getting entangled in such strange situations, depends on the individual. An extraordinarily important area of life in which we constantly encounter our missing element is the relationship. This occurs to such a degree that even without any previous knowledge and with a great degree of probability we can tell what element we lack on the basis of these encounters. Completely instinctively, and without having the slightest idea of this basic concept of the four elements, we tend to look for a partner who complements us by living what we have remained unconscious of, that we have suppressed. So if we would like to know what element, what structure of consciousness we are lacking, we just have to observe the people with whom we live or have lived in the most important relationship. The quality that these people personify for us is usually exactly what we are lacking. And this is why it is totally correct for us to admit from the depths of our soul to our "better half"—"You're Everything I Need!"

There are naturally other ways of finding out what our missing element is. The horoscope is a lucrative source of information, even if experience has shown that the great variety of formulae offered for determining the distribution of the elements fall short. However, as long as we are just interested in recognizing the missing element, it is often enough to determine which sign group has the least or none of the classic seven planets in it. The newer planets Uranus (⛢), Neptune (♆), and Pluto (♇) can be neglected in this way of looking at things because they move so slowly that they represent entire age groups in the same sign and the individual statement of their sign position is accordingly negligible.

If you would like to determine your missing element without any knowledge of your horoscope, you will find a brief description of the essential characteristics of the individual elemental types in the next chapter. This should make it easy to recognize the missing element, either directly or by using the description of your partner to recognize the missing element through which we feel ourselves to be complete.

Table 2. Distribution of the Four Elements in the Zodiac*			
Fire	Earth	Air	Water
♈ Aries	♑ Capricorn	♎ Libra	♋ Cancer
♌ Leo	♉ Taurus	♒ Aquarius	♏ Scorpio
♐ Sagittarius	♍ Virgo	♊ Gemini	♓ Pisces

*To determine the missing element, check the placements of the seven classical planets (and luminaries) in your chart: ☉ = Sun, ☽ = Moon, ☿ = Mercury, ♀ = Venus, ♂ = Mars, ♃ = Jupiter, ♄ = Saturn. Note the element that is missing or where you find few planets.

The Four Elements—
Who Fits with Whom?

Accroding to traditional teachings, there are two elements respectively that fit well together, while the other combinations are more difficult. Fire and air are considered to be masculine elements that are related to each other and harmonize well, as do the feminine elements of earth and water. Popular astrological partnership predictions, usually follow this simple basic pattern. It's obvious that we can get along well with the signs of the same element. After all, we are in our own element with them, which means we look at the world in the same way. Moreover, we have a good understanding of people with the related element so that in this very fundamental consideration of the twelve signs there are six masculine and six feminine signs, each of which harmonize well with the others of the same group. See Table 3.

Whether we should take a simplistic approach to an essential area of life such as partnership is an open question. Even everyday language has two extremely contradictory opinions about this situation. On the one hand it says that "birds of a feather flock together," but then there is also the following expression: "opposites attract." So which of these two elemental theories should we believe? "Birds of a feather flock together" is certainly a good basis for the friendships we cultivate, and for the experiences we have within a group. This is also where we can apply the statements about elements that harmonize with each other. By way of comparison, "opposites attract" is the

Table 3. Masculine and Feminine Elements			
MASCULINE		FEMININE	
Fire	Air	Earth	Water
♈ Aries	♎ Libra	♑ Capricorn	♋ Cancer
♌ Leo	♒ Aquarius	♉ Taurus	♏ Scorpio
♐ Sagittarius	♊ Gemini	♍ Virgo	♓ Pisces

motto for a relationship—or is there a greater contrast than between a man and a woman? This is why it is very questionable when astrological statements about partnership are made only according to this basic pattern. In fact, it has been demonstrated often enough that although we get along well with our own and the related element, such connections may not create enough excitement to keep a relationship full of life. Understood in this manner, relationships between all the elements—and all the astrological signs— are obviously possible without the difficult ones necessarily being any worse than others or even hopeless.

Since we can ultimately become whole only by developing the four elements within us, we must first understand the nature of each individual element, how it gets along with the other element, and how these complement it. In the following descriptions, each element will be described as if a person were to consist of just this element alone. However, there is no such extreme form, since we are all mixed types. One element is so strongly developed in each of us that we appear to primarily represent this type of element.

The Fire Element

The Strong-Willed Individual

The fire person lives in a world of optimism, enthusiasm, and has a great capacity for exuberance. His courage in taking risks and a strong belief in himself are the basis of his nearly inexhaustible drive. He trusts the power of his intuition, follows his will, his convictions, and at the same time, likes to place himself at the center of all events. Attention is simply important; this is why he also does a great deal in order to be seen. With his fire power, he may also spark other's interest and enthuse them for his goals. This is how he sets developments in motion, gives dynamic impulses, motivates and spurs others on, and is a master at playing to an audience. His passion is expressing his will. This is why he loves the still unstructured future, which he can form according to his own will. He likes to risk the big success or new beginning, which causes the blood to surge through his veins. He looks for challenges and, even if he happens to fail at some point, he quickly recovers, gets up, and tries it again. For him there is always a next time, a new try.

He is the master of the beginning, yet his fire sometimes flags when translating his projects into concrete terms. Impatience is his distinguishing feature, and the time between the sowing and the harvest often becomes a hard trial of patience for him. Fire ignites easily, but staying power and a careful treatment of energy reserves are not his strength. Routine work is not at all to his taste because it leaves no room for spontaneity, and also sets tiresome limits on his urge for freedom and desire for what is new.

The past is extremely uninteresting and boring for a fire person because it can no longer be changed, even with the best of will. This is why consideration means little since he prefers to charge forward and wants to be the first. Believing in the goal is the engine that drives him on.

Fiery people prefer to actively intervene in life instead of waiting and taking what's in store for them. More than any other element, fire individuals have a more difficult time tolerating inner tensions, which is why they translate impulses and drives into action as quickly as possible and work them off. This direct power of expression, the sometimes childlike spontaneity, and the uninhibited way of always claiming the entire pie has something very winning about it. However, the high degree of willingness to take a risk, the lack of self-control, and the deep aversion to any type of criticism—not to even mention self-criticism—in connection with fiery impatience can let some of the noble plans turn into an unimagined adventure that may also end with everything razed to the ground.

Fire has quite a difficult time with the earth signs, although their realism, deliberateness, and objectivity form a good counterbalance to it. But from the perspective of fire, earth is simply much too slow, too boring, always coming up with misgivings, constantly urging caution and, on top of everything else, even demanding facts that the fire individual should substantiate. All of this is much too arduous, too unimaginative and dry, especially since it threatens to stifle his enthusiasm.

However, fire also has its difficulties time and again with the emotionality of the water signs because water's lack of drive, connected with a frequently pessimistic keynote, could put out the fire. The sensitivity that sometimes lets the water individual be cautious and shy is often interpreted as cowardice by the fire person. Yet, it is precisely this opposite pole that could teach him to perceive what goes on around him instead of simply placing himself at the center of attention in a self-confident or high-handed manner.

On the other hand, air is the element that fans the flames of fire. Fire individuals love air types because the latter's breezy ideas constantly give their fiery will fresh nourishment. He loves them at least as long as they spare him of their smart-alecky questions and don't ask him to give reasons for his convictions. When ideas (air) and will (fire) connect in a positive way, this can naturally be the birth of some good projects; however, some things also just keep on being hot air or end up as a lot of noise (air) and smoke (fire).

The Earth Element
The Realistic Person

The world of the earth individual is the world of facts, experiences, order, and structure. She values and relies on everything that she can grasp and examine with her senses. The earth individual does not warm up to fiery speculations, elevated theories are too unfounded for her, and watery fantasies don't really appeal to her sense of reality. She will always prefer a bird in the hand to two in the bush! What counts for her is the bottom line, what she has in her pocket, and what she can take home with her. Earth-oriented people may be slow and deliberate in their actions, but they are persistent and have staying power as a result. Once they get involved in a plan, they will follow it directly and consistently until they reach their goal. Their strong trust in pragmatic values makes them the keepers of tradition and simultaneously suspicious of bold utopias. They value tried-and-true methods far more than modern solutions, in the same way that the past and present are more important than a fictitious future that is still unstructured and will ultimately always be unpredictable.

The rooted earth individual usually lacks the willingness—and sometimes just simply the necessary imagination—to warm up to the world of ideals, longings, or ideas. She lavishes care and attention on the familiar since this is what she knows and can depend on. This is why she loves routine and repetition, and has a difficult time with changes and innovations. Others are sure to have had a hard time with her stubbornness, lack of flexibility, and resistance to anything unaccustomed. However, when her need for security lets her hold on too tight to things proven and achieved, when she desperately clings to money, property, possessions, and reality, there is the danger of losing sight of life's meaning and that all of life's joys will be smothered because of her lack of inspiration and visionary strength.

The lively, restless air signs sometimes make too much fuss for the earth individual. Without further ado, they too easily stir up her clear structures, constantly come up with some sort of lofty and much too modern ideas that don't interest her at all. She cannot comprehend why she should get mixed up in such high-flown "mental acrobatics," especially since theory and practice seem to constantly contradict each other here. She only values perceptions when she can truly do something with them. Having a perception for perception's sake appears to be quite superfluous to her. At the same time, more receptiveness for the air world could actually be good for her, since the inventive spirit of air could actually bring easy solutions and make some things go more smoothly.

Earth has a very special problem with fire because fire has a carefree way of "burning up" all the reserves that earth has so carefully developed and leaves nothing behind it but scorched earth. The earth individual not only finds the impetuous forward-surging fire to be uneconomical, but also much too thoughtless in the face of uncalculated risks. However, the warming fire is good for the earth, since it can bring healthy excitement and intensity into her life through the momentum, joy, and constantly flaming optimism of the fire individual.

Water is the fertilizing element for earth. Its depth of feeling prevents the earth individual from becoming crusted and rigid. Water also makes the earth malleable. However, when a flood occurs, the fruitful soil is transformed into dangerous swampland.

The Air Element

The Intellectual

The air individual moves easily in the world of theories, thoughts, and abstractions. He possesses a quick grasp and nimble verbal ability to express himself. His need for contact and exchange drives him from one place to the next, but the desire for freedom and independence prevents him from spending much time anywhere. So the air individual approaches other people in an open and friendly way but usually makes an impression that is somewhat distanced and cool in the process. His train of thought frequently moves in leaps and bounds, primarily on the surface of things. These people are brilliant, informative, create ideas, impart knowledge, make connections, think in relative terms and question things, but usually manage to avoid commitment and depth, as well as emotional involvement. This light, lively, curious mood frequently leads to impatience, nervousness, and fragmentation.

Their inexhaustible interest (Latin = being in between) in everyone and everything prevents them from taking a clear position and makes them light-weights without a homeland. The future is the favorite playing field for their thoughts since this is where they can be devised and invented. Things that are new keep all the possibilities open and leave leeway for experiments and utopias.

Although the air individual constantly strives for clarity and objectivity, he may sometimes get lost in the elevated labyrinths of his own mental world. Then he is like the comical professor who experiments in his ivory-tower laboratory with high-flown theories that no one would know how to use, even if they ever did prove to be more than a flop.

Air often has a difficult time with earth in the truest sense of the word. Earth's unwavering sense of reality lets some of those lovely castles in the air smash to pieces on hard ground. On the other hand, however, this combination is valuable because airy ideas only become useful in the practical sense when they interact with earth.

The water signs are usually a closed book for the air individual as well. The world of feelings is too vague for him, he cannot comprehend it; it's not logical, at best psychological—and he can only smile about that. Yet, the water signs in particular are capable of breathing life into his abstract ideas and making them more human.

By way of contrast, air people value the warmth of the fire signs, as well as their capacity for enthusiasm and momentum, even if the impulsive, rash energy of fire sometimes moves too quickly even for the air individual.

The Water Element

The Emotional Person

The water individual intuitively attunes herself to her surrounding world. Her antennae are permanently set on reception, which gives her an excellent sense of empathy, on the one hand, but also makes it considerably more difficult for her to draw the line against outside influences. Water people take in a great deal and in this process let themselves be influenced by energies and forces that aren't even meant for them. Their sensitivity lets them always know what the other person expects from them. As a result of their great willingness to react to other people's wishes, these are the people with a thousand faces who are capable of appearing in whatever way the person with whom they are dealing at the moment wishes them to be.

In accordance with this, water people have difficulties in developing a feeling for their own identity and their own boundaries. Despite all this, it would still be wrong to underestimate their instinctive urge toward goals because nothing can ultimately stop water from following its true destiny, even if it has to make detours that appear very curious in the eyes of the other elements. A willingness to help, sympathy, sureness of instinct, empathy, and often a good deal of intuitive ability are the strengths of water, which is why these people frequently dedicate themselves to therapeutic tasks.

Although the water individual can tell beautiful stories, she has difficulties in expressing herself in formal terms and explaining something factually, since the world of sober rationality is not hers. She is much more at home in the rich world of images, of the imagination, and the soul. She is the born soul doctor who can listen to others, be truly sympathetic, and show deep understanding. And she is naturally also the teller of fairy tales, the poet, the artist, or the magician. Her sensitivity lets her be less daring than the other elements and sometimes even less able to cope with life. When the demands of the outer world become too hard, so that she no longer feels capable of coping, she often retreats into her own inner life or into a fantasy world, and hopes to somehow wrangle through on the outside. In extreme cases, this leads to escapism, stubborn denial of reality, a leap into the irrational, or flight into intoxication. Then the past, with its images, has a firm hold on her and her glance tends to wander more backward than forward. Her soul gets caught up in memories time and again, revealing old, familiar things in intensive dreams even years after everything has long been over. Like no other element, water draws into the depths and only becomes calm when it has landed at the bottom. Water does not move on its own power. To do this, water needs impulses from the outside or, even better, a slant that gives it a direction, as well as a setting that provides it with support.

This is why the water person values the proximity of earth individuals, who give her structure and security. However, this applies only as long as they don't start to dry out her water by, for example, trying to suppress the inner correlations that she senses with their unimaginative factual thinking.

From the deep water perspective, air tends to be a superficial element. When air approaches are too cold and hostile, water shuts itself off by forming a sheet of ice and thereby preventing the coldly analytical intellect from looking into the depths of her soul. But where these two elements connect well, we can find artists who know how to express the images of the soul in words or through music, as well as the true spiritual helpers and guides.

Water flees from the hot fire signs. The combination steams. Water quickly feels herself to be overpowered or easily has her feelings hurt by the heated directness. On the other hand, the momentum of a fire person—his optimism and joy in life—can sometimes rouse the water type out of her apathy.

The Achilles' Heel as a Center of Conflict

C. G. Jung suspected that there are two reasons behind the tendency to link ourselves with a partner who personifies everything that we lack: on the one hand, we believe that we have rid ourselves of the annoying problem forever with this completely unconscious move. Let the other person take care of it! On the other hand, such a relationship gives us enough occasions to mock, make fun of, and tease the other person. Seen in this light, although we may be quite glad to finally have found someone who takes over the area that we find so difficult, at the same time we often look down on this way of being in the world with a certain disdain since it seems so strange to us. To be totally honest, we actually can't understand why a person would seriously and truly want to be involved with this element and therefore—at least secretly—react with mild smiles or open ridicule.

Our strengths never lie in our missing element. This is our weak point, our vulnerable spot, our Achilles' heel. For this reason, it's great to have someone else protect this weak spot. On the other hand, we naturally need an immense amount of faith before we can entrust this most vulnerable spot to another person. The myths explain how this can go wrong. Siegfried, Achilles, Hercules, and Samson became victims because other people knew where their weak spots were.

As a result, we experience completion through our partner in an entirely conflicting manner. During the phase of infatuation, it is natural for us to experience the epitome of happiness because we have finally found what we've always lacked. Even people who hadn't consciously known beforehand that they were missing something feel extremely enriched during this time and begin to blossom. However, when the initial feeling of being in love starts to subside—and experience has shown that this is the case after six months at the latest—some of our partner's idiosyncrasies begin to strangely disturb us. Then it usually doesn't take long for the first deep disappointments to occur and the initially intact image of the beloved begins to crumble. However, none of these images are correct. Neither during the state of falling in love, nor in the phase of being disconcerted, nor in the disappointment do we really see the other person as he or she actually is. Our missing element allows a distorted picture to be created in all of these cases. The spectrum appears as follows, ranging from the light side to the dubious phase, and then on to the shadow aspect.

If we lack *fire*, we are naturally thrilled that a person enters our life who brings us momentum and optimism. We find it wonderful that this person is so spontaneous and full of "go," and we often praise the magnificent and self-confident impression he makes. We are completely enchanted by this awe-inspiring charisma, admire the courage, strong will and ability to take risks, and value the generosity that he displays. We enjoy "catching fire" when we are close to him and "warming up" to adventures that we otherwise would have never had thought ourselves capable of. As a result, we simply become more (physically) active.

Yet, after a certain period of time, it dawns on us that our peace and quiet is likely to have disappeared forever. This person constantly "makes things hot for us," and while we pant behind, we notice that all of this is much too strenuous. However, only when the shadow aspect constellates do things really become critical. Then we suddenly feel nothing more of the warmth and become increasingly aware that the other person just revolves around his own self, an inconsiderate egomaniac who steals the spotlight time and again with overly emotional gestures and impertinent obviousness. He bluntly rakes in all the attention, the entire applause, and simply takes the whole pie. Now, at the very latest, our "flame" has been put out and we are aghast as we ask ourselves what could have fascinated us about this partner.

If we lack *earth*, we are entirely enchanted at the start by finally having someone in whom we can place our entire trust, who is our refuge of peace and composure. We think this person is a rock of dependability upon which we can build, behind which we can hide, and against whom we can lean. We notice with relief that she actually likes to do all the boring things that have always spoiled everyday life for us. The partner brings regularity and structure into our life, excels at keeping everything in order, and is ingenious and truly skilled in dealing with the mundane matters of this world. Above all, she always keeps promises, has a sense of values, and practically loves thinking about and managing money.

However, with passing time we notice that this wonderful person can also have something very tedious about her, displaying qualities like being finicky, slow, and increasingly boring. The partner prefers to continually just do the same thing, develops no new interests, and doesn't want to get to know any new friends. As an utterly sober rationalist, she has a bone-dry approach and only considers what she can touch to be real. When the varnish has faded, we recognize that concealed behind it is actually just an unimaginative petty mind, an obstinate jackass, an extremely small-time Philistine, someone as exciting and lively as a sack of potatoes. The partner ultimately becomes just a millstone around our neck with her eternal misgivings, fear of everything strange and new, and slowness and penetrating perfectionism, which steal our entire momentum in life.

If we lack *air*, we are truly inspired at the start to have found someone who brings such a breath of fresh air, ease, and the smell of springtime into our life. This is someone who is so intelligent, knows so much, has apparently read all the books in this world, and, on top of everything else, knows all the encyclopedias by heart; someone who can analyze things with astuteness, who has a smart solution on tap for every problem; a person with whom we never get bored because he always has a story to tell, who provides us with so much information and gets us to read books that previously would never even have occurred to us. This is someone who knows how to express himself in a masterly way and can play with words, who has no trouble (and even enjoys) formulating letters and other texts, developing ideas, and never runs out of something to say, even in the most boring company, because he can even talk about the most off-beat topics and show interest in them, if this is absolutely required of him. This is a person who enjoys making contacts for us and—if necessary—even carrying out negotiations for us. It's simply wonderful that Mr. or Ms. Intelligence has entered our life in person, making so many things clear that we hadn't seen before and letting some things that we had previously never comprehended become clear.

But with time, it dawns on us that not everything that sounds clever is actually sensible, since many things are easier said than done, and sometimes a dramatic torrent of words only produces trivialities, or that even the most pleasant-sounding sayings can consist purely of empty phrases. It becomes increasingly clear that we have been taken in by a big mouth, a smart-alecky know-it-all. Once we have broken the spell that this angel once had on us, he gradually sinks down into the world of shadows and we now can see his dark side. We suddenly sense how ice-cold, two-faced, wily, heartlessly calculating, and alarmingly noncommittal air can be. With a shudder, we suddenly become aware that this person apparently has no values at all, that he writes everything on the wind, that everything is relative, that he can ridicule and make nasty remarks about anything, even our deepest feelings; even in the holiest, most touching and intimate moments, he can pour water over everything with a stupid saying. We notice that we have gotten involved with a windbag who actually thinks only about his freedom, his dearly beloved independence. He is a scoundrel and a traitor whose words and promises aren't worth a hoot.

If we lack *water*, we are intoxicated and enchanted at the beginning when this person with her thousand faces enters our life. We can hardly believe how deep water can feel, how devoted and sensitive this element is. We feel how we melt when this person senses and fulfills even our most secret longings. Never before has someone understood us so deeply, never before has someone been so affectionate, so close, so sensitive, so caring. Water lets our feelings overflow; water sweeps us away with it into a world of fantasy, a world we had never even dared to dream about. Water has an intuitive knowledge and speaks with self-evident truth about how future developments will unfold so that we often have the impression that this person is a sphinx.

But when the first wave of enthusiasm starts to fade, we recognize more and more that she is actually no different than anyone else, that some of the lovely dreams burst like soap bubbles, and that this person's imagination increasingly runs away with her. Once our sphinx has finally lost her luminosity to the point that we only perceive deep black, the original wonderful enchantment will have also been transformed into its dark opposite pole. Then we suddenly notice how little drive water has, how helplessly this individual—who can give other people so much help—is entangled in her own problems. And the beautiful world of fantasy turns out more and more to be a mirage, a treacherous net of pure wishful thinking in which our partner is hopelessly caught. Now it suddenly dawns on us how demanding water is, how it sucks everything that surrenders to it into the depths, how much we are in danger of being drawn into the entanglements. We start to panic when we realize that a rogue who truly knows all the tricks of the trade has emerged from behind the transfigured image we had of her at the beginning.

• • • •

For many people, the image of the person who has been dearly beloved up to that point collapses so intensively that we revile the loved one as "deceptive packaging," someone who has viciously deceived us. We wish that the person who had once had been our angel would now "go to hell" as quickly as possible. We make the mistake of believing that only now do we actually see the bare truth in the disappointment phase and everything beforehand was fraud and falsehood. This simply isn't true. To the same degree that the earlier state of being in love excessively elevated the image of the other person, it is now seen as diabolic. Reality lies somewhere between these two poles. The other person certainly possesses both shadow and light. When we are able to accept him or her as such, the actual relationship can begin.

To fall in love and float on clouds during the first six months is wonderful, but no challenge. Using this euphoria as a gauge for the depth of the resulting relationship is definitely a foolish thing to do. Being in love appears to be just a means of luring and bonding in order to bring us out of our shells. It takes us to the point where we can change. Being in love lures young people from the feeling of security within the parental home out into life; later, being in love entices adults out of the "adult" reserve so that we can once again open up to another person despite setbacks or emotional injuries.

Is being in love therefore just a mean trick, a nasty ruse of life that only leads us to new disappointments? Or is there something more behind it? It appears to be the longing of our soul for wholeness that drives to connect with what we lack. However, the naive idea that the path to wholeness is easy will only bring disillusion and disappointment. Wholeness must be achieved, and love and partnership plays a central role in this effort. The idea that we must often walk a narrow line is made clear by all the fairy tales that tell us of the search for the thing that is hard to find. The raising of the treasure, the freeing of the beautiful prisoner, or any other difficult work of deliverance are all analogies for becoming whole.

The development can naturally also go in the other direction. When we initially transfer the dark aspects of the missing element to another person, we see the enemy or a villian in him or her, a primitive person, or a despicable creature. Many people leave it at that and lastingly cement their personal enmities and animosities. But sometimes a change occurs as a result of a coincidence or a more conscious look. Then we suddenly comprehend that a truly fine human being is concealed behind this image that we despise and some-

Table 4. Light, Twilight, and Shadow in Encounters with the Missing Element.

	FIRE	EARTH	AIR	WATER
Light	Courage, self-confidence, dynamic force, momentum in life, joy of living, strong will, optimism, spontaneity	Steadiness, reliability, security, willingness to take responsibility, structure, repose, trust, composure	Agility, keen perception, clarity, solutions, ease, thirst for knowledge, alertness, flexibility	Empathy, sense of security, sixth sense, understanding, ability to be devoted, imagination, caring, spirituality
Twilight	Egotism, arrogance, pride, pushiness	Boredom, eternal routine, inflexibility	Noncommittal attitude, superficiality	Moodiness, lack of drive
Shadow	Unpredictability, inconsideration	Merciless severity, stubbornness	Icy coldness, inaccessibility, snobbishness, calculation	Emotional blackmail, escapism, telling lies, manipulation

times battle. We simply hadn't recognized this because of our distorted perception. We suddenly realize that love and hate actually belong together like light and shadow, for they are two sides of the same coin. We may also notice how much we also need this person that we hated and why we can't get free of him or her; or, put in more precise terms—why we don't let go. He or she may be part of our life so we have someone on whom to project our shadow, a scapegoat, someone who is "responsible" for the evil in the world.

As long as we only see the light *or* the shadow in this other person, we have a blurred picture that doesn't do justice to this individual, since the profile of a human being can only be perceived in a mixture of light *and* shadow. See Table 4 on page 17.

When encountering the element that we lack, we are usually enchanted by the light aspect at first, then we notice that the picture of the other person slowly becomes shady before we ultimately perceive the shadow aspects of this element.

Sometimes this path also goes in the opposite direction. Then we increasingly value a person to whom we previously had a reaction of vehement disapproval. We can only really see the entire human being, his or her actual profile, in a mixture of light and shadows.

Symbiosis or Self-Sufficiency?

Once we have found the person we need, for whom we have a "weakness" in particular because he or she has strongly developed precisely the aspects that we lack, then there are two typical ways of reacting. The most frequent reaction is the spontaneous: "Thank God, now I don't have to worry about that stuff anymore!" This leads to symbiosis, while the other reaction is either: "That's really too much!" or "I don't like this at all!" or even: "Anything but that!" These reactions conceal a flight into self-sufficiency, resulting in our making fun of the foreign element, complaining about and ridiculing its qualities, and even compulsively drawing the line at it because we—at least secretly—feel threatened by it. Both reactions are expressions of weakness. In the case of symbiosis, we flee into childlike dependence and behavior patterns, whereby self-sufficiency looks like strength to the outside world but is ultimately just a gruff facade hiding fear and a lack of self-confidence. The temptations that lead us to the deceptive solution of symbiosis appear in accordance with the missing element as follows:

If we lack fire, then we often also have too little motivation, momentum, or the ability to be enthusiastic and optimistic, but above all, spontaneity, courage, assertiveness, and self-assurance. We could say that our energy level is on a low flame and challenges easily become excessive demands for us. Although we know how to do something often enough, even have the "tools" to do it, and wish for nothing more than that it would get done, we don't have the momentum and simply can't get going on it. It obviously is a great relief when the fire individual appears, bringing dynamic force, impulses, liveliness, excitement, and confidence into our life; and, on top of everything else, gives his opinion to everyone who we never dared tell ours.

If we lack earth, we often experience problems with everyday reality. We have a hard time budgeting and dealing with money, or we just can't seem to take care of certain types of practical work because we are too impatient, unskilled, not ingenious enough, or simply don't have a way with tools and household devices. Although we often have the right idea, a noble intention, or a deep wish, it's terribly difficult to turn this impulse into reality and actually do the job. When an earth individual finally enters our life, we are not only relieved but also admire the ease with which she takes care of all the things that have always been so difficult for us. Thanks to our admiration, she naturally has the best motivation for doing even more of what she does so well, putting things in order and taking care of them for us without hesitation.

If we lack air, then we are often missing agility, but also clarity, mental adroitness, sometimes even words and often the right idea, the right solution. Yet, we still have the deep desire time and again to change something, to achieve something, or overcome a problem and really have good intentions. We also are persistent enough. But we simply can't find the right trick to do things, how to untie the knot. We also have difficulty in analyzing problems or reflecting on experiences and suffer from a lack of flexibility and improvisational talent time and again. If we then run into an air individual, for whom all of this is no problem at all and even enjoys solving these tasks for us, it's naturally no wonder when we move into his world with fluttering flags and love to let him take over all these unpleasant things for us.

If water is our weakness, then we haven't "the foggiest idea," strictly speaking. We don't have the right "antenna." Even though we can calculate things or even build on the basis of pragmatic values, approaching our plans full of optimism, we still don't have a nose for things with a sure instinct. Moreover, we lack depth in our soul. We are too dry for anything to penetrate into our soul or make it resonate. We have a hard time with anything irrational, with the world of feelings, as well as the image world of the soul. When a water individual suddenly enters our life, we are fascinated by the natural way in which this person understands, for example, how to interpret our dreams. She opens our eyes for worlds that we had never thought possible, giving us a feeling of emotional security that had never been there before. We sense that someone is looking deeper into us than even we have ever done, and feel ourselves to be understood by this person like never before.

What would be more logical than to take the comfortable path in all these cases, leaving what is so difficult for us up to the other person and trusting in him or her? As understandable as this impulse may be, it is also insidious because the symbiosis created naturally leads straight to dependency and a lack of independence. In the case of its failure, it also leaves behind a deep feeling of being unable to cope with life since when we are not confronted with our weak side for a longer period of time, we cope with this area of life even more poorly than before. It's like having a part of ourselves torn out, without which we can no longer live. Above all, symbiosis prevents us from becoming whole. If we simply let someone else live the qualities that we are lacking, then we will certainly never develop this aspect of consciousness and the abilities and behaviors that correspond with it. But this means that one color of the four-color print will always be missing within us; we will be capable of perceiving and shaping neither ourselves nor our life in all of its colorfulness.

The other typical reaction is the flight into self-sufficiency. This is often based in the fear of even admitting our own weakness or mistakes. The best way to do this is to immediately start by questioning the concept of the four structures of consciousness, the four elements, or the four types of character, and at the same time deriding the idea of wholeness with all its related themes, such as the development of the weak aspect, as ridiculous. The deeper this fear sits and the weaker the sense of self-worth, the more vehement, even hostile, this attitude will be. The person mimes the role of the superior individual with greater or lesser mastery, downplays the meaning of the missing quality, time and again makes fun of how the partner imagines that he or she possesses splendid qualities, and goes into the offensive in case of a conflict. The self-sufficient individual then explains to his or her partner that the latter's strengths are the ones that the world could most easily dispense with and he or she shouldn't imagine them to be worth anything since, strictly speaking, it would even be better for humanity when this element—this structure of consciousness, this way of being—didn't even exist.

An important opportunity, which every relationship offers, is wasted in both cases: taking learning steps on the path to our own wholeness. Instead of happily leaning back because someone else takes care of the things that are so difficult for us, or secretly even hating this other person for doing this, for constantly demonstrating how easy these things are, it would be much more intelligent to ask him or her: "Please show me how to do it." But this requires quite a bit of willingness to be humble, along with having good intentions. To do this, we not only have to admit our weaknesses to ourselves but to the other person as well. Furthermore, we must comprehend that we are missing something essential and that this is more than just a little flaw. We must be seriously willing to learn something that is tough, sticky, arduous, and difficult for us, at the same time that our partner is a virtuoso in this field.

How absurd symbiosis or self-sufficiency can be is illustrated by the following example. When two people move to a foreign country and one of them speaks its language well, but the other knows just a few broken phrases, then nothing would be more logical than the first person, who can express himself without a problem, speaking for both of them at every opportunity. With time, he will master the language that he already knows even better, while the other will gradually be left completely speechless as a result of this symbiosis. In contrast to this is the opposite pole, the self-sufficiency that can be compared to the behavior of members of the colonial "master class." In no case during colonial times would a respectable member of the ruling class (just like some insolent tourists of modern times) have learned the "primitive" language of the colonized countries, but naturally expected everyone else to learn their language. The price for this is high. Self-sufficient individuals never really participate in life and therefore cannot learn from life. At the same time, they become increasingly mistrustful because they don't understand what others are discussing with each other. This isolates them more and more to the point that, as misanthrops, they are imprisoned in the cold loneliness of proud resignation.

Dissolving and Binding—Alchemy in a Relationship

Self-sufficiency and symbiosis embody the extreme forms of two basic forces that—lived in a healthy balance—control every living relationship—dissolving and binding. In every relationship these two forces are in balance with each other. Whether this balance of power comes about in a relaxed and harmonious way, or whether it is achieved after repeated, hot wars petrify into a state of cold war, or clothes itself in apathy and indifference, is all the same. Both of these powers are balanced in every situation. In this process, it may look like one of these two forces has temporarily been repressed and the other has won the upper hand. But it is quite certain that the seemingly inferior power is only repressed into the unconscious and will re-form itself there in order to appear again sooner or later and win the upper hand. The roles belonging to this interplay of forces are often already given to the participants at the first moment of meeting each other, long before even one of them suspects that a relationship will develop from this encounter. From the very beginning, one of them takes the role of "binder" while the other takes over that of the "dissolver." And this is how it usually stays thereafter. Only in rare cases does an exchange of roles occur during the further course of the relationship.

The binder's task is to be responsible for the committed nature of the relationship, that the two people are together and do as much as possible with each other, while the dissolver must maintain the distance between them in order to guarantee that both of them have enough space to be independent. As long as both attend to their tasks to the right degree, the relationship will be healthy and develop in a lively way. Whenever two people can leave each other alone and then come back together again, in order to once again leave each other alone and come back together once more, both personal growth and the growth of the relationship are possible, since neither of the two is pressed into a rigid pattern or reduced to one mode of expression; instead, each of them is permitted to gradually appear as a complete human being. On the other hand, two people who just bind will stick firmly to each other in the symbiotic sense since there is little room for further development. And when only detachment prevails, where everything is just loose and relaxed, the friction for further development is missing.

Alchemists were aware of the secret of every higher development in the constant interplay of dissolving and binding. An extensive knowledge about the true laws of change is concealed within their time-honored tradition. Whenever a profound change becomes necessary in our life, whenever we feel that we must transform ourselves or when we discover that our growth has stagnated and our relationship has stopped developing, then it's helpful to take to heart the advice of this hermetic science, which C. G. Jung called the "psychology of the Middle Ages."

The interesting thing about this polarity of forces is that they are mutually contingent upon each other. In the proper mixture, this is a guarantee for the liveliness of the relationship. But if one of the two changes the rules of the game, he or she forces the other partner to take countermeasures. So if the dissolver suddenly asks for more independence, the binder can hardly do anything but demand more commitment. This gives the dissolver the feeling of now being definitively captured, which is why he or she then demands more freedom, whereby the binder sees the relationship so endangered that he or she demands more commitment. Two people can actually work each other up to the point that both are in a permanent state of alarm. In such extreme situations, the rather rare change of positions may take place. If, for example, the binder is so frustrated that he or she gives up and ends the relationship, it just might happen that the entire detachment of the dissolver breaks down, his or her holy freedom is suddenly insignificant, and the previous dissolver now becomes the best of binders. However, this reverse of polarity never works as a tactical measure, but only when the related steps are genuine. If the binder only acts as though he or she wants to leave, but inwardly hopes for the dissolver's turnabout, everything will remain as it is.

Considered in symbolic terms, the separating aspect is a masculine quality, whereby the feminine is seen as the binding power. Analogous to this, masculine thinking is oriented toward differentiation, whereby feminine thinking always recognizes and emphasizes the mutual factors. Even if this classification doesn't mean any type of compelling role distribution for the sexes, men still tend toward emphasizing the separating factors, the difference, and the details, while women primarily focus their attention on the connecting, the mutual factors, and the whole. Jungian psychology presumes that this is based on the respective initial human experience with the first person a child relates to—the mother. While the boy feels the difference based on the polarity from the start and must also develop his identity in differentiation from the mother, the girl first experiences the solidarity with the mother and can very well orient herself toward her mother while developing her own identity. Accordingly, a boy has much more difficulty in developing his own nature than a girl. However, there is "compensating justice" in the fact that the boy is used to satisfying his desires and needs with the opposite sex starting at the mother's breast while this becomes a challenging learning task for the adolescent girl.

A further compensation is illustrated in how the opposite of what has just been stated can be seen on the unconscious level. Here, the man reacts in a feminine manner and the woman in a masculine way, usually without even being aware of this. The archetypal forces that cause this are called the anima and animus in analytical psychology. What this means and the deep significance found here can be seen in the following section.

Anima and Animus—The Inner Beloved

It is in the nature of the unconscious mind to always behave in a manner that is compensatory, or balancing, in relation to our conscious mind, thereby forming an opposite polarity to everything with which we identify consciously. This is why complications often arise when we are committed to everything that is good, light, noble, and true. Marie-Louis von Franz warned about idealistically having one-sided wishes of only acting in a good and proper way because we then involuntarily put ourselves into the hands of evil. She drew the following conclusion: "To do good may still be the goal, but it makes us more modest to know that the compensating destructive side constellates when we want to be too good."[1]

For this reason, we know that where there is light, there is always shadow. As illuminating as this phenomenon may be, and as easily as we can recognize it in others, our ego would prefer to hear nothing about this principle when it comes to ourselves, and we constantly want to apply special rules. But we are all exceptions! This is why people who are completely convinced that they are thoroughly "light" and certainly don't have any shadow aspects often feel themselves to be so "unappreciated" when, to their surprise, they are criticized by others, or when their goodness is even questioned. But, unfortunately, the others must experience and endure these shadow aspects of which the supposed "light being" is so completely unconscious. This idiosyncrasy of the unconscious mind explains some of the contradictions in life. For example, why do people violently fight for peace, or why are the moralizers of the nation entangled in dirty affairs time and again? The unconscious mind has the truly thankless task of forming the dark opposite pole to the vainly brilliant feeling of self, leading the self-righteous ego into temptation time and again so that it becomes aware of its own unconscious dark aspects. To damn it as the work of the devil, as frequently happens in narrow-minded religious circles, doesn't show a more profound insight into the important significance of this opposite pole.

As C. G. Jung recognized when researching the unconscious mind, its contents include elemental images inherent to every human being. These

---

[1]Marie-Louise von Franz, "The Redemption of the Feminine in the Man," in *A Psychological Interpretation of the Golden Ass of Apuleius* (New York: Analytical Psychology Club of New York, 1970).

include the hero, the dragon, the virgin, and the old wise man. Jung called these inner pictures *archetypes* or primordial images of the human soul. There are two among them that, according to his observations, play an important role. They are mediators between a person's conscious and the unconscious mind, as well as the inner, initially unconscious opposite pole to his or her conscious sexual behavior. Jung called these "forces," which see to it that the unconscious mind of a man reacts in a feminine manner and that of a woman reacts in a masculine way, the *anima* and *animus:* The anima is the female aspect of a man, and the animus is the inner masculinity of a woman.

One phenomenon that makes it easy to recognize the effects of these archetypes is the conflict situation familiar to us in so many relationships: while the man constantly talks about his holy need for freedom, his urge to be independent, and the impossibility of being truly committed, the woman swears on what they have in common and is willing to give her anything for the committed nature of the relationship. This is at least the outer reality on the conscious level. On the other hand, the opposite poles are forming in the unconscious mind. The anima, the inner femininity of the man, does her best to counteract this conscious urge for independence. The result is impressive. Instead of really pursuing his supposed yearning for freedom, the man feels himself drawn to his partner to the same degree that he talks off her ears about his need for independence, since his feminine aspect, his (unconscious) anima, binds him to the relationship to the same extent to which he consciously strives to remain free. Since we like to project unconscious forces onto others, this man will naturally blame his partner for his supposed lack of freedom, accusing her, and insinuating that she won't let him go, when it really is his anima that binds him. For her part, the woman wonders why this man comes back to her time and again when he actually just wants to tell her that he will certainly leave again. But while she consciously struggles for the continuance and committed nature of the relationship, attempting to bewitch and beguile him, her inner opposite sexuality reacts with increasing intensity and one fine day, as if out of the blue, her animus draws the sword and lets her—to her own surprise—break up the relationship for which she had fought so long.[2] The more unconscious we are of these inner forces, the more we are at their mercy and the less we understand our behavior in moments when these unconscious forces determine what we do.

Obviously this example isn't the only way in which the anima and the animus work. Instead, their actual intent is to guide a person. In the language of myth and fairy tale, they are the guides of the soul accompanying us. The

---

[2]All relationships don't end in this way. In something like the "mother-son relationship," described on page 57, a man may roam, while his increasingly bitter wife waits for him at home with more or less patience and understanding, and this may go on for years.

anima and animus can also be described as the inner beloved. We believe the right partner should be just like the anima or animus inherent to our unconscious mind. Whenever we encounter a person who enchants us, the anima or animus is involved in the situation since only the unconscious mind has the power to cast a spell on consciousness. In other words, we meet someone in the "outside world" who fascinates us, and this person offers a suitable projection surface, a "hook" on which we can hang our soul image, the picture of our inner partner. If this succeeds, then we are—at least for a while—convinced that the right person has finally entered our life. However, there is a tiresome problem here in that the power of the projection diminishes with time, the beloved picture starts to crack, and the true contours of the other person shows through with increasing clarity. But since only our inner soul image can be perfect, and the outer reality always comes along in an imperfect form, this disillusionment invariably brings with it disappointment and sadness at the loss of the idealized image. In her work on the anima and animus, Emma Jung put this into very apt terms: "When this discrimination between the image and the person sets in we become aware to our great confusion and disappointment, that the man who seemed to embody our animus does not correspond to it in the least, but continually behaves quite differently from the way we think he should."[3] Is there any woman who isn't familiar with this? And any man in his own way?

All soul images have a polarized nature, meaning that they have a light and a dark side to them. Whenever we think an angel enters our life, we naturally have transferred the light side to this person. In as far as this is a purely unconscious projection, it can very quickly turn into its opposite because, when we feel boundless enthusiasm about a beloved person, and overlook all his or her shortcomings, and just want to see the angel in him or her, it usually doesn't take long before the angel plunges into hell and turns into a devil or a witch. This dark image naturally corresponds as little to the outer reality as the angel did before. But it is experienced with the same intensity and battled with the same vehemence with which the desired image had been longed for. This is why it is so important to become aware of this inner person and the fact that we project it. Otherwise, there is the danger of destroying something valuable out of ignorance.

It is apparently the intention of these soul guides to lead people into the area of life where they can learn more about themselves than in any other: the relationship. Only in the intimate and constant confrontation with the other sex can we become aware of our unconscious opposite sexuality and comprehend the anima and animus as forces that ultimately want to lead us to

---

[3]Emma Jung, *Animus and Anima* (Dallas: Spring/Analytical Psychology Club of New York, 1957, 1972, 1978), p. 11.

wholeness. Just simply projecting the inner image onto the other person, believing that we have finally found the right partner, and hoping that we will now have peace of mind forever after, means making things somewhat too easy for ourselves and getting taken in by the cheapest wish dreams. The initial feeling of infatuation that enchants us at the moment of the successful projection is certainly a beautiful, uplifting state. But, according to everything that psychology and life experience have discovered, how much we are in love just says something about the degree of disappointment that must follow sooner or later; interestingly enough, it says absolutely nothing about the depth and durability of the relationship that can result from it. A fall can even occur from the rosiest seventh heaven, taking the entire relationship with it into an abyss while, on the other hand, a deep relationship can grow between two people even without infatuation at the beginning.

This amorousness, which can stimulate our inner partner, is apparently something like a magic potion that inspires our consciousness, lets us go beyond our limitations, and brings us together with another person. But this love-intoxicated exaggeration of reality is no more the goal in itself, or meant to be a permanent state, than any other form of intoxication. The actual relationship starts only after we have become sober, when we no longer worship the other individual as the Dream Woman or Prince Charming, but increasingly see who he or she actually is. To swear eternal faithfulness is easy, just as easy as the frequently heard protests of chronic singles or aging Casanovas that they long for nothing more than to immediately commit themselves for all eternity, if the right person would just come along.

The right person certainly exists. But definitely not in the way that we longingly dream about him or her in the years of our youth. He or she does not exist in a "completed form," and can only become the right person if we make the decision to be with him or her. This doesn't mean that it doesn't matter with whom we bind ourselves. There are certainly people who are more meant for each other and fit together better than others. But as long as we only get involved with each other with the reservation that the other person should not disappoint us, or that he or she eliminates as quickly as possible the "shortcomings" that we have already recognized, we have not truly gotten involved. Even if we—above all during the phase of infatuation—are so totally convinced of our love, this always applies: a love with reservations never is intended for the other person but always just for our own inner soul image, for which the other person is a possible candidate. Nothing is easier than loving the *idea* that we have of a person since it corresponds to our inner partner image. At the same time, we are only loving our idea that we have of the other, the inner image that we project on him or her. It's only natural that we don't notice what we are doing at first. A projection continues to be experienced as pure reality until—if at all—it slowly dawns on us that we are once again being taken in by our own idea.

And it's quite inevitable that disruptions attempting to make us aware of this will come sooner or later. Whether we will recognize their causes and comprehend this correlation remains to be seen. These disruptions cannot be avoided even in the most traditional of marriages, those marriages that still serve as evidence that today tradition, morality, and commitment have gone downhill. Even if this is true, the patriarchal marriage, which begins with at least the woman as a virgin and remains respectable until death doth them part, is not particularly suited as a laudable role model. When it truly "functioned," this primarily occurred because the man, thanks to his instruments of power, could manipulate the woman and force her to personify his anima. Whenever a woman does this, she can be certain that her husband will cherish her. Naturally this is very tempting, at least for a woman who is financially and socially dependent upon her husband. In most cases, she will not even be aware that she has been "purchased" since she is pampered and experiences his affection and generosity to the extent that she is his sweet girl, sweetheart, or, since the 50s, his baby. The price for this is high. It is the price of self-denial. Whenever a woman tries to personify the anima, her partner's searching image, she can naturally only do this at the expense of developing her own true nature. Instead of developing her own personality, she is just a sum of outside expectations. When she is not conscious of this, and doesn't break out of the corset of an identity determined by someone else, sooner or later this act of self-betrayal may become evident in the form of emotional disorders or physical afflictions. Hysteria and migraines are two typical forms of expression[4] here, which is why it was no wonder that these disorders were dismissed as being purely women's diseases in the heyday of the patriarchal marriage at the beginning of the 20th century.

Of course, not only men succumb to the temptation of forcing their wives into the patterns of their anima with skillful manipulation and more or less gentle force. Enough women also try to seduce a man and use a lot of coaxing to make him personify their inner ideal image, their animus. In all these cases, the love is always directed at the inner image, while the supposedly beloved partner is just a candidate granted a framework within which he or she must prove capable of worthily filling the garment and role of the animus.

When we accept and love our partner as the human being that he or she really is, and we can generously promote and support the development of his

---

[4]There are also obviously many other causes for these disorders.

or her individual nature, then we have something quite different. However, the necessary precondition for this step is that we are truly interested in the partner. As obvious as this may sound, we are frequently unwilling to do this as soon as our "image" of the other person threatens to crumble. Only when one person recognizes and loves the other as the living original that he or she is can we genuinely speak of love. Everything else doesn't deserve the name because it arises from egotistical motives, such as the desire to grace oneself with a partner, to never be alone, or to have someone take care of our material and erotic needs.

In order to achieve a real relationship, it is not only important to become conscious of our own inner beloved, but also to take an intense look at this inner image. The cause of many problems in a relationship is not—as people would like to believe—the other person, but these inner figures. C. G. Jung made this very clear when he said: "It is a mistake to believe that one's personal dealings with one's partner play the most important role. Quite the reverse: the most important part falls to the man's dealings with the anima and the woman's inner dealings with the animus."[5] However, the friction with the partner is indispensable in so far as we can only become aware of our anima and animus in relation to the opposite sex. Only in relationships do our projections become effective.

This book offers guidance in this process of consciousness, for in the next section we describe the twelve feminine and masculine types and their strengths and weaknesses. In connection with the horoscope, the personal character can be sketched, creating a sort of an "identikit" picture of the anima or animus and we can use this information to become aware of how our soul image is constructed within.

---

[5]C. G. Jung, *The Practice of Psychotherapy*, vol. 16 in *The Collected Works of C. G. Jung*, Bollingen Series XX, R. F. C. Hull, trans. (Princeton: Princeton University Press, 1954), ¶469.

The Searching-Image Conflict

Our inner opposite sexuality (anima/animus) is composed of a four-part structure, just like the four aspects of our consciousness that correspond with the elements of fire, earth, air, and water. Only when these four aspects are fully developed can the anima or animus mature into wholeness. However, at first they may "simply" lie dormant in the double sense of the word—sometimes they already have a second aspect—within us and wait for their development. These are simple and dual in as far as depth psychology teaches and astrology demonstrates that only one or two sides of this inner four-part group are emphasized within each human being at the start. The missing aspects only become conscious during the course of life when they are lived out and developed in the encounters and experiences with the opposite sex. The searching-image conflict—whose profound significance is largely unknown and which is considered by many people to just be an annoying, troublesome, or disappointing experience—proves to be a vital driving force in this process of development.

With the help of astrology, both the significance of this development and the reason why a searching-image conflict must occur sooner or later in many relationships can be easily perceived. Seen in astrological terms, the element that we lack is most likely identical with the one corresponding to the sign group that either has no personal planets or the fewest personal planets in our horoscope. It is generally known that we prefer to link ourselves with a person who strongly embodies precisely this missing element to compensate and complement this situation. Yet, at the same time we bear within us a searching image that tells us what our partner should ideally be like. This inner imprint, with which we have become familiar as the animus and anima, can also be perceived with the help of astrology. The coloration of the animus as the searching image of the woman is displayed in her horoscope in the position of the masculine planets Mars (♂) and the Sun (☉) within the signs, whereas the anima as the searching image of the man can be read in the sign position of the feminine planets Venus (♀) and the Moon (☽) within his horoscope. However, it is very improbable[1] that both of the searching-image planets are located in the signs that belong to the group of

---

[1]This case cannot be completely excluded because although the position of the planets' signs are the most important, they are not the sole indicator for the distribution of the elements.

the missing element, since it would hardly be a missing element in this case. In other words, when you read the distribution of the elements within the seven personal planets (Sun (☉), Moon (☽), Mercury (☿), Venus (♀), Mars (♂), Jupiter (♃), and Saturn (♄)) from the position of the signs and learn that none of these planets are located in the corresponding sign of the missing element, then you will know that it is mathematically impossible for two planets to be located in the missing element. No matter how the seven planets are divided into four groups, there will always be a group with one planet at most.

We therefore tend to link up with a person who complements us because he or she corresponds with our missing element, but who doesn't embody—or only partially embodies—our inner searching image. This is why we experience him or her, as soon as the joy of the successful complementation subsides, increasingly as an insult to our inner image, as an affront for the animus or anima. And then comes the day when we start accusing him or her of not being the way we think a real man or woman should be.

If we lack fire, and our planets of the opposite sex[2] are located in earth, air, or water, after the initial enthusiasm about our partner's dynamic nature, temperament, and all the other fiery qualities, we will start to complain that he or she is not as down-to-earth (earth), cool and inventive (air), or imaginative and sensitive (water) as would correspond to our inner image.

If we lack earth, and our planets of the opposite sex are located in fire, air, or water, after the initial enthusiasm about our partner's down-to-earth nature, reliability, and all the other earthy qualities, we will start to complain that he or she is not as spontaneous and capable of enthusiasm (fire), as smart and clever (air), or as tactful and devoted (water) as would correspond to our inner image.

If we lack air, and our planets of the opposite sex are located in fire, earth, or water, after the initial enthusiasm about our partner's lighthearted nature, breeziness, and all the other airy qualities, we will start to complain that he or she is not as warm and temperamental (fire), as practical and steadfast (earth), or as romantic and caring (water) as would correspond to our inner image.

If we lack water, and our planets of the opposite sex are located in fire, air, or earth, after the initial enthusiasm about our partner's depth of feeling, sureness of instinct, and all the other water-related qualities, we will start to complain that he or she is not as interested in doing things and being dynamic (fire), as clear and carefree (air), or as objective and uncompromising (earth) as would correspond to our inner image.

---

[2]The planets of the opposite sex are the Sun (☉) and Mars (♂) in the horoscope of a woman and the Moon (☽) and Venus (♀) in the horoscope of a man.

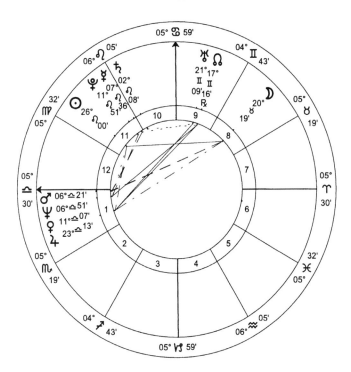

Chart 1. Bill Clinton. Born August 19, 1946, 08:51:00 CST, Hope, AR
(093:35:00W 33:40:00N, 14:51:00 GMT). Koch houses. Birth data: mother.
The personal planets indicate the following distribution of elements:

Bill Clinton		
PLANET	SIGN	ELEMENT
☉ Sun	♌ Leo	Fire
☽ Moon	♉ Taurus	Earth
☿ Mercury	♌ Leo	Fire
♀ Venus	♎ Libra	Air
♂ Mars	♎ Libra	Air
♃ Jupiter	♎ Libra	Air
♄ Saturn	♌ Leo	Fire
Dominant Element		Air
Missing Element		Water
Searching-Image		Air (♀) and Earth (☽)

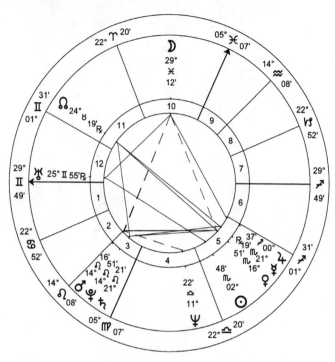

Chart 2. Hillary Clinton. Born October 26, 1947, 20:00:00 CST, Chicago, IL (087:39:00W 41:51:00N, 02:00:00 GMT). Koch houses. Birth data: from Hillary Clinton.

The list of personal planets results in the following distribution of elements:

Hillary Clinton		
PLANET	SIGN	ELEMENT
☉ Sun	♏ Scorpio	Water
☽ Moon	♓ Pisces	Water
☿ Mercury	♏ Scorpio	Water
♀ Venus	♏ Scorpio	Water
♂ Mars	♌ Leo	Fire
♃ Jupiter	♐ Sagittarius	Fire
♄ Saturn	♌ Leo	Fire
Dominant Element		Water
Missing Element		Air and Earth
Searching-Image		Air (♂) and Water (☉)

A look at the horoscopes of Hillary and Bill Clinton should illustrate this searching-image conflict. (See Charts 1 and 2, pages 33 and 34.)

While there are no planets in water signs in Bill Clinton's horoscope, this element is strikingly strong in his wife's horoscope, meaning that she complements him in the best way. On the other hand, he can give her the air that she's missing, as well as a bit of earth.

The searching-image conflict now arises from the situation that Bill Clinton obviously looked for a woman with a strong water emphasis, yet his inner femininity has imparted a different image of a woman to him. In his case, this is a mixture of air and earth since his Venus ($\female$) is located in the air sign of Libra ($\libra$) and his Moon ($\leftmoon$) in the earth sign of Taurus ($\taurus$). As a result, he will sooner or later have become irritated by, and most likely have reproached Hillary about, her lack of straightforwardness and an uncompromising approach (earth) and not being as clear and diplomatic or as carefree (air) as his anima makes him believe a woman should be.

In the reverse direction, things are not as crass since, with his Mars in Leo ($\mars$/$\leo$), Bill Clinton can easily correspond to the fiery portion of Hillary's searching image with its many fire planets. In contrast, he lacks the water quality that is also part of her searching image on the basis of her Scorpio Sun ($\odot$/$\scorpio$). In this respect, she will certainly have accused him on more than one occasion of lacking in depth, intuitive understanding, sureness of instinct, and other water qualities.[3]

There are naturally also cases in which the path to a relationship runs differently. Then the partner is truly and lastingly experienced as the personification of the soul image. Astrologically, this corresponds to an extensive harmonization of the searching-image planets of one's own horoscope with the same planets in the partner's horoscope. But as good as this may sound, and as much as these relationships may be praised in some books on astrology, they are lacking in something quite decisive. In more precise terms, these people have not yet found what they are missing. They lack the complementation through the missing element and thereby also frequently lack the opposing tension that we need in order to clash with it and get the best out of ourselves.

All this doesn't mean that relationships must fundamentally be dramatic, or that it would be naive and pointless to strive for a harmonious life together. Yet, particularly in difficult phases, it is extraordinarily helpful to perceive the basic meaning and significance of the conflicts inherent to almost every relationship, the conflict between the searching image that we

---

[3] In this and similar examples, we should always keep in mind that the problems that these two have with each other are not necessarily identical with what the media reports about them.

carry within us as the anima or animus and the person with whom we prefer to link ourselves because he or she embodies what we lack. The following section makes it clear that this isn't really a dirty trick of fate or a mean prank by Creation, but rather that a very significant portion of our process of maturation lies within the solution of this conflict.

The Development of Anima and Animus

B ecoming aware of and developing the anima and animus is important because these archetypal forces can cause many problems on the purely unconscious level, or even consciously when they are poorly integrated. It is as if they bother us and lead us into conflicts until we become aware of them and recognize them as inner persons. Typical anima problems that men have are moodiness, moaning and sulking, pompousness, and the capricious sensitivity of the prima donna who knows how to tyrannize his entire world by being constantly insulted. A woman's animus problems are often displayed as thought processes that do not penetrate through to the solution of a problem, getting stuck in the description of the problem, or concentrating on proving that this problem will never be solved. Calculated pessimism, suffering from life, frequently being unhappy, and even attacks of depression, are the consequences. Another typical characteristic of the animus are those opinions that are dressed up as theses, and recited with a metallic ring to the voice in a discussion or debate. Replies frequently lack inner coherence, and are reminiscent of broadly spread attacks that don't sound like specific replies to the statements being made.

As long as the animus or anima are undeveloped, we will just have a biased and distorted image of the other sex. Despite this fact, almost every man believes he knows what a woman is; in the same manner, there is hardly a woman who questions her image of a real man. Particularly in partnerships (but not just here), we tend to make ourselves an image of reality and overlook the reality behind this picture. We are absolutely convinced that we know what our true partner is like. We even go as far as to hold up our inner picture as objective, while claiming loudly that we are only dealing with reality. We very rarely become aware of the fact that we underestimate, violate, and do injustice to other people when we maintain this inner image.

Perhaps this human tendency is the basis for the Old Testament ban on making an image of "anything that is in the heaven above, or that is in the earth beneath, or that is in the water under the earth."[1] This prohibition is still so much alive in the Islamic faith that few devout Muslims will allow their photographs to be taken. The picture that we make of other people all too easily becomes a fixed pattern into which we want to force them. The

[1]Exodus 20.4

more we believe in the misconception that the other person is more or less like ourselves, the more likely we are to engage in this behavior. Even if it's emphasized time and again that each individual is different, we give little thought to what this actually means. How different people really are, how unique they are, can be shown through astrology. The horoscope illustrates the individual character of each human being. The astrological chart can let us know the differences and no one can ignore these differences.

In order to truly comprehend the other sex in its different nature, it is necessary to develop our own inner opposite sexuality. As long as animus and anima are effective only within the unconscious mind, we will never do justice to our partners but will only perceive our own projections of this person. Only with the gradual increase of consciousness do we slowly recognize more and more of how our partners actually are. We can learn to differentiate between him or her and the image that we have had up to now. When our inner "searching image" begins to develop as a further step toward consciousness we can grow beyond the biased constriction of our initial perceptions and begin to comprehend and value the other sex in its complete state of being different from us. This step toward consciousness is incredibly significant. Anything outside of our consciousness remains unexpressed and we don't recognize it, or we completely overlook it until perhaps one day it slowly dawns on us and becomes clear to us. Then we start to see something in the "proper light"; we begin to comprehend, we can begin to recognize and value its individuality and intrinsic worth.

That this inner confrontation can bear fruit far beyond the bounds of the relationship is illustrated by the following thought. For the feminine aspect, the human being is always at the focus of attention. This is why the feminine aspect within us can never understand why someone (a man) would respond to a cause or principle. However, the masculine aspect within us feels that structure and order are threatened when important principles are not carried out uncompromisingly and their observation is not supervised. Seen in this light, a mature person would be someone who unites both aspects within himself or herself. This person would know how to live with strict consistency (because of the cause) and merciful leniency (for the sake of the individual) to the proper degree in his or her life.

Only when we can deeply approve of and positively experience how both sexes are fiery, earthy, airy, and watery in their own individual ways, without anyone having an exclusive lease on one of these aspects as a personal domain, can we accept and also support our partner as he or she develops personal uniqueness. The opportunity to do this has certainly never been greater than today, at the beginning of the Age of Aquarius. At its heart is the androgynous individual, uniting the masculine and the feminine aspects as treasured human qualities.

As long as we—despite enlightenment and liberal ways of thinking—continue to believe within ourselves that men can actually get along quite well without the water world of feelings, or that women should at least leave the fire world of self-assertion, power to be authoratative, and claims to leadership to the men, if not the world of thought (air), then our inner opposite sexuality is still in its infancy, and we are still far away from true maturity. Among other things, this is expressed by granting each sex the freedom to experience and shape reality in its own way, or, put in other terms, to approach each element in its own way. What this actually means is explained in Table 5, which is certainly not meant to be a role restriction, but rather something to think about. The masculine manner described here is naturally open to the woman as well, just as a man can also choose the feminine approach. But if differentiating and setting limits are classified as qualities symbolically masculine, and we recognize the emphasis on what we have in common to be a feminine tendency, then we can very well experience the four elements and shape them in different ways from this perspective. One further distinctive feature would be equating something like the strength of

Table 5. How the Elements Relate.			
ELEMENT	MUTUAL LEVEL	MASCULINE APPROACH	FEMININE APPROACH
Fire	Will, ideals, goals, enthusiasm	The pioneer, fighting spirit, competition, conquest, rivalry	Creativity and dance; enjoying mutual interests
Earth	Body, fertility	Safeguarding what has been achieved; limiting, protecting	Tilling fertile ground; taking care of people and things
Air	Mind, perception	Causal thinking, analysis of detail	Analogous thinking, perception of the whole
Water	Soul, world of emotions, intuition	Artistic expression; willingness to help	Sureness of instinct; healing power, caring

the masculine directed toward the outside with the extroverted attitude, while the feminine would correspond to the powers that are introverted, inwardly directed, and active in secrecy.

This model has an interesting parallel in C. G Jung's typology, for he differentiated between an extroverted (outwardly directed masculine) and an introverted (inwardly directed feminine) form of expression for each of the four basic characters.

The four basic aspects of the masculine and feminine can also be naturally described on the collective level as archetypal representatives of fire, earth, air, and water. In the process, they show themselves in primordial images that—like all inner images—have a light side and a dark opposite pole. Tables 6 and 7 show these four elemental forms of expression of the feminine and the masculine as basic aspects of the anima and animus.

In order to understand how significant the development of anima and animus is for a relationship, consider the example of a woman who, as a result of her maturation process, has become aware of her wholeness and the four

Table 6. The Four Elemental Aspects of the Anima.				
PERSON	FIRE	EARTH	AIR	WATER
Archetype	Amazon	Mother	Lorelei	Sphinx
Characteristic	Temperament	Steadfastness	Lightness	Devotion
Light	Energetic	Clever	Wide-Awake	Sensitive
Shadow	Hurtful	Hardened	Untenable	Moody
Quality	Strength of will	Vigor	Inventiveness	Intuition
Problem	Lack of tact	Inflexible	Too mental	Hypersensitive
Opens Eyes For	What's positive	Reality	The light side	The Soul
Mythological Figure	Artemis	Demeter	Athena	The Muses
Type	Wild	Practical	Intellectual	Mysterious

THE TWO CENTERS OF CONFLICT 41

aspects of her femininity—the Amazon, the Mother, the Intellectual, and the Sphinx—within herself and is so well developed that she can appear in each of these four facets and express them.

If this woman now meets a man who still has an underdeveloped or atrophied anima, which at best lets him perceive two aspects of a woman, let's say fire and earth, then this man will perceive her as a being with whom he can do many different kinds of things (fire), who is available for some sensual pleasures (earth), but he won't see that she also has an intellectual side (air) and gives and seeks emotional depth (water). This woman will naturally tell him sooner or later that she really likes to go skiing (fire) with him and to bed (earth) with him, but that she only really feels partially seen, understood, and accepted by him when he doesn't relate to her emotional depth (water), or that he has no use for her mind (air). But as long as his anima hasn't developed these aspects, he actually doesn't even know what she's talking about, or why this is so important to her. He's satisfied with experiencing her fiery

Table 7. The Four Elemental Aspects of the Animus.			
PERSON	FIRE	EARTH	AIR	WATER
Arthetype	Warrior	Shepherd	Scholar	Magician
Characteristic	Self-confidence	Responsibility	Cleverness	Emotional insensitivity
Light	Courageous	Protective	Ingenious	Understanding
Shadow	Ruthless dare-devil	Incorrigible jackass	Smart-alecky know-it-all	Greasy rogue
Quality	Strength of will	Energy	Inventiveness	Imagination
Problem	Unpredictable	Inflexible	Noncommittal	Unreliable
Strives For	Breakthrough	Materialization	Freedom	Depth
Mythological Figure	Prometheus	Pan	Hermes	Poseidon
Type	Athlete	Pragmatist	Intellectual	Artist

and earthy characteristics. If his anima doesn't develop any additional aspects, then he cannot perceive his partner in her entirety. Until he does, he will simply be lacking in perception, and thereby in appreciation for these additional, feminine aspects. Because of this he will consider these qualities dispensable in his partner—and ultimately, in all other women.

For this reason, the precondition for a mature, lively, and harmonious partnership is that both partners develop their unconscious opposite sexuality, meaning that the man must become conscious of his anima and the woman of her animus. These developed human beings give us the feeling of being truly understood and accepted, and when we each have begun to develop this kind of maturity we are able to see our partner in his or her own individuality and are thus able to love unconditionally.

So how does the development of the anima and animus occur? According to Emma Jung, the character of these two figures is determined not only by the respective disposition for the opposite sex, "it is conditioned by the experience each person has had in the course of his or her life with representatives of the other sex . . ."[2] At this point, the fundamental significance of the searching-image conflict is revealed. The disposition of the opposite sex that Emma Jung speaks about shows itself, as previously described, in the position of the signs of a person's searching-image planets. Because of our tendency to form a bond with a partner who may personify our missing element but doesn't (or only partially) personify our searching image, a conflict arises in which we clash until, in the best case, a light goes on within us, meaning that we become aware of something. The searching-image conflict offers us the opportunity to crack the previously constricted image, the anima or animus experiences an episode of development, and our consciousness of the nature of the opposite sex is enriched. This is an opportunity for growth—but not a guarantee!

We can try to solve the searching-image conflict in another way. For example, we can insist on our narrow perspective while at the same time doing everything to force our partner into our much too constricted fixed pattern. Or we can separate from this person in disappointment and indignation, and continue to search for the right partner, for that someone who finally is exactly like our presently naive and undeveloped searching image whispers he or she should be.

The purpose of the conflict gives us new impulse for inner growth. Without the conflict, the animus and anima would hardly have an opportunity to develop, since we would then simply become involved with a person

---

[2]Emma Jung, *Animus and Anima* (Dallas: Spring/Analytical Psychology Club of New York, 1957, 1972, 1978), pp. 1–2.

who reflects our searching-image planets. However, becoming the mature partner of a mature human being would then be impossible since it is only the conflict that tears us out of the paradisiacal simplicity and stimulates our growth. It would also be just as unlikely that we could mature within such a relationship without the danger of growing beyond the partner's narrow perceptive borders and thereby increasingly alienate him or her.

What can be done to support the development of the animus and anima? We don't need to search for situations that force us to learn and grow. Life provides us with adequate opportunities. The most essential factor can be found in observing what we experience in dealing with the opposite sex in a way that is attentive, alert, and open to new perceptions. Particularly important here is everything that bothers us, makes us insecure, causes us to get worked up time and again—everything for which we would like to send all men (or all women) to the Moon. Concealed behind these troubles and nuisances are usually valuable perceptions that are waiting to be had. Just like the enchanted prince and princess of the fairy tale, they are waiting for release. But as long as they are in the unconscious mind pressing against our threshold of consciousness, we can only perceive them in a distorted, bewitched figure, and we cannot truly comprehend their significance. This is why they draw attention to themselves by leading us into conflicts as their only chance of reaching our consciousness. Once they have succeeded at leaping over the threshold, they become conscious and immediately show themselves in a different light. This larger, more complete picture naturally also includes the shadow aspects we have previously experienced, which will now lose their "absolute" claim and move from the center of our perception to the place they actually deserve. This frees our perspective for the actual, valuable meaning of what we had previously fought against, despised, and feared.

In addition to all the considerations of expediency, this appears to be a very important reason why marriage is entered into as a bond for life and considered to be indissoluble in most cultures. Since becoming whole is the life goal of the soul, and this goal cannot be achieved without an active confrontation with the opposite sex as the opposite pole, marriage is considered indissoluble. Otherwise, many people would be quick to take to their heels in the phase of disappointment at the end of infatuation, or when the searching-image conflict becomes clear. However, the solid framework offered by the bond for life at least guarantees that both poles remain in contact, that disappointments are talked about, and conflicts carried out, knowing that both people will probably clash with each other, and therefore have the opportunity to change and grow as a result of these confrontations.

However, when relationships become increasingly noncommittal, and marriages everywhere end in divorce, the question naturally arises as to what this means in terms of the compulsion for confrontation. We could see an undesirable development in our culture and complain that everything is much worse today than it was in earlier times. We can also trust the change and realize that profound changes mean something because they correspond to a new consciousness and contain a new set of tasks. In this case, this could mean that the need to have confrontations, which the indissoluble marriage brought with it, has been superseded today by the *freedom* to have confrontations. We may not understand the meaning of this freedom, or know how to deal with it, but that doesn't refute the supposition. In order to truly understand this train of thought, we must take a brief look at the last two centuries.

Since the French Revolution (1789), we have broken out of the narrow structures of the Middle Ages and have achieved a freedom that has never been experienced before. For this new freedom to be suitably put to use, a greater consciousness of the meaning and purpose of life is required. While people of the Middle Ages were satisfied with the "pray and work" task in life, and religious doubts were countered by religious dogmas, individuals of modern times demand other, more personal answers. The narrowness of medieval doctrine robbed us of the air to breathe and we now feel the urge to experience personal meaning in our lives. At the same time, the face of astrology is also changing. Astrology was almost exclusively used as a tool for discovering the best moments in time and for prediction during the Middle Ages; today people want different information. Prediction is only reliable when the framework conditions and the possibilities of "living an astrological constellation" are very narrow and limited. In view of the virtually enormous freedom of development available to modern individuals, the purely prognostic medieval astrology was bound to fail and increasingly fall into disrepute. When things looked as bad as possible for it, so that hardly anyone could take it seriously anymore, it entered into a new marriage in the middle of the 20th century. It united with psychology, a child of the 20th century, winning back not only its credibility in the process, but also finding a fundamentally different set of tasks. Instead of presenting people with an inevitable fate, the horoscope now shows us the nature of our tasks in life. Instead of telling us whether we have good or bad aspects, it provides us with a consciousness of our situation and lets us perceive what the "bad" aspects are about, what they are good for, and what we can learn from them.

This knowledge, for which we can thank psychology and psychological astrology, increasingly opens up insights into the depths, and to the indispensable meaning of conflicts, which had earlier been endured as God-given in the best case, but never truly understood. If we take this knowledge to heart and also become aware of our responsibility, we actually no longer need to be forced into a confrontation with the other sex through an indissoluble marriage. Considered in this light, the significance of marriage is changing.

If life is concerned with developing the four aspects of inner opposite sexuality in the encounter with the opposite sex, the question naturally arises as to why there aren't four different relationships, since that may be the only way to experience the quality of the four elements in the opposite sex. In general, this question can't be answered with "yes" or "no." There is obviously the possibility of experiencing and developing the various aspects within one single monogamous relationship. However, the precondition for this is that both partners, either voluntarily or forced by the compulsion of outer circumstances, take the alchemical formula of higher development to heart, known as the principle of "dissolve and bind." Whenever two people stick to each other in an indissoluble way, no individual development can take place. But when they let go of each other time and again, or must let go because of their living situation or other circumstances, and then find their way back to each other again, form a bond, and then leave each other again, and then form a new bond, each partner has the opportunity to develop further facets of his or her individuality during the periods of letting go, becoming a bit more himself or herself, and thereby reflecting another aspect to the partner the next time they bind again. This dissolving and binding naturally doesn't mean permanently questioning the relationship, constantly separating from each other, or being noncommittal in some other way. Instead, it means accepting other people completely as they are, not nailing partners down to the picture that we have created of them, but leaving them as they are, letting them continue to become what they are, and not only permitting them their own continuing development, but also supporting them in it. This is all much easier said than done!

Perhaps we believe today that we can avoid some of the related difficulties if we increasingly understand the dissolving and binding in literal terms and actually dissolve one relationship and enter into a new one. But whether we actually spare ourselves problems is an open question. However, this path can also lead us onward, in so far as we take it consciously. The important thing to understand is how past relationships have taught us what they were "good" for. In this context, C. G. Jung spoke of a functional relationship and meant this to be a relationship that becomes exhausted as soon as it has fulfilled its function. If, for example, this function is a step in the direction of becoming conscious for one or both of the partners, then the excitement between the two dies out the moment that this step has been taken. In addition, such a relationship can no longer be kept alive, even with the best of will.

While looking at these considerations, some readers will say that they wish for nothing more than to take this step of growth within the life of a relationship, but that a suitable partner is always lacking since, unfortunately, there are no longer any real men (or real women) in this world and because all of them are just . . . (and then some sort of platitude follows). Anyone who complains in this manner should be reminded that each person always finds the relationship for which he or she is truly ready (since that's the only thing that works). Truly willing means more than just wishing to get out of the current situation, longing for something other than the state that one suffers at the moment. This means opening up without a guarantee and being vulnerable in the process. But, above all, it means dealing with the person to whom life has led us instead of arrogantly looking beyond him or her to an unreachable horizon where all the wonderful people appear to be romping around. It's clear that we would immediately open up if we could only catch this person's attention. But someone who isn't available, who sits in a fortress and waits for the prince or princess to come sometimes has to wait patiently, like Sleeping Beauty, for 100 years. This isn't a problem for a fairy-tale child, but it is terribly long for a human life.

In summary, it can be said that if the two conflicts so typical of relationships are properly understood and lived out, they make an essential contribution to becoming whole. The phenomenon that we bond with an individual who personifies the element that we lack makes us conscious of our Achilles' heel, and offers us the opportunity of getting to know this element. When we get in touch with this element, we can balance out our errors, heal our sore spots, and achieve a holistic consciousness.

The searching-image conflict that this kind of growth brings—that the person who "elementally" complements us doesn't (or only partially) correspond with our searching image—pressures us to expand our searching-image and develop the anima or animus as the feminine quality within the man and the masculine quality within the woman. Even if we would like to have things differently, this just happens to be our nature since "nothing changes without necessity," said C. G. Jung, "least of all the human personality."[3]

---

[3]C. G. Jung, *Development of Personality*, Basic Work, vol. 9, p. 13.

The Relationship Quartet

If we consider the animus and anima to be an inner person, then every relationship has four actors appearing in it respectively: the man with his inner woman and the woman with her inner man (see figure below). C. G. Jung described this relationship quartet as the *marriage quarternio*.[1] Each of the "persons" involved in this can come into contact with any other member.

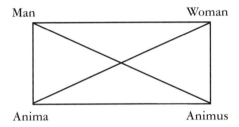

On the conscious level, the man and the woman encounter each other. This is the level at which we best know ourselves and can most clearly perceive our partner. It is therefore considered to be the least complicated.[2] On the level of experiencing the self, the man becomes familiar with his inner femininity (anima) while the woman encounters her animus, her inner masculinity. But there is also a relationship between the man and the woman's animus, as well as between the woman and the man's anima. Through this axis, each of the two can win the others for him- or herself. Whenever a woman senses the inner beloved of a man and tries to personify the anima, he will become soft, melt, and let himself be wrapped around her finger. The same applies in the opposite direction as well. The woman's animus can become an "ally" for the man. If he knows how to personify this inner image in his appearance and his powers of assertion, but above all in the way that he thinks and expresses himself, he will deeply impress the woman.

Of course, this isn't meant to say that both partners should betray their own uniqueness and from this time on fool the other person by constantly

---

[1] C. G. Jung, *The Practice of Psychotherapy*, vol. 16, *The Collected Works of C. G. Jung*, Bollingen Series XX, R. F. C. Hull, trans. (Princeton: Princeton University Press, 1954), ¶425.
[2] In transactional analysis, this corresponds to the adult level.

miming his or her searching-image as much as possible! The issue here is actually quite different. In most relationships, a paralyzing poison creeps in sooner or later—established habits! Whenever we believe that we have a right to the other person or the right to demand something in particular from him or her, it is time to remember an important principle: we have no right to any another human being, not even our companion in life. However, we may win this person over to our cause and are permitted to do so. This happens most easily—but not always and not exclusively—when we turn to the anima or animus as our ally in the other person. This background emphasizes once again how important it is that the anima and animus are differentiated and developed. It's understandable that a mature individual will not always enjoy personifying a very simple and half-baked searching-image in order to win over the partner.

The most difficult level in the quartet is the encounter between the anima and the animus, especially when these inner forces continue to be lived in a completely unconscious and undeveloped manner. Then the animus will draw the sword of his power and the anima will spray the poison of deception and seduction. Although the fire of passion also burns on this level, bringing the people together and welding them to each other, dangerous and no less passionate entanglements also lurk here. "One of the most typical expressions of both figures," commented C. G. Jung, "is something that has long been called 'animosity.' The anima causes illogical moods, and the animus produces irritating platitudes and unreasonable opinions."[3]

It's not difficult to recognize the issues that take shape sooner or later in most relationships. Their most outstanding feature is that, despite the most vehement skirmishes and conflicts, they don't change one fraction of an inch. Whenever the provocative topic arises, a small and insignificant remark is often enough to start a new war and everything is on the line once again. According to the temperaments involved, it can be fought in a heated, ice-cold, silent, or tearful way. In time, at the first signal both partners go into the more and more familiar trenches of war as an increasingly foregone conclusion so that the old battle starts a new round. In this process, there is soon no argument that hasn't long been said and no accusation that hasn't been made a hundred times. "Anyone who still has the humor to objectively listen to the conversation would probably be extremely astonished at the overwhelming amount of platitudes, inappropriately applied truisms, phrases from newspapers and novels, vulgar insults, and shocking displays of illogical thought," is how C. G. Jung characterized this hopeless level of commu-

---

[3] C. G. Jung, *Psychology and Religion: East and West,* vol. 11, *The Collected Works of C. G. Jung,* Bollingen Series XX, R. F. C. Hull, trans. (Princeton: Princeton University Press, 1958), ¶48.

nication and added: "It is a dialogue which, irrespective of its participants, is repeated millions of times in all the languages of the world and always remains essentially the same."[4]

Whenever we participate in this kind of conflict, we should keep in mind that two unconscious forces are battling with each other. Neither of them is interested in insight; neither of them is willing to make an honest compromise. Because each is 100 percent certain that they are completely and exclusively right, neither can give in; both just want to win, and this is why nothing works out. Even if we realize how completely pointless these wars are and how good it would be to avoid them, it still isn't easy to translate this insight into action the next time. The only promising method consists of immediately bailing out of the discussion; the best thing to do is change to another level, something like: "Hey, how about going to the movies tonight?" It's obvious that the other person won't immediately break off the argument that is just getting started because of this. After all, the tried-and-true arguments are freshly polished and waiting to be used. Instead, he or she will—according to temperament—swear, sigh, be cynical, or ask silently with an ice-cold glance: "How did you come up with the idea of going to the movies, just when we . . . ?"

At this point it is extremely important to remain very clear and unwaveringly decided to not continue the battle in any case. Despite all the insight, this is much more difficult each time than we believe. Our partner in the conflict will obviously first press our most sensitive buttons to see if we actually do want to climb into the ring, whereby all the enlightened resolutions about definitely wanting to do things differently this time are blown away once again.

This doesn't mean to imply that the best way to cope with conflicts is to successfully suppress them! The issue at hand here is sparing ourselves of some of the quarrels that are not only completely hopeless and purely destructive, but which also exhaust and wear down a relationship in time. The differences of opinion that start the argument rolling should be calmly clarified and settled at a later point in time.

Lived in the more mature form, the relationship quartet resembles a balanced play of forces, as it is familiar in the form of the Tai Chi symbol from the Far East, uniting two principles that each bear the heart of the other within themselves. This also illustrates the connection between man and woman, whose unconscious minds form the pole of the opposite sex as the anima and animus.

---

[4]C. G. Jung, *Aion*, vol. 9, II, of *The Collected Works of C. G. Jung*, Bollingen Series XX, R. F. C. Hull, trans. (Princeton: Princeton University Press, 1959), ¶29.

The Tai Chi symbol (☯) connects yin and yang, the feminine and the masculine force, both of which bear the heart of the opposite pole within themselves.

PART II

SEARCHING-IMAGE
and SELF-IMAGE
in the HOROSCOPE

The Relationship Quartet
Seen in Astrological Terms

Relationship conflicts start within ourselves. If we recognize the parties to the conflict as inner persons of our own emotional landscape and understand their problems with and affections for each other, then familiar relationship disputes suddenly appear in a new light. If we comprehend how our inner persons love and hate each other, form alliances, and contradict each other, then we no longer wonder about some of the inconsistencies in our relationship. And when we find new solutions for our inner contradictions, then we will also overcome the corresponding crises in our relationship life.

According to the original teachings of C. G. Jung, the shadow of the human being is shown on the dream level in the form of someone of the same sex. The anima, on the other hand, appears in the dreams of a man as a mysterious female stranger, while the animus usually shows up in the dreams of a woman as a number of men, such as a council of elders. Today, as a result of their research, leading Jungians[1] have discovered that this concept is too constricting. Instead, they assume that the animus and anima belong to the "inner person" of *every* human being, and therefore an animus is also at work on the unconscious level in a man and an anima is effective within a woman.

We have a changed understanding of the shadow to thank for this enrichment of our inner soul images. The dream figures of the same sex, with which the shadow has been associated up to now, is interpreted by Jungians today as the animus of the man or the anima of the woman, while the shadow corresponds to all the themes and images experienced by the ego as foreign or hostile. Examples of typical figures appearing as the animus or anima on the dream level are: king and queen, brother and sister, the unfamiliar boy, the unknown girl, mysterious strangers, such as water-nymphs, vagabonds, wayfarers, or the wise, old man or woman.[2] There is also an expanded understanding of the function of the animus and anima. They play a central role when it comes to detaching us from our parental images and helping us become mature adults.

---

[1]Such as Joseph Campbell and Verena Kast.

[2]This also shows a new understanding by the current Jungians. The wise old man or woman is no longer seen to be the archetypal image of the self, but as all symbols that overcome opposites.

This more comprehensive and newer concept resembles the picture also depicted of human beings by astrology. In his or her horoscope, every human being has four personal planets, which correspond to the "relationship quartet," so that this not only takes place *between* people, but also *within* each individual human being at the same time. These are the masculine planets of the Sun (☉) and Mars (♂), as well as the feminine planets of the Moon (☽) and Venus (♀), of which the Sun and Moon correspond to the inner parental image while the anima is initially personified by Venus and the animus by Mars. The inner "relationship quartet" is illustrated by Table 8.

The important thing to know about this is that the anima and animus, as archetypal forces, is that they separate us from our parental images and let us become mature adults. In pictorial terms, they are concerned with becoming mature. The hot-blooded Mars boy (♂) must win the prudent fatherly power (☉) if he wants to do justice to the animus function as an intellect-engendering principle. The same applies to the connection between the girl (♀) and the mother (☽) so that the anima doesn't just function in a partly cool and coquettish, partly moody manner, but also in its mature, caring way, as one of the forces that guides human beings. This is why the detachment from our "parents" involves the true parents only in a minor way. At best, the outer level is a reflection and a gauge for how far the much more significant confrontation with the inner parental images has flourished.

How important this step is may be illustrated by astrology, which recognizes the inner parents as the Sun and Moon within the horoscope. In childhood, these planets (luminaries) can be compared to glasses through which we perceive our parents, completely apart from how they actually are. This is why significant statements about how an individual experiences his or her parents can be made on the basis of the person's horoscope, without even looking at the parents' horoscope. However, since the Sun and Moon in the horoscope of an adult primarily make important statements about the nature of his or her *own* being, the two more significant planets cannot just be experienced as parental images. Instead, we are meant to become mature and increasingly personify these placements in ourselves. At least in terms

Table 8. The Inner Relationship Quartet.	
MASCULINE SIDE	FEMININE SIDE
Parental Level: ☉ Sun—Father	Parental Level: ☽ Moon—Mother
Animus: ♂ Mars—Boy	Anima: ♀ Venus—Girl

Table 9. From "Little Man" to Man—From "Little Woman" to Woman.						
☉ Sun Father King	Fatherly Level				Motherly Level	☽ Moon Mother Queen
+	+	Mature Man	Mature Woman		+	+
♂ Mars Boy Prince	"Little Man" Level				"Little Woman" Level	♀ Venus Girl Pincess

of the same sex, this occurs somewhat on its own with increasing age, particularly when we ourselves become fathers or mothers. However, frequently enough, even the development of our own gender behavior gets stuck in a half-baked step, to make no mention of developing the inner opposite sex aspect. And as long as this is the case, the basic psychological rule applies that we initially have two possibilities in our relationship life: either we imitate the marriage of our parents, or we do exactly the opposite. In the process, it doesn't matter whether we do the same or the opposite because both of these still occur in childlike dependence on the role model. Only when we have found a third way as a new, personal possibility of dealing with each other in the partnership have we separated, become independent, and grown to be a free adult.

How can this developmental model be understood astrologically? In pictorial terms, it looks like this: the Sun (☉) corresponds to the father, the Moon (☽) to the mother, Venus (♀) is the beauty, the fair one, the graceful temptress, and Mars (♂) is the boy, the hothead, the conqueror. In a fairy tale, these four figures always appear as the king, queen, princess, and prince. And just as the fairy tale deals with how the prince and princess finally find each other, and then become the king and queen themselves, this is also how it is in real life. A fully-grown man can be seen as someone who unites the prince (♂) and the king (☉) within himself and turns from a "little man" into a real man; while the "little woman" turns into a mature woman if she understands how to combine the princess (♀) and the queen (☽) into one image in her life (Table 9).

Table 10. Male and Female Characteristics.		
	FATHERLY CHARACTERISTICS	MOTHERLY CHARACTERISTICS
Light	Willingness to be responsible; stability, prudence, kindness, strength of will, firmness	Gentleness, mercy, caring, devotion, understanding, forgiveness
Twilight	Hardening	Fickleness
Shadow	Merciless strictness, doggedness, tyranny	Moodiness, scheming, creating emotional dependency
	CHARACTERISTICS OF THE "LITTLE MAN"	CHARACTERISTICS OF THE "LITTLE WOMAN"
Light	Desire to conquer, independence, spontaneity	Tempting, inspiring, brightening and refining
Twilight	Prowling around	Seductive flirting
Shadow	Brutality, roughness, audacious, inconsiderate	Falseness, slyness, the *femme fatale*

In order to develop from a "little man" into a man and a "little woman" into a woman, the themes of the parental level must be connected with those of the youthful level. Table 10 shows which qualities are related to these individual concepts.

A mature person is someone who has not only succeeded in combining both aspects in his or her own gender behavior, but has additionally united the aspects of the opposite sex into a searching image—someone who has developed the entire inner quartet. The imbalances that can result when even one aspect of the inner quaternity remains underdeveloped are illustrated by the following scenarios. However, the behavior patterns described as typical here should only be seen as examples. There are naturally also many other possible forms of expression.

If you would like to take a look at the following descriptions of the various aspects in the horoscope, remember that the horoscope is lived out at a level beyond every statement possibility. It's therefore impossible to say to what degree a person will develop, or has developed, the quality of a planet. It's only possible to recognize whether or not the development takes place easily or with difficulty, but not whether the person is even striving for it at all. This means that—independent of the aspects of the four planets discussed here—the youthful side will most likely be lived in a very air-oriented horoscope or when Uranus is strongly placed (for example, at the Ascendant), while an adult attitude can be assumed early on, perhaps even too early, in a very earthy horoscope, or in one with a strongly positioned Saturn.

The Masculine Side

Mars urges the young man to conquer a woman. In contrast, his Sun shows the manner and the power with which he takes responsibility for the relationship that results.

A strongly developed Mars and a weakly developed Sun represent a man who is a professional "son." He always remains a boy, doesn't want to take on any responsibility, and, as a result, isn't taken really seriously by anyone. But the reverse constellation has its problems as well. If there is a lack of Mars power, the man lacks in punch, in assertiveness, in his willingness to deal with conflicts, perhaps even in potency. With a strong Sun, he will then be the fatherly friend, a type of "nice guy" who shows understanding for everything and everyone but who is less of a partner for his wife than a father. Which is why it's no problem to allow her to call him "daddy" in front of anyone.

Strongly developed Mars ♂, weakly developed Sun ☉

Weakly developed Mars ♂, strongly developed Sun ☉

In the horoscope, Venus is primarily a symbol of a man's anima, his inner searching-image that tempts him. Whenever he encounters a woman who personifies this image, or who may stimulate it in some other way, desire awakens within him. His Moon is the expression of his mother image. If he doesn't know how to unite Venus and the Moon into an overall image and recognize and develop his anima in this expanded image, there will be a disruption of his relationship life as a consequence of the tension between the inner mother and the inner beloved.

When there is a strong Moon position and a weakly developed Venus, this can be seen by how he actually remains faithful to his mother and—insofar as he doesn't uncompromisingly avoid other women completely—tends to treat his wife like a sister, whereby it's obvious

Strongly developed Moon ☽, weakly developed Venus ♀

that she must obey his mother's instructions. If he brings in more of his own fatherly Sun side, then he will wish that she becomes a mother herself as quickly as possible so that they can imitate his parents' marriage together. Above all, when there is a weak Mars level, such a marriage will soon be quite drab. If, in contrast, his Mars youth side is more strongly characterized, he will act in a rebellious, uncouth, or overpoweringly know-it-all manner toward his wife, just as he had done with his mother during adolescense.

With a strong Sun ☉

With a strong Mars ♂

If the Venus side of the man is more strongly developed and the motherly lunar qualities have remained underdeveloped, he will love his wife's girlish aspects and want her to remain like this forever. Her natural aging process can also irritate him, as well as the moment that she becomes a mother. If he has primarily developed his fatherly solar side, he will preferably have a father-daughter relationship; this type of marriage is typical of patriarchy, in which the woman is not permitted to grow up and shouldn't develop any individuality of her own; instead, she remains reduced to being the personification of the man's anima. If, on the other hand, the man remains a boy lacking in prudence (☉) who solely identifies his masculinity with Mars potency, then he will love women, but always more than one. He will not understand why he should be true to one when there are so many of them. Even if he becomes involved in an apparently committed relationship despite this, he will turn his partner into his "mother" sooner or later, for he will probably demand, in all seriousness, that she understand that he "must" be unfaithful to her time and again. As an adolescent boy he was allowed to ask, and had to ask, his own mother to understand that he was interested in other women. But this makes an infantile and grotesque impression when an aging boy forces his partner into the mother role by expecting the same understanding from her. This sometimes happens when his wife actually becomes a mother and therefore better serves as a projection for his own devalued Moon. As long as his step toward maturity, which unites his Venus and Moon into one anima image, has not yet taken place, this change of roles by the wife causes his Venus to become

Strongly developed Venus ♀, weakly developed Moon ☽

With a strong Sun ☉

With a strong Mars ♂

"free." So when his wife has a child, other women suddenly attract him and he actually doesn't understand why he shouldn't give in to this attraction.

The Feminine Side

Venus shows herself to be the temptress and—according to the sign—the coquette, the vamp, the aloof lady, the woman who wants to be courted, the source of inspiration, or simply the beauty who bestows her favors on the best man. In contrast, the Moon personifies the motherly side of the woman: her understanding, sensitive nature, a willingness to be there for other people, to look after, nourish, care for, as well as hold onto them, that sometimes borders on selflessness.

If the Venus side of the woman is strongly expressed, and the Moon is weak, she will enjoy the eternal game of love. She will like to flirt and do it with grace; she may even provocatively approach being desired and courted. Whether she does this as the cool beauty, the hot-blooded dancer, the sensual woman, or the devoted muse, it always remains a game in which beauty and eternal youth are the highest trump cards. But when one only knows the trump card, one must lose sooner or later. This is the configuration of the eternal daughter who recoils at the leap into being a mature woman, who doesn't develop any motherly qualities, and instead prefers to let herself be pampered by a "sugar daddy." The price of all this is never being taken seriously as an adult, self-determined woman. Instead of maturing, she wilts, and for the rest of her life always remains a girl in a body that constantly ages.

Strongly developed Venus ♀, weakly developed Moon ☽

In the reverse, when the Moon is strong and Venus is weak, there may be a lack of loveliness, charm, grace, and erotic excitement. Such a woman is the understanding friend who often maintains many friendships with both men and women, all of whom like to pour out their hearts to her and seek her understanding. Seen in this way, she often takes over this form of the mother role at an early age. But the desire to have children of her own as soon as possible is also typical of this configuration. The problem here is usually that although she is quite

Strongly developed Moon ☽, weakly developed Venus ♀

appreciated by her many friends, she isn't desired as a woman; even when a partnership comes about, she is easily pushed into the mother role described above, meaning that she should be understanding of her partner's unfaithfulness.

In a woman's horoscope, Mars is primarily the symbol of her animus, her inner masculine nature. Whenever a man personifies this image, he thereby stimulates her searching-image. Whether she desires him, fights against him, or despises him as a result can be seen in how well Mars is placed within the overall picture of her horoscope.[3] On the other hand, the Sun shows the fatherly aspect of her inner masculinity, its prudent, intellectual side. If she doesn't know how to develop both, then she will lack either in assertiveness (Mars ♂) or insight and mental power (Sun ☉). If she doesn't want to unite both aspects within herself, the result will be disruptions in her relationship life because she divides the male sex into young men and fathers or—put in more casual terms— into "bad boys" and "good daddies."

When the Sun is strongly developed and Mars is weak, she will always judge men according to her inner father image, valuing them above all for their generosity and cleverness, as well as their ability to personify security. She tends to experience the physical sexual nature of a man in an irritating way because it is taboo for the father. She prefers to seek this level—if at all—in forbidden adventures that inspire her imagination. If her Moon is in a strong position, she will quickly want to experience her partner as a father in order to personify the parental role strongly inherent to her nature. The erotic/sexual excitement between them may fade quite quickly, especially when he says "mommy" to her for the first time. *(margin: Strongly developed Sun ☉, weakly developed Mars ♂)* *(margin: With a strong Moon ☽)*

If, on the other hand, Venus is strongly developed, then she may be the typical "daddy's girl." To get her partner to fulfill her wishes, she will seduce him with all her charm and eroticism, but only flirtatiously put on a show without fulfilling the wordless promises she has made. As long as she sees the man in the role of father, *(margin: With a strong Venus ♀)*

[3]For more on this topic, see the section called "The Inner Relationship" on page 192.

she feels "secure," since a father is not permitted any sexual infringements despite all of her daughterly arts of seduction. She will be all the more amazed, if not outraged, when her fatherly friend doesn't agree to this role but wants her to see him as a man.

With a strong Mars and a comparatively weak Sun, the woman finds a macho, brash, direct, and potent masculinity to be appealing. She loves the enigmatic boyishness in the man. Strength, courage, and initiative impress her, but she sees little of the man's maturity, doesn't really know how to appreciate it. If her Moon is strongly developed, she may tend toward a mother-son relationship. If so, then she may look for a partner she can take care of with love and a great deal of understanding, but who will play the boy role for the rest of his life. He is permitted to, and should, play the role of the hero for her, take risks for her sake, and try to do many things in which she indirectly participates, without having to do it herself. At the same time, she may treat him like a child, which eventually lets him become a "stupid old boy" with advancing age. On the other hand, if her Venus is more strongly developed, Beauty and the Beast encounter each other since she seeks the passionate relationship or loves the thrill of a forbidden affair. On this level, things will certainly be the hottest and most carefree, but also the least stable. Eternal young love counts here, a love that isn't permitted to mature and dies bit by bit with every symptom of aging, with every new wrinkle and gray hair.

Strongly developed Mars ♂, weakly developed Sun ☉

With a strong Moon ☽

With a strong Venus ♀

When we look at these imbalances, it becomes clear that development of our masculine and feminine qualities is an important step for maturity. If purely intellectual insight would suffice, this problem would certainly be quickly solved. But, unfortunately, it's not enough to understand the correlations. Instead, there is a great danger of falling prey to the illusion that the problem has already been overcome if we just perceive it or give it a fine-sounding name. Perceptions gained from books and conversations are certainly helpful. However, the necessary steps of development must be taken—in an active confrontation with the opposite sex.

A successful unification of the masculine/feminine parental level with the child level is illustrated on the tarot card "The Lovers" in the Crowley deck. It is the Holy Wedding; the wise old man gives the "relationship quartet" his blessing here, and the quaternity becomes whole. The king, queen, prince, and princess can be recognized as the four aspects of the searching-image and self-image in the horoscope of an individual. This is discussed in detail in the following section.

The Lovers. From the Crowley Thoth tarot deck. *The card "The Lovers" in the Tarot of Aleister Crowley shows the successful maturation step, the combination of the quarternity into a whole, with the image of the Holy Wedding.*

Masculine and Feminine Planets as Searching-Image or Self-Image

From the position of the masculine planets Mars (σ) and Sun ($\odot$), as well as the feminine planets Venus ($\circ$) and the Moon ($\mathcal{D}$), a person's individual searching-image or self-image can be read from the horoscope. This certainly doesn't exhaust the astrological significance of these four planets. However, this book is not concerned with showing the entire spectrum of their equivalents but solely with making visible their role as the searching-image or self-image within the partnership.

In a woman's horoscope, Venus ($\circ$) shows how she brings herself to a relationship as a young woman, while the Moon ($\mathcal{D}$) complements her feminine self-image with the aspect of the mature woman and shows how she expresses the motherly side of her personality. These two planets not only let us recognize how she feels as a woman but also how her self-image changes during the course of her life. On the one hand, based on the relationship between these two planets, we can read how the young woman views the mature woman, whether and how her feminine sense of self will change; on the other hand, aspects involving Venus and the Moon will clearly show increasing and decreasing values, strengths and weaknesses, problems and solutions that are connected with her role as a woman in the various phases of life.

A woman with a Cancer Venus ($\mathfrak{S}/\circ$) may want a family and children of her own at a very young age, but if her Moon is in Aquarius ($\mathcal{D}/\approx$), she may increasingly value independence in her role as a mother during her more mature years. A woman with Venus in Aries ($\circ/\Upsilon$) may experience herself as an Amazon, as a biker queen, or as a tomboy, but if her Moon is in Taurus ($\mathcal{D}/\forall$), her belligerent element and her willingness to engage in conflict will give way in time to her good-natured, peaceable, and pleasure-loving side. Additional information about how aspects work is discussed on page 183.

In a woman's horoscope, Mars (σ) and the Sun ($\odot$) correspond to the masculine side of the woman, her animus, which is initially experienced in a more or less conscious manner as her masculine searching-image. At the same time, Mars (σ) personifies the youthful side of the masculine, and the Sun ($\odot$) represents the fatherly aspect. In keeping with what has been previously said, we can naturally also read here how the two themes complement, contradict, or even appear to exclude each other.

By way of contrast, Mars (♂) in a man's horoscope shows how he approaches a woman as a young man and involves himself in the relationship, while the Sun (☉) expresses his own fatherly, mature masculinity. On the other hand, Venus (♀) and the Moon (☽) illustrate the feminine side of the man, his anima, which he more or less consciously experiences as his searching-image. Venus personifies the youthful aspect, and the Moon the motherly side.

Similar to what has been said about these planets in a woman's horoscope, the developmental themes can also be read in these configurations. This means that an Aries Mars (♂/♈) with a Capricorn Sun (♑/☉) will be a young hothead who turns into a man with a great deal of integrity, willingness to be responsible, and prudence in his mature years. A man with Mars in Pisces (♂/♓) and Sun in Leo (☉/♌) will move from being a rather shy youth to someone with more self-confidence as he matures.

On the basis of a diversity of horoscope factors—like positions of the houses and aspects in particular—the influence that the "youthful planets" Venus and Mars exercise on the searching-image or self-image can only be theoretically differentiated in terms of their coloration from the more "mature planets" of the Sun and Moon. We are generally unaware of our searching-image, and even our self-image, especially as young adults. These energies flow into each other and allow a masculine image to be created from Mars (♂) and the Sun (☉) and a feminine image from Venus (♀) and the Moon (☽). Keep in mind that the horoscope cannot tell us how mature or developed a person will be. For this reason it would not be productive to try to differentiate between the mature and immature forms while describing individual characters in the following sections. The twelve masculine and feminine characters are portrayed in their complexity, and readers will have to determine how the energy is being expressed.

Searching-Image and Self-Image— Projection or Self-Realization?

When we encounter our searching-image, this doesn't necessarily mean that we encounter this person with open arms. It very much depends upon how well—or how problematically—the theme of the searching-image is integrated into the rest of the horoscope. If we read that the Sagittarius Venus seeks the man of the world, this is simply because expansiveness and sophistication are Sagittarian qualities that open her heart. But if her horoscope shows a Cancer Mars, then her personal searching-image is the preserver of regional traditions who feels that there is no place like home, and has no idea what would make him go out into the world, or why he should travel to distant, unknown lands. It is therefore important to differentiate between what is good for a Sagittarius Venus and what special searching-image is shown in her horoscope.

Although a man with a Leo Venus looks for a classy woman, if the rest of his horoscope is completely dominated by the sign Virgo, he will naturally have enormous problems with her. On the one hand, he avoids the limelight in which she naturally prefers to bathe herself, but on the other hand it's obvious that he is constantly afraid he cannot afford her lifestyle—in his eyes totally exaggerated and nonsensical—and ruin himself.

In the same sense, the Aries Mars in a woman's horoscope stands for the macho type, whom she seeks. But whether she greets him with enthusiasm, experiences him as a rival who she must constantly battle, or absolutely rejects this type of masculinity with total indignation, can be seen in how this Aries Mars gets along with the rest of the aspects in her horoscope.

The less a planet appears to fit in with the rest of the horoscope, the more it will tend to be suppressed and projected onto others. A projection in and of itself is a totally natural process. Since we are far more used to looking toward the outside world instead of what's inside of us, we initially recognize some things that are a part of our own disposition only in an outer manifestation. Just like a small child with dawning consciousness first just speaks about itself in the third person before it learns to say "I," we also initially become conscious of things during the further course of life when we experience them as something foreign, about which we then prefer to converse in the third person and get agitated about: "Did you hear about what this person said, did, thought, wanted to do?" But if we don't get stuck on this level of consciousness, we will increasingly comprehend in life that many of the phenomena we perceive in others with admiration or indignation are just reflections of our own, yet unconscious, dispositions—something to which we could very well say "I" to. "Projections," explained C. G. Jung, "change the world into the replica of one's own unknown face."[1] When we recognize that the assumed quality isn't in the other person, but within ourselves, psychology calls this "taking back a projection." So every act of taking back a projection is a step in the direction of self-knowledge.

From childhood on, we are always quick to take back projections whenever we subsequently achieve a better position and think we are fantastic as a result. However, we clearly have a more difficult time with images of the enemy that we have found in our surrounding world and which we pursue and battle with great passion. If people take it upon themselves to perhaps point out to us that this could have something to do with us personally, we find it unacceptable. And we are right in reacting like this; in fact, this is generally a characteristic within us, an inner person, which has not been heard from up to now. Whether we are suppressing something that had already been conscious at some point or wanted to become conscious of just now (meaning letting it become unconscious once again), or whether we project something, in all cases this represents important protective measures by our consciousness. If we didn't have this possibility, we would be so flooded by all the images in our memory, all the external impressions, and above all, by the contents of the unconscious mind, that we couldn't tolerate it; our consciousness would break down in the face of this onslaught. It's as if the wheel of time distributes all the necessary steps of perception along our path in life so that only one experience after the other enters our threshold of consciousness. With this "appetizer," it becomes possible for us to cope with, digest, and thereby integrate one perception after the other.

So projections aren't inful or wrong, as we may occasionally hear. After all, we don't even create them. We find them, so to speak, since our unconscious mind projects its contents so perfectly that we could swear all the related qualities were exclusively and undoubtedly to be found in the other person. This makes it particularly strenuous when it comes to getting wise to ourselves. "He must be convinced that he throws a very long shadow," commented C. G. Jung, "before he is willing to withdraw his emotionally toned projections from their object."[2] If we fail to do this, but stubbornly insist instead on the illusory reality suggested by the unconscious mind,

[1]C. G. Jung, *Aion: Research into the Phenomenology of the Self*, vol. 9/II of *The Collected Works of C. G. Jung*, Bollingen Series XX, R. F. C. Hull, trans. (Princeton: Princeton University Press, 1959), ¶16.
[2]C. G. Jung, *Aion*, ¶16.

although the time has long come to take back the projections and integrate them, then they will become a genuine problem. They develop the idiosyncrasy of increasingly isolating us because they move us away from the reality of things. They even let us believe so intensely in the images that we make of reality, that it doesn't even occur to us that there could be another reality *behind* our images. The more we estrange and isolate ourselves from the world in this way, the more we will project onto our environment that it is withdrawing from us because of malice. This drives us deeper and deeper into isolation, and others appear even more evil to us, causing further isolation—and so on and so forth. "It is often tragic to see how blatantly he bungles his own life and the lives of others yet remains totally incapable of seeing how much the whole tragedy originates in himself, and how he continually feeds it and keeps it going," is how C. G. Jung describes the dilemma and additionally explains: "However, his consciousness is not doing this since it whines and curses at a disloyal world that retreats increasingly into the distance."[3]

We naturally prefer to project socially outlawed themes like violence, abuse of power, wiliness, betrayal, or cowardice onto others. If there is a scoundrel who tends toward such disgraceful deeds in our horoscope, and particularly among the four inner persons who form the relationship quartet, then we will probably live it in the form of a projection for a long time. This is easiest for us to do when it is a planet of the opposite sex. Then "all men" are chauvinists, or "all women" are evil, and so forth. And when a shadow falls on the parent of the same sex, we can also easily project it. We also manage to do this in the most difficult cases when it comes to the inner persons who personify our own gender role. An example of this may be in the horoscope of a young man whose Mars is colored in such an "outrageously cruel" manner that he totally suppresses his dangerous side and plays it down since he believes that he couldn't hurt a fly. The same applies to a young woman who quickly makes a vow of chastity because her Venus has such an "outrageously lascivious" disposition, and she does not want to become conscious under any circumstances.

Yet, such once-and-for-all solutions all have one big problem. Whatever we do not let into our conscious mind doesn't disappear; it remains unconscious, but also draws attention to itself from the outside in order to achieve consciousness. The "harmless boy" will come into contact with acts of violence and will be provoked to the point where he perhaps blows up one day and comprehends that he has been sitting on a highly explosive time bomb in terms of his personality. Time and again, the chaste young woman will be

---

[3]C. G. Jung, *Aion*, ¶18.

confronted with sensuality in an outrageous way and led into the temptation of dirtying her snow-white dress. But until this happens, both of them will cling to their "intact" image that they have of themselves, and they are deeply indignant when others express doubts about it because these other people have heard the time bomb ticking or have discovered a lustful look in the young woman's eyes.

When it's time to have such insights, the unconscious mind leads us into every conceivable situation to make us aware of the theme that wants us to pay attention to it. When we are willing to comprehend this correlation, and if we do, depends upon our willingness to open up to self-knowledge that doesn't particularly flatter our ego consciousness. The more difficult, the more unpleasant the perception, the more stubbornly we will project it onto others, and the more we may be indignant about situations in which we encounter this theme. Experience has shown that the degree of our indignation is a reliable gauge for the intensity of suppression, and for our refusal to take back the projection. In order to prevent an obvious misunderstanding at this point, it should be said that there is plenty enough wrong in the world, and our condemnation is completely justified. When people are tortured, or the environment is polluted, it's not enough to just look at our own belly button, to ask what this is trying to tell us, what this probably means in relation to us, and thereby slink away from the responsibility of courageously intervening and taking a stand. It is also just as inadequate to pillory the evil without comprehending that it also corresponds with one side of our own, previously suppressed nature. And taking back the projection naturally in no way means recognizing the torturer within ourselves in order to subsequently live it out without any scruples. Instead, this is a matter of becoming aware of a trait that has let us do certain things up to now, for which we had no explanation because we were unconscious of this characteristic although we had lived it out. If we become conscious of a disposition that we have suppressed up to this point, we can study it in its variety of forms and then find a way of expressing it for which we can truly assume responsibility. Astrology provides excellent support in this process, since it illustrates our disposition and at the same time shows that there is a broad spectrum of possibilities for living out the respective theme.

For example, the torturer mentioned above could correspond to a difficult aspect of Pluto (♇) and Mars (♂). However, by the same token, Pluto-Mars aspects cannot be reduced to the level of a torturer. Among the many forms that this constellation may assume are a hunger for power, sadism, sexual obsession, and a virtually black-magical will to destroy. Yet, in the conscious encounter, a person with the same aspect can also perceive magical powers, with whose help he or she can heal and stimulate, support, and accompany truly profound changes. The transformation of a disposition that tends to be destructive into a valuable, helpful power only becomes possible when we deal with it consciously. However, as long as it must draw attention to itself in a suppressed manner from the unconscious mind, it will primarily show itself from its problematic side.

When the Description of the Searching-Image or Self-Image Appears to Be Inappropriate

If you don't immediately recognize yourself in the following description of one or more inner persons, you may want to explore this further by seeing an astrologer. According to our experience, the explanation lies in one or more of the following possibilities:

A) Another description appears to be more appropriate than the description of the actual planetary aspects. Possible causes are:

1. The corresponding planet disrupts the overall tenor of the horoscope by playing a special role, which conflicts with a number of other personal planets, or with the Ascendant. In pictorial terms, the planetary majority can so push the eccentric planet to the edge that the person has a hard time in becoming aware of this "peculiar" disposition.

   For example, let's assume that a woman has an Aquarius Moon and experiences herself, in crass opposition to our description, as an absolute homebody. But if many of her planets are situated in home-loving signs like Taurus (♉), Cancer (♋), or Virgo (♍), then they imprint the domestic behavior of this woman and may repress her urge for independence, her desire for individual extravagances to the point that this tendency remains largely suppressed in the shadows.

2. The described portrait of the planet isn't experienced because other planets form such powerful aspects to it that its own image becomes eclipsed.

   For example, let's assume that a man has the feminine planets of Venus (♀) and the Moon (☽) in Libra (♎), but doesn't find the light-footed muse or the innocent angel particularly appealing. Instead, he is much more fascinated by an aggressive, tomboyish woman who knows how to hold her own, or a sly, disreputable, or deeply passionate woman.

   In the first case, the strong Mars aspects (♂) have shaped his searching-image; in the second case, these may be aspects of Pluto (♇). The more precise the degrees of these aspects, the more it appears that they truly change the coloration of the searching-image. And yet, it is still important to recognize the actual primordial image behind this aspect in order to understand one's own disposition—and thereby oneself.

B) A person constantly experiences what is described in the searching-image as the image of his or her enemy. Possible causes are:

1. The searching-image planets are engaged in conflict with the self-image[1] or another strong configuration in the horoscope. Square aspects, as well as oppositions and even neighboring signs, can initially awaken the impression that the themes are mutually exclusive of each other and can only be experienced as hostile. The challenge is certainly greater here than for other types of aspects; however, this is also naturally a matter of finding a synthesis and turning discord into harmony, exactly like in all the other tensions in the horoscope.

   For example, a man with a strong Pisces emphasis has a very intuitive nature and feels many correlations in life that other people wouldn't have the slightest idea about. If his searching-image is located in Gemini (square) or Virgo (opposition), then it may easily turn into an image of the enemy, because a total Gemini person must naturally have doubts about correlations that are purely sensed but not intellectually comprehensible, or may even rip them up with biting irony; on the other hand, only what's tangible counts for a Virgo person, and he or she tries to disprove anything supernatural with such hair-splitting mania that it hurts the Pisces deep down inside.

2. Or a woman with a strong Sagittarian emphasis might have a Scorpio Mars (neighboring sign). Then she will tarry in Olympian heights with Sagittarian loftiness and believe herself to be good, noble, and pure, far above all the earthly depths and drives; at the same time, she contemptuously looks down on the dark abyss of the Scorpio world as being dominated by physical urges, immoral, and dirty.

C) There appears to be no inner image at all, or it is so spongy that all the descriptions seem to fit it. Possible causes:

1. Neptune (Ψ) is involved and fogging up the picture. This is primarily the case when Neptune forms a conjunction, square, or opposition with a planet. The more precise this aspect is, the more numb the feelings may be when a person wants to track down the inner planetary theme.

2. The respective planets are situated in the 12th house of the horoscope. Planets in the 12th house only become conscious—if at all—late in life. It's as if they stood behind a veil that only let's us perceive a very vague impression of their contours.

---

[1] For more about this, see the section "The Inner Relationship," on page 192.

How the Searching-Image and the Self-Image can be Recognized in the Horoscope

If you want to find the masculine and the feminine within yourself, or within another person—your searching-image and your self-image or that of the other person—you should first study the individual imprints based on the position of the signs of the masculine planets Mars (σ) and the Sun ($\odot$), as well as the feminine planets Venus (φ) and the Moon ($\mathcal{D}$), as they are described in the following section. The man will recognize his masculine sense of self in the descriptions of Mars and the Sun, while his searching-image (his anima) results from the respective position of Venus and the Moon. The woman will find her self-image represented by Venus and the Moon, while her searching-image (her animus) is concealed within Mars and the Sun. As previously explained (see page 63ff.), the following descriptions only differentiate between masculine and feminine, but not additionally between the Sun ($\odot$) and Mars (σ) or between the Moon ($\mathcal{D}$) and Venus (φ).

Inasfar as the two masculine ($\odot$ and σ) or the two feminine planets ($\mathcal{D}$ and φ) are not located within the same sign, the respective image will be composed of two masculine or two feminine descriptions. Each of these read as if there would only be this one configuration within the horoscope. However, it would be wrong to mistake one part for the whole. Every characterization is a phantom image that helps us understand the actual idea, the archetype that the respective planet in the sign embodies, along with its contribution to our searching-image or self-image.

The descriptions of the masculine and feminine types have the following structure:

FEMININE (φ AND $\mathcal{D}$)	MASCULINE (σ AND $\odot$)
Outer profile	Outer profile
Basic emotional mood	Strengths
Her world	Distortions and weaknesses
How she can be won	Professional themes
Behavior within a relationship	His way of courting a woman
Faithfulness and eroticism	Behavior within a relationship
Conflict behavior	Sexuality and faithfulness
Domesticity	Conflict behavior
Role as mother	Father role

The different structures of this description are not meant to dictate something like the traditional role behavior or an inequality between man and woman. Instead, the typical astrological correlations of the Moon and Venus are listed under the feminine types while the determined Sun or Mars themes are found under the masculine descriptions. However, since the horoscope of every human being displays these four planets, both men and women have the possibility—and ultimately also the task—of finding, living out, and expressing all the related themes within themselves.

• • •

In order to develop the searching-image and self-image, it's best to proceed as follows:

1. Read the following character descriptions according to the sign positions of your planets Moon, Venus, Sun, and Mars.

2. Once you have studied the portrait of the inner images, the next thing to do is take into consideration the—in some cases—substantial, sometimes even overlapping shading that is triggered by the aspects of other planets. On the one hand, this will result in the upgrading and downgrading of certain aspects that let us experience specific individual images as noble and valuable while others appear in a worse light (see page 177). On the other hand, these aspects can color an image, a᠁ even discolor it, to the extent that the original idea can hardly be perceived (see page 183).

3. When you have taken a look at every trait of the Sun, Moon, Venus, and Mars in all of their nuances, when each of the four inner persons has attained its own profile, then it will naturally be interesting to consider the inner relationship, the way in which they deal with the others and with each other—virtually like an inner relationship drama (see page 193).

PART III

The TWELVE

FEMININE TYPES

♈	Aries As the Feminine Searching-Image or Self-Image.
♀	In the **feminine** horoscope as the self-image of the young woman; In the **masculine** horoscope as the main symbol of the anima and the searching-image.
☽	In the **feminine** horoscope as self-image of the mature/motherly woman; In the **masculine** horoscope as the motherly/complementary portion of the anima and searching-image.

ARCHETYPE: The Amazon.	ELEMENT: Fire
TYPE: The wild woman, the vagabond, the tomboy.	STYLE AND TASTE: Prefers strong colors and striking forms with a signal effect. Loves action art and everything experimental.
MATURE FORM: The independent lady, the courageous woman.	NAIVE OR DISTORTED FORM: The virago, the shrew, the fresh girl, the blabbermouth.
STRENGTH: Willing to engage in conflict, straight-forward, direct, spontaneous, cheerful, carefree, daring, adventuresome.	PROBLEM AREAS: Restless, explosive, irritable, impatient, one-sided, pushy, crude.
RELATIONSHIP STRENGTHS: The woman who's game for anything.	RELATIONSHIP PROBLEMS: Competitive behavior and lack of empathy.
BASIC MOOD: Hot-blooded, lively, and carefree. Immediately reacts to outside stimuli.	EROTICISM: Fiery and passionate. Loves ticklish situations and love at first sight.

PLACES AND SITUATIONS WHERE SHE MAY BE ENCOUNTERED:
At the fitness center, in the motorboat club, at end-of-season sales, passing on the freeway, at the race track, bungee jumping, dancing rock'n'roll, in the sauna, at the snack bar, in the sporting goods store, at the express counter, in the betting office, at the campfire, at sunset, at the very front, at the political party congress.

BASIC PRINCIPLE:
To be alive means to burn with passion!

Aries

Interpreted as the feminine searching-image or self-image, the sign of Aries stands for an active, tomboyish woman who stands her ground. Her behavior is resolute and self-confident, her glance is spirited and brash, and she has a powerful voice. She is an athletic type and her appearance reflects a carefree, youthful freshness. She feels best in jeans and a tee-shirt or in similar comfortable clothing that doesn't limit her freedom to move. Her taste in clothing tends toward strong red tones that draw attention to her like a signal, even from far away.

On the scale of spontaneous, direct, effusive, as well as vehement, expressions of emotions, she has no problem achieving the top grades. Her spectrum ranges from storms of enthusiasm to aggressive outbursts of rage. She is so impulsive that every kind of emotional pressure is immediately released to the surrounding world. The words patience, reservedness, and modesty are foreign to her ears because her inner fire simply blazes too high for such well-mannered behavior. Yet, even the heftiest emotional storms subside just as quickly as they appeared. However, these alternating baths of hot and cold can be very strenuous for the people around her, particularly because they occur so unexpectedly and are also blunt, direct, and sometimes even hurtful. On the other hand, she doesn't wallow in sulking or ill will and rarely holds a grudge.

Her world is an arena in which she can prove her strength. She feels best where something is happening. Independence and self-sufficiency strengthen her feeling of self-worth. She loves to prove her abilities where her improvisational talent is required. She basically believes she is capable of everything and sometimes takes hurdles just to try something out without giving it much thought beforehand. This, among other things, can make her a real challenge for many men. She enjoys contending with them in many aspects of everyday life as a matter of course, and naturally in her professional career, as well. Here she often walks away as the victor. With her strongly pronounced desire nature and her thirst for adventure, she prefers to live according to the pleasure principle, which she freely yields to at any time. She is interested in everything new, thrilling, and exciting, or anything for which she can fight with commitment. Although she likes to take over the leadership role herself and starts new projects time and again, some things remain unfinished because she lacks the necessary staying power.

The heart of this spirited woman must be taken by storm—or not at all. Her idea of a romantic time can best be found in films about the wild west, in which the hero slugs it out for the sake of the lady or risks dangerous adventures in order to prove his love to her. Men who are shy or don't know what they want make life very difficult for her. She is important down to the tips of her toes, and very quickly loses interest in an indecisive to and fro. This woman wants to be conquered quickly, and when it takes too long, she will take the initiative herself. "Ladies' choice" is something she could have invented because the role of the patiently waiting, devoted female was never written for her.

She has a hard time with a traditional relationship because her impetuous wildness, self-reliance, and brash directness are hard to reconcile with the image that most people still have of a woman today. She may sometimes even deny her need for closeness just to protect her independence. Within a partnership, she likes to take the lead and makes sure that not too much everyday routine arises. She gets up early and can also be quite unpleasant with her activism. She likes to make decisions, and doesn't hesitate much when it comes to energetically pitching in somewhere. Her life totally takes place in the here and now. In her uncomplicated direct manner, she has such a refreshingly honest quality that she's like an open book; other people always know where they stand with her. Although her sometimes vehement declarations of love are heartfelt and genuine, they are usually valid just for the present moment. Someone who wants to maintain her affection in the long run should always come up with something new to keep her interest alive.

This doesn't mean that she can't also be faithful, but when her routine or everyday monotony gets to be too much, she sometimes looks for new adventures to bring tingling excitement back into her life. She's doesn't worry about the risk of burning her fingers now and then, since she experiences ticklish situations as erotic, and her flaming passion is kindled by playing with fire. At the same time, her strength lies in the absolute devotion to the moment and the perfect presence of all her senses.

When there are problems with love, she's the last person to avoid a conflict. To the contrary, she may experience a vehement confrontation as something stimulating, and so the sparks may frequently fly in her relationship. To what extent this changes something depends primarily on her partner, since she isn't really willing to make compromises. In her opinion, conforming is always something the other person should do. Despite all this, she's also very good about forgetting the fight, and even the agreements reached afterward.

Someone looking for four quiet walls has reached the wrong number with her. The many impulses she needs and loves will turn her home into more of a pigeon loft than a cosy nest. Her household must be uncomplicated and easily managed since she can truly imagine something more exciting than polishing the silverware. Since she also is rarely a great gourmet, but a friend of quick cuisine, don't wonder when the invitation to dinner reveals itself to be nothing more than a simple picnic. She loves change more than other people, so she moves the furniture around so that no boring habits develop. She frequently loves to live out of a suitcase so she can yield to her spontaneous impulses for a change of scenery at any time.

She doesn't let the role of mother really restrict her, either. She is good at setting limits for her children in terms of her own interests. Patience isn't her strong point here, and particularly with an infant she may feel somewhat helpless at times. Instead, she's good at motivating others and empathizes with the needs of younger people throughout her lifetime. Based on her convictions, she supports her children's sense of initiative, understands their need for exercise and movement, and raises them to be independent at an early age. She will also get involved in some adventures, passionately loves to run races with her offspring, and maintains an impetuous, youthful soul up into ripe old age.

Someone desiring a sensitive, devoted partner who radiates calm or loves stability will be hopelessly overtaxed with this woman. But someone who loves spontaneity and variety and desires a courageous companion who is a great sport can experience great excitement with her.

Taurus
As the Feminine Searching-Image or Self-Image.

In the **feminine** horoscope as the self-image of the young woman; In the **masculine** horoscope as the main symbol of the anima and the searching-image.

In the **feminine** horoscope as self-image of the mature/motherly woman; In the **masculine** horoscope as the motherly/complementary portion of the anima and searching-image.

ARCHETYPE: The Earth Mother.	ELEMENT: Earth
TYPE: The natural beauty, the warmhearted and sensuous woman.	STYLE AND TASTE: Prefers natural materials and warm colors. Has a heart for antiques and loves the richness of baroque.
MATURE FORM: The steadfast woman, the preserver of tradition.	NAIVE OR DISTORTED FORM: The ponderous person, the lazy girl, the stingy or greedy woman.
STRENGTH: Good-natured, trusting, patient, natural, calm, able to enjoy things, sensual, warm, content.	PROBLEM AREAS: Envious, self-indulgent, inflexible, awkward, prejudiced, obstinate, indolent, mulish.
RELATIONSHIP STRENGTHS: The sensual, faithful, and understanding companion in life.	RELATIONSHIP PROBLEMS: Tends to be intensely jealous and clings to what is familiar.
BASIC MOOD: Usually in a good mood and friendly, with an unshakeable basic trust.	EROTICISM: Strongly pronounced sensuality and deep sensitivity. Loves a relaxed, quiet atmosphere in a familiar setting.

PLACES AND SITUATIONS WHERE SHE MAY BE ENCOUNTERED:
On the farm, in the great outdoors, in the kitchen, at the florist, at the archeology seminar, at the antique trade fair, in a painting class, at the flea market, at an auction, at the bakery, in the bank, making pottery, in the garden, where a house is under construction, at the collector's exchange, meeting the same friends at the same place every week, on a picnic, in the wine cellar.

BASIC PRINCIPLE:
Take your time to do it well.

Taurus

Interpreted as the feminine searching-image or self-image, the sign of Taurus represents a warmhearted, sensual woman who appears to be at peace with herself in her femininity and radiates a natural beauty. Her behavior is charming, her friendly glance reveals a good heart, and her voice is soft and melodious. She loves form-fitting clothes that highlight her feminine charms, but doesn't show off. She prefers natural fabrics, soft materials, and warm, calm earth colors.

This woman doesn't experience any extreme emotional fluctuations, and has a practically unshakeable composure. Her pleasant confidence and her warm, sensible manner also have a calming effect on her surrounding world. She likes physical closeness and needs a sense of security and stability. Sudden changes throw her off track and make her feel deeply insecure. This is why she loves structure and the traditions that have grown over time. She lavishes care on everything that is near and dear to her. It's a true pleasure to absorb the beauty of this world and everything that she loves with all her senses, enjoying it as she makes it a part of herself. If someone wants to take something from her that she is familiar with, her apparently boundless good nature disappears for the moment. She then shows her possessive side and makes clear where the boundaries are.

Her world is nature, her own garden, a workshop, or a studio—simply a place in which she can express herself through her hands or which she can shape with her hands. Her experienced eye for proportion, color, and form makes her a talented artisan. She loves everything beautiful, as long as it has a sensual touch to it. On the other hand, she shows no interest in an aesthetic that is perfect but cold. She stands with both feet on the ground of reality and has an express sense for a practical lifestyle. Careful planning means more to her than making spontaneous decisions. This is why she likes to have a solid job in which nothing needs to be rushed and the products and projects can gradually mature. Anything she loves is what she wants to have, and so she collects whatever appeals to her. This can become a problem when her attention is directed more toward quantity than quality and she simply hoards everything that's offered to her.

The way to this woman's heart is naturally through her stomach. Anyone who wants to win her over should invite her to a good meal. She's interested in a candlelight dinner in an elegant and dignified atmosphere, as well as a picnic in the great outdoors; the main thing is that it tastes delicious and there's enough of everything. A man who knows how to pamper her with his own cooking skills naturally makes a big impression on her. But in other ways as well, she is extremely receptive to the bodily and material pleasures of life. However, it is still advisable to have enough perseverance since it could very well take a bit longer until she warms up. She is fundamentally cautious and doesn't like to get involved in adventures. If she had her way, she would even demand a guarantee of faithfulness. But once she has decided on someone, her love is steadfast, hearty, and deep.

In a relationship, she expects the physical presence of her partner since air alone doesn't satisfy her. In a certain sense, she sees it as her partner's duty to be with her and be there for her. She wants a man who is there, one she can touch, feel, taste, and smell. Men who are unreachable, distant, and unreliable don't interest her, which is why she doesn't like separations of place or time. Weekend relationships are taboo for her. She loves rituals that take place on a regular basis, long-term planning, and insurance against everything and anything. Abundance simply gives her a sense of well-being, and she doesn't like living from hand to mouth. For this reason, she puts away enough reserves in due time to bridge meager phases. If it's necessary, she can even exercise restraint, but not at the expense of pleasure.

For her, clear situations are an urgent need, which is why she is a faithful person in the depths of her soul. It's not hard for her to make binding promises, and it's obvious to her that marriage is a decision for life. As Baroque as her taste may be, her experience of eroticism also ranges from satisfying to effusive. In this sense as well, she isn't a vagabond but needs an atmosphere of familiarity so that her warm sensuality can blossom.

When problems are encountered in the love relationship, she proves her strength. Even though she hates conflicts and desires nothing more than a peaceful, harmonious relationship, she remains steadfast and doesn't let herself be irritated all that easily even by vehement confrontations. To the contrary—when a relationship threatens to dissolve, her possessive side emerges as fierce jealousy. She simply has a difficult time parting from anything that she has considered her own at any time, no matter whether this means people or things, and she defends her property vehemently and with an unmistakable determination.

She loves her own four walls, especially since no one can take them away from her. And this certainly gives her a deep sense of satisfaction. Once she has set up a home, she would prefer to add onto it three times before she would move for additional space. So quite a few things collect in her home with time, and her preference for antiques fills up her living space as well. Moreover, she doesn't like to throw anything away because she doesn't want to part from things that she may be able to use it again. And yet, there's always a cosy atmosphere in her home. Her friends appreciate her as a warm-hearted host and know that she's an excellent cook. People like to come to her home for intimate gatherings, which she very much appreciates.She loves a cozy home and doesn't have to go to every party.

In the role of mother, she distinguishes herself with the patience of a saint. She is nurturing and giving in her entire being and knows how to create an atmosphere of sensual security. She is the mother to touch and cuddle with, who experiences physical nature and closeness as an obvious need. By always making sure that there's enough of everything, she conveys a basic trust in the abundance of life to her children. But when the time comes for her children to leave the nest, she usually has a hard time letting them go. Separating from the familiar daily life of the family and looking for new tasks means a readjustment that is extremely difficult.

She certainly isn't the most flexible or daring woman, and someone looking for excitement and variety will be irritated in the long run by her tendency toward the familiar. But anyone who knows how to appreciate her earth qualities will find her to be a sensual connoisseur and a faithful, understanding companion in life.

Gemini
As the Feminine Searching-Image or Self-Image.

In the **feminine** horoscope as the self-image of the young woman;
In the **masculine** horoscope as the main symbol of the anima and the
searching-image.

In the **feminine** horoscope as self-image of the mature/motherly
woman; In the **masculine** horoscope as the motherly/complementary
portion of the anima and searching-image.

ARCHETYPE:	ELEMENT:
The woman of letters.	Air

TYPE:	STYLE AND TASTE:
The intellectual, the bookworm, the clever woman.	Prefers playful forms and light color tones, likes airy arrangements in the manner of Art Nouveau.

MATURE FORM:	NAIVE OR DISTORTED FORM:
The wise woman of the world, the all-around woman.	The shrewd person, the eternal girl, the gossip monger, the prude, the smart aleck

STRENGTH:	PROBLEM AREAS:
Open-minded, sociable, carefree, imaginative, flexible, friendly.	Superficial, cold, moody, fickle, non-committal, chatty.

RELATIONSHIP STRENGTHS:	RELATIONSHIP PROBLEMS
The uncomplicated, cheerful companion with whom one can talk about anything.	Can be very cool and aloof and remain noncommittal.

BASIC MOOD:	EROTICISM:
Cheerful and carefree, with quickly changing emotions.	Playful and artful. Loves the passing flirtation and the excitement of something new.

PLACES AND SITUATIONS WHERE SHE MAY BE ENCOUNTERED:
Looking for an apartment, at the newsstand, in the bookstore, on the staircase,
at the sidewalk café, at the secretary's desk, on the telephone, at the post office,
in the editorial department, in the language lab, at the book fair, in the seminar,
at the reading circle, at the information counter, juggling.

BASIC PRINCIPLE:
I'm not confused, I'm just well-mixed!

Gemini

Interpreted as the feminine searching-image or self-image, the sign of Gemini represents an intelligent woman who is clever, wide-awake, and rarely at a loss for a response. Her behavior is very smooth, sometimes even saucy. Her glance is curious and quite lively, and her voice sounds light and clear. In appearance, she is the eternal youngster who stays mentally active up into old age and goes nimbly through life. She prefers dressing in pale spring colors, wearing light-weight, casual materials, and changing her style time and again.

With her rather vivacious temperament, she resembles a butterfly that's now here and now there, participates in everything happening around her with lively curiosity, and also has an opinion about everything. Her emotional landscape sometimes has changeable moods, but she generally is good at subjecting her inner state to her intellect. She can talk about everything that moves her in a carefree, light, and open manner without giving the impression of truly being touched by it. Her joy in the lightness of being doesn't permit her to be overcome by ardor or brooding thoughts. On the inside, she always maintains enough independence to be able to adjust to a new situation at any time. Rarely does she experience this lack of independence as an emotional homelessness. And should this occur at some time, she will escape this feeling by quickly making new, exciting and stimulating contacts.

Her world is the world of words. She reads the daily newspaper during breakfast and the crime thriller at night. In between, she browses through the bookstores and antiquarian departments and constantly increases the number of books that remain unread in spite of all the speed-reading courses. She is a wandering soul, driven by her thirst for knowledge and certainly not interested just in trivialities. She likes to participate in intellectual and cultural life, visits art exhibits and openings, loves street theater and cabaret, cinemas, and literary circles, and knows how to make contacts everywhere in a masterly way. Since she is full of curiosity about life, she is naturally always well informed and knows where something is happening and what the current issues are.

So she usually loses her heart in a passing moment. An interesting contact in the train, a brief conversation at the bakery, a flirt at the sidewalk café—simply any airy encounter can be the beginning of a great love for her.

Someone who knows how to play with words, who can win her attention by being smart, nimble-minded, and verbally brilliant, will have the best chances. On the other hand, someone who is at a loss for words won't have much of a chance with her. She loves talking on the telephone for hours, ingenious faxes, and love letters pasted together from the headlines of the daily newspaper. Here as well, she always maintains enough relaxed, airy distance since her breath gets taken away in the truest sense of the word when passion becomes too intensive.

A light, fresh breeze always blows in the relationship with her. She makes sure there is enough change and a variety of contacts. Her circle of friends is therefore large, but also changeable. As much as she may love a man, her curiosity is simply too pronounced for her to do without the many interesting encounters that she desires from life. So she doesn't feel good alone as a couple for very long. Instead, she blossoms in the middle of a group of cosmopolitan, well-read, and witty people. Some men feel irritated by her changeability and experience her light, relaxed manner as a friendship that is too cold and non-committal. Yet, someone who can properly appreciate her will be fascinated in particular by her many facets, her independence, and the liveliness she brings into the relationship. But anyone who believes he has a right to her has made a fundamental error. All her actions are of her own free will because she does not respond to pressure. This is why, even after she has said "yes," she considers an intimate partnership to be a voluntary togetherness.

In this way she always remains open for new acquaintances, even when she is in a committed relationship, and studies—purely to be informed, but on a regular basis—the personal ads in the newspapers and magazines. In her eyes, this has absolutely nothing to do with being unfaithful. Just mentally playing with the possibilities creates an erotic tickle for her, and even if she imagines something in theory, she doesn't have to live it out in practice. Her eroticism awakens most quickly in a witty conversation and develops playfully and easily into a communicative ping-pong match. Her carefree sensuality is characterized less by deep passion than by the joy of playing with the possibilities.

When there are problems with love, she becomes cold, juggles arguments skillfully, and with a cynical undertone in her voice, usually has the last word. In the process, she becomes perceptibly aloof on the inside. It's not that she immediately runs away, but it certainly isn't possible to threaten her with emotional blackmail. She isn't willing to make exaggerated compromises because of a fear of loneliness. However, she always has an open ear for a good suggestion, and is also always interested in a fair and well-considered compromise so that the conflict can be worked out.

There is a draft in her home, so to speak, since she lives with the doors open in every sense. Loneliness isn't her thing, and she hardly seems to need a change to retreat and be silent. She loves rooms flooded with light and air and a great deal of space, and her furnishings are a colorful collection of oddly assorted individual pieces. She rarely understands domesticity to mean "home sweet home," since a too settled way of life is lethal for her vital spirits. This is why she frequently likes to change residences. Thanks to her sociable nature, she knows how to quickly create a casual connection to her new neighbors and participate in the life of the part of town where she lives. However, after the next move, these contacts will usually be forgotten again; there are neighbors everywhere.

As a mother, she finds it exciting to observe the mental development and learning progress of her child. She promotes and supports her child's curiosity from the start and is very understanding of the child's thirst for knowledge. Although her light, carefree manner doesn't permit too much emotional closeness, she is an uncomplicated mother who exudes cheerfulness. Actually, she tends to see herself as a big sister, and later, as a friendly advisor to her children. The role of the solicitous mother is too binding and contradicts her urge for independence. She needs her freedom as often as possible. Early on, she will look for another task outside the house and shows a lot of inventiveness in managing both the family and the job at the same time.

A man who desires a dreamy woman for himself alone or a practical housewife is better off not getting involved with this airy being. But someone who knows how to appreciate a variety of social contacts, playful charm, and pleasant ease, who loves things casual and likes the feeling of a fresh breeze, will be inspired by her.

Cancer
As the Feminine Searching-Image or Self-Image.

In the **feminine** horoscope as the self-image of the young woman;
In the **masculine** horoscope as the main symbol of the anima and the
searching-image.

In the **feminine** horoscope as self-image of the mature/motherly
woman; In the **masculine** horoscope as the motherly/complementary
portion of the anima and searching-image.

ARCHETYPE: The mother.	ELEMENT: Water
TYPE: The caregiver, the romantic.	STYLE AND TASTE: Prefers soft forms and colors, sometimes also ruffles and trims, and loves the style of romanticism.
MATURE FORM: The mama, the artist	NAIVE OR DISTORTED FORM: The Lolita, the motherhen, the cry-baby, the eternal daughter, the pouter.
STRENGTH: Emotionally profound, imaginative, warm, empathetic, family-minded, flexible, artistically talented, sure of her instincts, easily touched.	PROBLEM AREAS: Thin-skinned, self-pitying, indolent, easily seduced, moody, too willing to blame others.
RELATIONSHIP STRENGTHS: The motherly woman who lovingly looks after emotional and physical well-being.	RELATIONSHIP PROBLEMS: Can be extremely touchy, quickly insulted, and bears grudges.
BASIC MOOD: Very sensitive, changeable, and dependent on outer circumstances.	EROTICISM: Likes tender cuddling, is devoted and highly sensitive. Loves a snugly, cozy environment.

PLACES AND SITUATIONS WHERE SHE MAY BE ENCOUNTERED:
At home, at kindergarten, on the baby ward, in the mothers' society, at cooking class, baking bread, in a furniture store, at the ocean, in front of the fireplace, at her parents' home, in the folklore museum, on the hotline, at the theater for popular plays, at the society for local history and culture, at the poetry reading, at the family celebration.

BASIC PRINCIPLE:
Remembrance is the only paradise from which we cannot be driven.

Cancer

Interpreted as the feminine searching-image or self-image, the sign of Cancer stands for an empathetic, motherly woman. Her behavior is reserved, sometimes shy, her glance is dreamy, and she has a melodious voice. Her appearance is very feminine, and she likes to dress in soft, flowing materials in pastel tones. Because of its lace and ruffles, a hint of nostalgia wafts through her clothing.

Her temperament is quiet, but moved by strong emotions. Whenever warm memories or images of earlier days or good times rise up within her, her heart overflows. Like ebb and flow, her moods are subject to the "whims of Luna," the rhythms of the moon, and can often lead to vehement baths of alternating hot and cold emotions. If she doesn't have a private place she can use as a retreat in order to come to terms with her emotions, she will feel herself at the mercy of the surrounding world and its harshness without any protection because of all her sensitivity to its vibrations. Things that are familiar and comfortable to her can then lure her out again. But if she feels like she has been treated harshly or misunderstood by other people, she can—deeply disappointed by the entire world—retreat and need a long time before she risks coming out again. If she doesn't find enough solace, understanding, and a sense of security, then self-pity will turn her into a defiant, pouty, childish woman with whom it's better not to tangle. She finds the best protection against a world that she experiences as coarse and hostile within the family, the bonds of which give her such a strong support that her own clan always remains more important in life than friendships could ever be.

Her world is the inner life and the realm of imagination. Strictly speaking, she never stops believing in fairy tales, but hopes within the depths of her soul throughout her entire lifetime that princes will conquer evil dragons and that everything will turn out all right in the end. With this romantic wishful thinking, as well as with her passionate defense of her childhood ideals, she naturally clashes severely with reality time and again. But in connection with the extremely lively image world of her soul, this also inspires her to creative work, above all, painting and lyric poetry. In spite of all her softness, she knows exactly what she wants and frequently also what other people need. Particularly because of her deep emotional experiencing and vast empathy, it's possible for her to help others in need and be an extremely understanding advisor for them. With her big, motherly heart, she may often be the point of contact for people who trust themselves to her care. Because of this, she frequently looks for a profession in the social services or nursing area, and working with children also very much suits her. In addition, she is interested in everything related to her homeland and origins.

The heart of this woman can only be won by a fairy-tale prince, whereby her romantic powers of imagination can substantially contribute to the possibility of a quite earthly person having this magic for her. But this must be a man who understands how to breathe life into her dreams and who is willing to believe in their fulfillment as well. Something like a walk in the moonlight is a wonderful setting for her to open up to a new love, even if she tends to act rather hesitant and reserved at the time. Although steamy declarations of love deeply impress her, when they become too stormy she feels pressured, becomes insecure, and is put off. She likes to take her time, not because she's so shy, but more so that she can enjoy the unique enchantment of the beginning as long as possible. She only opens her soft and sensitive soul very carefully with growing intimacy. What she needs is the recognition effect, which only results with time or when the "suitor" reminds her of someone from her past. And it's only natural that she may meet her sandbox friend after many years again and immediately realize that he's the man for her life.

Life with her is very domestic, for she loves the privacy and familiar intimacy more than a large circle of friends. Once she has taken someone into her heart, she will feel her unconditional solidarity with this person and won't hear anything against him. If it becomes necessary, she will defend him rigorously and courageously with all available means. Once she has taken her loved one under her wing, her caring glance won't let him go very easily. By letting him have all her love and attention, she gives him the feeling of being her one and only. However, should he defend himself against this invariably well-meant mothering, she will be deeply indignant and make it clear that she knows exactly what's good for him. She loves family celebrations, never forgets a birthday, and maintains contacts with all her relatives. Time and again, she makes an effort to settle disputes that arise in order to keep the family clan together.

This is why she needs a home-loving partner who, like her, believes in eternal love and a cozy family bliss. It's not difficult for her to be faithful. Her sensual eroticism develops in an atmosphere of security and tender togetherness. The more intimate and protected she feels, the more her warm femininity will come to light. She is an extremely devoted woman who loves to unite with her beloved if the ambience is right. As a seductive, tenderly playful Eve, she always searches for Adam and the lost paradise.

When there are difficulties in love, she can suppress these so well that she overlooks them for a long time and can continue to believe in an intact world. However, to her great annoyance, problems treated in this manner unfortunately have the peculiarity of growing until they become totally obvious. Then she is desperately unhappy, has a falling out with the world, and withdraws in disappointment into her shell—or her parents' home. A great deal of tact and patience is then required to get her to come out again in order to find a true solution that doesn't just produce a hollow peace.

Her home is the place where she feels protected and safe against the harsh outside world. She knows very well how to make a warm nest for the others and create an atmosphere of comfortable security and familiar intimacy. Her past is present everywhere, and she sinks into dreamy thoughts and feelings of longing time and again when looking through photo albums and old love letters. Financial aspects mean little to her—instead, she clings to every object that has a personal meaning for her. The result is that her taste, which is good in itself, is frequently outdone by the value of remembrance: a present from her favorite aunt doesn't have to be attractive. Even if it's absolutely kitschy, it gets put in a conspicuous place. And the stuffed animals from her childhood are naturally nestled on her bed.

No one has a more pronounced need for family and children than she. She blossoms in her role as mother since it does her good to be needed. When she doesn't have her loved ones around her, she frequently worries and is concerned with keeping them all together. She knows how to build such a warm and pleasant nest for her children that they never want to leave. But this is also her problem. She can turn into a mother hen in her loving care, only letting her children become independent with a heavy heart. Even when they are adults, she likes to continue mothering them.

Someone who thinks that friends are more important than family bonds, who prefers to take to his heels instead of being in the family home, has come to the wrong person. But someone who can love from the depths of his soul, who values children and domesticity, as well as an intense romantic vein, will find her to be a sensitive, caring, imaginative partner, who is sometimes even in need of protection.

Leo
As the Feminine Searching-Image or Self-Image.

In the **feminine** horoscope as the self-image of the young woman;
In the **masculine** horoscope as the main symbol of the anima and the searching-image.

In the **feminine** horoscope as self-image of the mature/motherly woman; In the **masculine** horoscope as the motherly/complementary portion of the anima and searching-image.

ARCHETYPE: The queen.	**ELEMENT:** Fire
TYPE: The self-confidant lady, the star.	**STYLE AND TASTE:** Loves everything decorative, luxurious, and resplendent, as well as sumptuous scenery in the Renaissance style.
MATURE FORM: The magnanimous individual, the big-hearted woman.	**NAIVE OR DISTORTED FORM:** The primadonna, playgirl, luxury-loving lady, diva, egocentric person.
STRENGTH: Hearty, open, loves life, has talent for the show, has power of representation, is optimistic, creative, charismatic.	**PROBLEM AREAS:** Proud, snobbish, engages in self-indulgent introspection, snooty, ignorant, loves ostentation, craves extravagance.
RELATIONSHIP STRENGTHS: Generous, friendly, capable of solidarity, supportive.	**RELATIONSHIP PROBLEMS:** Can be very presumptuous, extravagant, and haughty. Quickly feels neglected, reacts stuck-up and cold.
BASIC MOOD: Very extroverted, zestful, usually in a contagiously good mood, with a tendency toward being theatrical.	**EROTICISM:** Lustily playful. Loves an elegant, animating ambience.

PLACES AND SITUATIONS WHERE SHE MAY BE ENCOUNTERED:
At the theater, on stage, in the circus, on the promenade, in the South, in the casino, in the castle, on the catwalk, on the board of directors, at the microphone, in the convertible, at the state reception, on the golf course, in the deck chair, at the solarium, at the jewelers, on the dance floor.

BASIC PRINCIPLE:
Always be the star in your own film!

Leo

Interpreted as the feminine searching-image or self-image, the sign of Leo stands for the hearty, self-confidant woman of the world. Her behavior is proud and stylishly independent, her glance open, and her deep voice melodious and sometimes a bit loud. Her overall appearance is impressive and dignified. She loves to dress up like a diva in velvet and silk, wears her hair in a thick mane like a lion, and likes to adorn herself with gold and diamonds. But even without all the glitter, she may have the same effect of being a queen just because of her warm, winning charisma and her striking self-assurance. Things that look inconspicuous on others develop a surprisingly exquisite effect when she wears them. She isn't a child of sorrow, but rather a playful being who likes to enjoy herself and move on the sunny side of life. Her feelings are warm, steady, and truly sincere. It's easy to forget sober everyday life around her and be swept away by her cheerfulness. Her ability to be enthusiastic is so convincing that it's difficult not to be infected by it. The totally natural way in which she lets her surrounding world participate in her strong emotional life proves that she knows neither an exaggerated sense of shame nor a false modesty. Her distinctly desirous nature knows few compromises when it comes to satisfying her own needs. With a sure instinct, she not only knows where the best things can be found, but also how to indulge in them.

Her world is a stage. She is spontaneous by nature and has an obvious predilection for skilled staging. Her joy in creative self-expression is much stronger than a possible fear of disapproving criticism. Wherever she appears, she succeeds in winning people for herself through her openness, or, in the worst case, she simply awakens envy. Both reactions ultimately lead to her being on other people's minds, and this is exactly what she wants. This makes her the born and worthy representative for the public; she loves the limelight and knows what the audience wants to see. Work in the leisure industry, in theater, film, or television suits her, as well as leadership positions of all types. She is interested in everything beautiful that life has to offer, and she can't find one reason why she should let herself be kept by unnecessary restraint from delighting extensively in the riches and luxury of this world, which she also generously shares with others.

If she wants to capture a man's attention, she knows how to put herself in the right light without much further ado and flirts with unmistakable openness. Above all, when she is seeking admiration, she may develop such bewitching sex appeal that a man will have a hard time resisting. Anyone who wants to win her over should know that love is not only a magnificent game for this woman, but primarily a drama as well! She seeks an imposing hero, with whom she can really be seen. She is impressed by a masterly appearance and aggressive wooing. This means that her heart can be won through big presents or little tokens that give her the feeling of truly being loved and valued.

Her demands and expectations of a partnership are naturally quite high. However, she is convinced that she deserves great things since, after all, she is something special and the chosen one at her side can simply feel lucky to be there. Provided that he can afford it! What she cannot stand at all is mediocrity and miserly behavior. Small-mindedness meets only with her contempt. She loves the good life, is rarely in a bad mood, and now and then has an envious self-assured attitude. She knows how to combine work and leisure in such a way that she's never stressed, but also doesn't give the impression of being idle. In addition, she supports her partner with friendly attention and is completely on his side, no matter what he does.

She is faithful to the man who knows how to continually express the required admiration to her, but can also share a generous lifestyle. Her playful eroticism awakens when she is seen, respected, and—even better— admired. She develops her sensuality creatively and in a distinctly lusty way in an elegant ambience appropriate for her. If there are problems in love, she is at first somewhat irritated. Problems actually don't belong in her everyday life. She is accustomed to avoiding possible difficulties through a generous heart and also does this within a relationship. If she doesn't succeed, she may show her claws and can also be loudly indignant. She knows how to fight for her rights and refuses to tolerate any type of insult. She defends her standpoint with vehemence and decisiveness and doesn't give in.

She has little interest in really fastidious, long-winded quarrels and profound discussions or solutions that require a great many self-critical insights. She understands domesticity to mean less a comfortable nest or the retreat into the private sphere than a place that, with its generosity, offers a prestigious framework for conviviality and social contacts. She needs an adequate amount of space in order to feel good. In addition, she has an exquisite, and usually quite expensive, taste when it comes to her furnishings. Castles, fortresses, and palaces, simply everything splendid and pompous, would be the ideal backdrop for her dreams of how she would like to live. However, even in more simple surroundings, with her design talent, she knows how to make more of something. She is a master of decoration and magnificent staging. As a born hostess who likes to have frequent company, it is easy for her to create a hearty, warm atmosphere.

She is a mother lioness in the truest sense of the word, going all out for her children and proudly showing herself everywhere with them. Sacrificing herself for their sakes would never enter her mind, but she enjoys pampering her loved ones with everything that she likes herself. Naturally only the best is good enough for her offspring, and she quite obviously makes sure that they also play the leading roles as early as possible. For this reason, she shows them at an early age how to behave in public and how to stage a successful performance. If enough time remains for her own needs as well—and she knows how to make sure of this—then she also likes to exuberantly play and fool around with them. Once they are adults, she naturally suns herself in their success, in the conviction that she has also done her part to contribute to their laurels.

Someone who shies away from the public eye and would prefer to sit comfortably at home sorting stamps shouldn't get involved with her. But a man who loves to pamper a woman, has a feeling for her theatricality, and welcomes her strong sense of self-confidence, will feel lucky to have this spirited woman at his side, with whom he can be seen everywhere.

Virgo
As the Feminine Searching-Image or Self-Image.

In the **feminine** horoscope as the self-image of the young woman;
In the **masculine** horoscope as the main symbol of the anima and the searching-image.

In the **feminine** horoscope as self-image of the mature/motherly woman; In the **masculine** horoscope as the motherly/complementary portion of the anima and searching-image.

ARCHETYPE:	ELEMENT:
The craftswoman.	Earth

TYPE:	STYLE AND TASTE:
The reliable woman, the skillful housewife.	Prefers practical, simple elegance of high quality. Loves living in clear functionality without frills.

MATURE FORM:	NAIVE OR DISTORTED FORM:
The person who copes well with life, the mindful individual.	The prude, the governess, the pedant, the cleaning maniac.

STRENGTH:	PROBLEM AREAS:
Precise, careful, has organizational talent, genuine, modest, efficient, thrifty, thorough.	Fussy, anxious, constantly critical, unimaginative, a perfectionist.

RELATIONSHIP STRENGTHS:	RELATIONSHIP PROBLEMS:
The woman who delivers more than she promises.	Sense of order, perfectionism, and a cleanliness quirk can become more important than being together in a comfortable way.

BASIC MOOD:	EROTICISM:
Usually quiet but may also be in high spirits, sensible, and usually disciplined with a high frustration threshold.	Gentle and reserved but also unexpectedly frivolous. Values a calm and secure setting.

PLACES AND SITUATIONS WHERE SHE MAY BE ENCOUNTERED:
At the health-food store, in the archive, in the laundry room, at the employment office, cleaning, at the research lab, in the pharmacy, doing a puzzle, at the health-resort hotel, in the household store, at the notary's office, in analysis, at the gym, in the bookkeeping department, in class, in the handicraft workshop, in the editorial department.

BASIC PRINCIPLE:
Caution is better than leniency!

Virgo

Interpreted as the feminine searching-image or self-image, the sign of Virgo corresponds to a clever, efficient, practical woman. Her behavior is simple and matter-of-fact, her glance firm, very interested, as well as critical, and her voice pleasantly calm, sometimes a bit pert. Because of the naturalness of her appearance, she is beautiful in a subdued way, even when unadorned. Her sense of the appropriate combinations is also reflected in her clothing, which must be practical and comfortable. She likes to wear classical elegance and pays attention to quality, even in her everyday wardrobe.

Her moods are pleasantly moderate and subject to few whims and fluctuations. She doesn't trust effusive emotions, which she considers too unpredictable and also frequently contradictory to her otherwise sensible way of thinking and acting. This restraint, as well as her enormous self-discipline, sometimes let her appear quite sober, cool, or even austere to the outside world. But this attitude usually conceals the fear of losing control and being at the mercy of situations that become extremely complicated. As a result of worrying about losing the ground under her feet, she may be overly cautious. But whenever she trustingly opens up, she shows others a true willingness to help and provides attentive loving care. She can look after others selflessly, without attracting attention, and doesn't hesitate long to help out wherever she is needed.

Her world is everyday life, which she masters and knows how to shape more brilliantly than anyone else. She would much rather accept a concrete project and immediately deal with it than take great risks and answer for their success or failure to the outside world. She is a skilled organizer, a clever tactician without any major illusions and exaggerated expectations. With joy and diligence, she dedicates herself to the practical, clearly defined tasks that she completes punctually and with a love for detail. She knows that an organism can only function when its components work well together, and she possesses an instinctive sense for healthy organized structures. For this reason, she is interested in social work, as well as in education and public health. Wherever she gets involved, she is not interested in cheap showmanship, but prefers to use understatement because a lasting, convincing, long-term effect is more important than a sensational but fleeting sham success.

A bit of endurance and serious intentions are required to lure her out of her reserve in order to win her heart. A quick adventure doesn't interest her.

She is much more impressed by someone who is able to cope with life and who has a distinct sense of reality. A man with ideas that are out of touch with reality, who has dreamy, visionary ideals shouldn't even bother approaching her. Her searching gaze sees every swindle. Sometimes, it also appears to be somewhat critical, but with this she just signals that she has no illusions about love and relationships. She isn't interested in either the entanglements of passionate affairs or the dreamy ecstasies of love. She knows what it's like to wake up the morning after and see that a beautiful dream turns out to be a humbug in the light of day.

This is why the phase of infatuation doesn't take unnecessarily long with her. She values living together in an orderly way since only mutual everyday life can convince her that the relationship is good. As soon as possible, she wants to land on the sober ground of reality so that she knows what she has and what she can reckon with. Sometimes she has already known her future mate for a long time and has thoroughly observed and tested him before an acquaintance or friendship turns into a serious partnership. It's not rare for her to live with a man with whom she is professionally involved. A functional relationship that fulfills some sort of practical aspect is more her style than a romantic love match with little basis in everyday life. She is frequently envied, and greatly appreciated by her partner, for the ease with which she moves through the regularly occurring routines of life. She knows how to make the best of everything, is willing to cooperate with the inevitable, and can therefore smoothly shape their life together.

She may take longer than others to examine the situation, but once she has made a decision, it becomes a commitment. Then she shows herself to be a completely faithful partner who is willing to walk the mutual path with all the consequences, and who has no problem in limiting her demands to a minimum during difficult times. Eroticism is a natural component of everyday life for her, and she doesn't need any extravagant backdrops or fantasies to turn her on. Ordinary, simple things stimulate her natural sensuality. So her desire can awaken in moments when hardly anyone else would consider it and sometimes in a surprising frivolity that others wouldn't think she is capable of.

When there are problems in love, she doesn't immediately run away. She knows that a solid relationship requires commitment, concessions, and compromises from both partners, and is gladly willing to do her part in this. However, she also expects her partner to work on the solution to the problem with the same thoroughness and seriousness as she does. But when agreements that have been reached are disregarded, she will respond by withdrawing her trust and making accusations. In order for her to open up once again after such a crisis, her partner must bring more than a little evidence of his reliability, and it must stand the test of her critical scrutiny.

She knows how to furnish her home in a way that is both tasteful and practical. Since she can easily separate from unnecessary ballast, her place is seldom cluttered. Instead, it is a mirror of her fine, simple, and stylish manner. As in other parts of her life, no exquisite pomp will leap out at her guests. It takes even an experienced eye some time to notice the beauty in the fascinating simplicity there. Behind all of this is a perfect housewife who has no problem with the monotony of everyday life, but who experiences its clarity as satisfying and comforting. When she sets out to defend this world against chaos and laissez-faire, she can also be very fussy in her love for fastidious order and pedantic cleanliness.

Before she decides on a family and children, she will soberly and objectively consider the obvious consequences involved. In the process, she certainly isn't in danger of losing herself in transfigured wishful thinking or idealized concepts. But once she has decided on this life, she is an efficient and reliable mother who raises her children to be cautious, helpful, and master life in a practical way. Well-regulated routines and meal times are maintained as a self-evident truth, and work naturally comes before play. It doesn't really bother her that she sometimes appears to be old-fashioned since she is convinced of the value of a practical lifestyle and healthy discipline. Despite all this, she isn't a brusque, unyielding, or embittered mother. Instead, she imparts these values to her children in a loving matter-of-fact manner and convinces them primarily by also adhering to her rules in a totally exemplary manner. She is always there when her children need her, and naturally looks after all the small and large worries with an understanding attitude.

Someone who dreams of an exciting *femme fatale* will find this woman too dry, and a man longing for a truly devoted yes-woman will stumble over her critical scrutiny. But someone with an eye for refinement, who values conscientiousness and diligence, who looks for a true companion in life who delivers more than she promises can be happy with this woman.

Libra
As the Feminine Searching-Image or Self-Image.

In the **feminine** horoscope as the self-image of the young woman;
In the **masculine** horoscope as the main symbol of the anima and the searching-image.

In the **feminine** horoscope as self-image of the mature/motherly woman; In the **masculine** horoscope as the motherly/complementary portion of the anima and searching-image.

ARCHETYPE:
The dancer.

ELEMENT:
Air

TYPE:
The ballerina, the beauty, the charming lady.

STYLE AND TASTE:
Prefers harmonious form and color combinations. Likes designer art, as well as the elegant style of Art Deco.

MATURE FORM:
The unflappable woman, the peace-maker, the esthete.

NAIVE OR DISTORTED FORM:
The doll, the fake, the overly sensitive person, the affected woman.

STRENGTH:
Friendly, elegant, obliging, charming, well-balanced, appreciative of art, sociable, diplomatic, graceful.

PROBLEM AREAS:
Craves harmony, aloof, indecisive, ingratiating, apathetic.

RELATIONSHIP STRENGTHS:
The partner who is well-balanced and always concerned with fairness.

RELATIONSHIP PROBLEMS:
More illusion than reality since she frequently is very interested in outward appearances.

BASIC MOOD:
Cheerful and poised, with a great ability to adapt and distinct need for harmony.

EROTICISM:
Graceful, coquettish seduction and light sensuality. Loves a stylish ambience.

PLACES AND SITUATIONS WHERE SHE MAY BE ENCOUNTERED:
At the fashion show, at the art academy, in the garden at Versailles, at the registry office, in the cosmetic salon, at the ballet, in the hotel bar, at the peace demonstration, in the perfumery, at the art opening, at the reception, at a concert, dancing.

BASIC PRINCIPLE:
I become who I am through you.

Libra

Interpreted as the feminine searching-image or self-image, the sign of Libra corresponds to an esthetic, elegant, well-groomed woman who looks like a ballerina. Her behavior is graceful and charming, her glance friendly, and her voice light and pleasant-sounding. Her likeable, cultivated appearance reveals her good taste. With a skillful hand, she understands how to appropriately combine colors, materials, and fashion styles, and she naturally always knows what is currently being worn in Paris, London, and New York. Her temperament is cheerful and carefree. With her winning, sociable manner she is popular and welcome everywhere. Her basic mood is good and sparkling with charm. She generously hands out compliments and is also receptive to all types of flattery herself. Inner equilibrium and harmonious concord with the world around her are her fundamental needs. She feels best when things are also going well for other people. Whenever emotional annoyances threaten, she is immediately concerned about bringing things back into balance. She is the master of lovely illusions. She is unequalled when it comes to perfectly shaping the outer appearance of things. On the other hand, she has a hard time coping with discord and sometimes suffers greatly because of this world's imperfection. This is why she does everything to avoid the hidden, deep, dark, and eerie aspects of life.

As the queen of good taste, the world of fine arts and esthetics is her world. She has a gift for combining business with pleasure wherever she is, and so her preferences and abilities often become her profession. Fashion, film, and architecture are areas where she feels at home. From the casual party to the banquet, she loves social events where she can nimbly and charmingly make and maintain contacts, and engage in relaxed conversations without having to commit to anything. She loves cultural life, likes to be invited to the theater, a musical, or a evening of chansons, and enjoys chatting in cafés on the boulevard or having a glass of champagne at a piano bar. Her appearance is very decisive for her self-confidence and this is why she does a great deal to correspond to her ideal of beauty. At the same time, she skillfully knows how to discreetly improve wherever Mother Nature wasn't quite attentive enough.

In order to win the heart of this woman, a man should be able to please her eye, in addition to having good manners. A well-groomed appearance, skilled courtesy, and a self-evident sureness of taste and style very much impress her. On the other hand, rugged masculinity repels her, and she finds blunt overtures to be practically shocking. Her idea of how a woman should be wooed is reminiscent of the courtship of the troubadours or the knights of King Arthur. However, a man doesn't have to take singing lessons if he knows how to show himself to be a gentleman and remembers to bring her roses and help her into her coat.

Life with her is pleasant, relaxed, and characterized by a spirit of partnership. She feels love to be an art that shouldn't be permitted to crash into the depths of human existence. For this reason, she constantly tries to make life together harmonious. She tends to have a hard time being alone since she needs someone else to be around just like she needs air to breathe. However, this need for contact shouldn't be misunderstood as the desire to merge with another person. She can't at all stand being pressured but needs—as in anything else—a balance between contact and freedom. She keeps away from the trivialities of everyday life as much as possible and prefers to enjoy her time with friends.

She loves to flirt, especially since she enjoys having her attractiveness confirmed time and again. A man who reacts with jealousy to this will have a hard time with her. However, if he is understanding about it, she will be a faithful partner for him. Eroticism is a graceful dance for her. The titillating mixture of flirting, grace, and a harmonious game of closeness and distance arouse her lightly playful sensuality. In such a *pas de deux*, style, form, and lovely illusions should be paid just as much attention to as anywhere else in her life.

When there are problems in love, she quickly shows herself willing to make a compromise, diplomatically avoids confrontations, and easily complies with her partner's wishes and suggestions. Because she may only truly feel well in an environment without conflicts, she may prefer a superficial and false peace to open confrontation. Being well-received and liked may be more important than asserting her own needs and concerns. As pleasant as this may appear to be for her partner in many cases, this attitude is very difficult to deal with when it comes to solving deep-rooted problems. Her indignation or inability to bear tension frequently causes her to look for premature solutions in which the actual problem is just avoided or temporarily glossed over.

Her style of living reflects her sense of beauty and perfection. Her home is a calling card for her elegant taste and could come directly out of a high-gloss brochure. The stylishly furnished rooms are always so well cared-for and neat that they may sometimes seem a bit impersonal as a result. She loves the company of other people and maintains friendships with much love and attention, even if there isn't a great deal of commitment involved. As the perfect hostess, she understands how to create a light, sociable atmosphere at any time and, practically in passing, pampers her guests with wholesome and delightfully arranged delicacies. Since she succeeds in mastering housework, her profession, and partnership with such ease, without ever appearing to be stressed, she is admired by other people for this quality.

As a mother, family peace is naturally very important to her heart. Difficulties or unpleasant things are simply faded out for as long as possible. She is the balancing power, always making sure that everyone is doing well. In terms of her children, she also tries to be as fair as possible and bring their interests into harmony with her own. At the same time, it's very important that she remains an attractive woman for her partner in addition to all the family obligations. When raising children, she promotes their interests in the areas of music, language, and art, making sure that they know how to behave themselves wherever they are and at any time. From early on, she permits them enough freedom and always has an open ear for their concerns and desires. She also likes to be a good friend to teenagers, and never meddles in their affairs without being asked to do so.

Someone who seeks commitment and passionate emotionality will experience this woman to be cool and smooth. But a man who values the charming and elegant atmosphere that this woman can create will find her to be a well-balanced partner who always strives to be fair.

Scorpio
As the Feminine Searching-Image or Self-Image.

In the **feminine** horoscope as the self-image of the young woman;
In the **masculine** horoscope as the main symbol of the anima and the
searching-image.

In the **feminine** horoscope as self-image of the mature/motherly
woman; In the **masculine** horoscope as the motherly/complementary
portion of the anima and searching-image.

ARCHETYPE: The female shaman.	ELEMENT: Water
TYPE: The mysterious woman, the Circe, the unfathomable one.	STYLE AND TASTE: Prefers strong contrasts and has a tendency toward things that are eerily beautiful. Likes provocations and the style of surrealism.
MATURE FORM: The female healer, the emotionally strong woman.	NAIVE OR DISTORTED FORM: The woman without scruples, the vamp, the obnoxious person, the *femme fatale*.
STRENGTH: Passionate, emotional depth, charismatic, committed feelings, inner stability, lack of tabus, power of suggestion.	PROBLEM AREAS: Need to control others, manipulative, compulsive, calculating mind, jealous, sexually dependent, masochistic.
RELATIONSHIP STRENGTHS: The committed partner who is willing to give everything.	RELATIONSHIP PROBLEMS: Emotionally unpredictable, provocative, hurtful, vindictive, and jealous.
BASIC MOOD: Frequently in turmoil on the inside but outwardly controlled and inscrutable.	EROTICISM: Passionate devotion and lustful, intensive experiences. Loves a touch of the disreputable and forbidden.

PLACES AND SITUATIONS WHERE SHE MAY BE ENCOUNTERED:
In secret archives, in the laboratory, at rituals, in the research lab, in the operating room, in the underground, at graveyards, watching crime films, on the black market, at the second-hand dealer, studying psychology, at the seance, at power places, in grottoes and caves, in the alchemist's kitchen, in the house of horrors.

BASIC PRINCIPLE:
The only way to get rid of a temptation is to give in to it!

Scorpio

Interpreted as a feminine searching-image or self-image, the sign of Scorpio correlates with a mysterious woman, a Circe who radiates dark fascination. Her Sphinx-like glance can fixate, hypnotize, and seduce. Her voice is suggestive and often whispers so quietly that she forces people to give her their full attention for this reason alone. Her appearance is accomplished and she often looks like a mysterious sorceress. She prefers to dress in dark colors, tends toward strong contrasts, loves provocative accessories, and also likes to appear in patent leather and leather.

Her temperament displays both passionate vehemence and controlled reserve, for the spectrum of her emotions primarily ranges between extremes. She is hardly acquainted with nuances. Her feelings have something uncompromising about them and resemble an ultimatum, circling time and again within the dark depths of emotional dependency and around the abysses of human weakness. Her immense sensitivity is penetrated with a basic mistrustful tone, whereby she rather quickly feels herself to be attacked and threatened subliminally. She comprehends dangerous situations more instinctively and quickly than other people. However, in her efforts to avoid abysses and dangers, she may develop compulsive behavior to which her surrounding world must also subject itself. This is because she leaves nothing to chance— even when it comes to her feelings—and outwardly makes a reserved and unapproachable impression. Concealed behind all this is an enormous vulnerability and constant fear of rejection. She is also primarily afraid of losing control and thereby being helpless and at the mercy of life's adversities.

Her world is the realm of shadows. Where others may shudder and turn away full of fear, horror, or revulsion, she stares as if spellbound with a mixture of abhorrence and fascination. She would find believing in an ideal world to be hypocritical and also terribly boring. Anything subversive awakens her interest, whether it is found in art or within public life. The shadow realm of society magically attracts her, as do the dark aspects of the human psyche. She frequently finds her calling here. Anything that is prohibited, frowned upon, and disreputable lets her heart beat with excitement. With her penchant for everything extreme, she loves what is slightly morbid and eerily beautiful, as well as being able to provoke others splendidly with it. She is fascinated with overstepping the line, fathoming secrets, violating tabus, being enchanting and bewitching, and knows very well how to manipulate others. Whenever this becomes easy for her to do, she quickly loses interest. However, she respects anyone who appears to resist her magic; and yet, she will constantly make a new attempt to beguile him with her power.

Anyone who tries to win the favor of this woman should use an unusual approach. This may be completely droll, obscure, disreputable, or even extreme, but don't bother going to her in a harmless and all too apparent manner. If you risk it, you will either win her completely or not at all. Nuances are foreign to her and she certainly can't be won with half-hearted attempts—the fire of her passion is too hot. Her demanding intensity makes her attractive and at the same time so unpredictable that approaching her isn't everyone's "cup of tea," no matter whether she shows herself from her mysterious, reserved side or is seductively luring.

Life with her is extraordinary. When she opens up, she does this in a way that is more committed and decisive than anyone else. And when she gets involved with someone, it is no longer called a relationship, but a pact, an irrevocable connection that must stand up to all the extreme experiences like power and helplessness and love and hate. Although she will do everything so that a man submits to her, at the same time she despises those who surrender and become spinelessly enslaved to her, which means that she may also run hot and cold at times.

This woman seeks intense experiences and likes to test the resistance. She doesn't tolerate it well when love becomes too peaceful and all conflicts give way to a great harmony. In order to create new tensions, she knows how to phenomenally enchant, beguile, and bewitch her beloved, "lulling" him until he completely gives himself up to her in order to provoke him so extremely the next moment that he startles out of his trance in a flash. She frequently becomes a slave to her uncompromising exclusiveness, which lets her endure and put up with whatever she has started.

Wherever her love has fallen, she no longer sees an alternative to it. Yet, she can be unfaithful—not in order to leave a relationship, but because she feels herself terribly drawn to secrecies. And, if she is openly unfaithful, this is one of her many provocations. In contrast, she herself is so wildly jealous that she would never forgive unfaithfulness. She knows how to use her erotic attraction in a conscious, bewitching, shocking, or even completely subtle but effective manner, whereby she is always in control. She is the epitome of the woman that many men fear because they could become enslaved helplessly by her spell of love. Her eroticism blossoms in the twilight, on the borderline of taboos, and gives her a magically fascinating charisma. She is the mysterious vamp, the *femme fatale* with the irresistible touch of the forbidden.

It is only natural that not every man will share this passion with her, and so problems will also come up in the love relationship time and again.

However, although this woman appears to initiate the relationship conflicts herself with her dark, sometimes also destructive side, she would go through hell in the truest sense of the word should a separation threaten. This is why she will hardly surrender even in the most difficult situations, but let things go to extremes time and again. Her tendency toward extremes drives her to do this. Only when she is completely shattered does she feel a regenerating energy that lets her rise from the depths once again, strengthened and purified.

Her home doesn't necessarily appear to be a cozy nest, but tends to resemble a mysterious fortress with an absolutely private realm. When decorating it, she tends toward breaks in style that bring tension and a change of pace, making her home into an unusual place with a certain something. The slightly wilted bouquet appeals to her aesthetic sense much more than any classical ideal of beauty. Being invited to her place should be understood to be a privilege that only good friends enjoy, and there are very few people who fit this description for her.

Either she wants a family and children at any price, or she feels a deep fear and rejection of this responsibility. As a mother, she leaves nothing to chance. Power and helplessness alternate back and forth between her and her children. They appear to be mutually at each other's mercy and thereby spin an inseparable bond of the most intense attachment. She can hardly be accused of a lack of effort, particularly not when it comes to defending her loved ones against attacks from the outside. Even if she can't always openly show her affection, she usually loves her children from the depths of her soul and, if need be, is unconditionally willing to sacrifice everything for them.

Those who shy away from extremes and deep passion, who prefer to sail in smoother waters and always want things to be comfortable, should keep well clear of this dark Eve. But those who seek intensity, who are fascinated by the disreputable and the forbidden, who are tired of superficiality and strive for depth, will find in her an exciting, extraordinary woman who is willing to give everything within a relationship.

Sagittarius
As the Feminine Searching-Image or Self-Image.

In the **feminine** horoscope as the self-image of the young woman;
In the **masculine** horoscope as the main symbol of the anima and the
searching-image.

In the **feminine** horoscope as self-image of the mature/motherly
woman; In the **masculine** horoscope as the motherly/complementary
portion of the anima and searching-image.

ARCHETYPE: The high priestess.	**ELEMENT:** Fire
TYPE: The liberal-minded woman, the well-traveled individual.	**STYLE AND TASTE:** Prefers everything comfortable and generous from exotic mixes to free style; likes the high-flying aspiration of the Gothic.
MATURE FORM: The scholar, the philosopher, the cosmopolitan.	**NAIVE OR DISTORTED FORM:** The snob, the hypocrite, the phony, the moralist.
STRENGTH: Confident, trusting, has spiritual beliefs, liberal-minded, zestful, tolerant, visionary, dignified, prudent.	**PROBLEM AREAS:** Presumptuous, conceited, has an expectant attitude, arrogant, dogmatic, haughty, complacent.
RELATIONSHIP STRENGTHS: The supportive partner who always knows how to make the best of everything.	**RELATIONSHIP PROBLEMS:** High levels of expectations that are quickly disappointed. Tends to moralize.
BASIC MOOD: Optimistic, cheerful, and sustained by hope and trust.	**EROTICISM:** Easily inflamed. Enjoys her experiences. Loves everything exotic and unfamiliar, as well as an unconstrained atmosphere.

PLACES AND SITUATIONS WHERE SHE MAY BE ENCOUNTERED:
On a trip around the world, in the lecture hall, at the ethnological museum, in the cathedral, at the open-air festival, in New York, on the observation tower, at the travel agency, in the foreign department, in the Chinese class, studying philosophy, in the courtroom, at the missionary station, in an airplane.

BASIC PRINCIPLE:
Human beings are noble, helpful, and good!

Sagittarius

Interpreted as the feminine searching-image or self-image, the sign of Sagittarius corresponds to a very tolerant, bright, and cosmopolitan woman who knows and loves the yearning for faraway places and the excitement of things exotic. Her self-confident behavior is casual and urbane. Her searching glance is directed into the distance, a hopeful keynote always rings in her lively voice, and her appearance—independent of her height—has something both noble and nonchalant about it. She has a distinct sense for everything comfortable and likes to dress with an exotic flair, cultivates an "independent" style, and thereby evades the dictates of fashion.

With her cheerful disposition, she radiates a great deal of joy and hopeful confidence, which others find contagious. It's not too easy to ruin her good mood. She has a basic trust in life and rarely fears getting the worst of the deal because she is convinced that there is plenty of everything. Since she fundamentally believes in the good in every person, she can openly approach others. If she does happen to be in a bad mood, she doesn't take long to get over her aggravation. Even in difficult situations, she rarely lets her head hang because she still feels herself sustained by an inner fire of hope. She is a generous woman who is very capable of enthusiasm and loves impressive, far-sighted plans and projects. She has little use for small-mindedness and mundane things. This gives her a certain tendency to exaggerate and have visionary ideals, and occasionally even a somewhat smug tone when she advocates her lofty convictions using overly emotional gestures. She can evoke the good in the world with ardent zeal, and if necessary, may also quickly reach for the stars in a utopian way.

Traveling is something she likes to do, and she does it often because her world is the wide world. Both outer and inner journeys are the elixir of her life; she is at home on all continents, and is always interested in anything that promises to expand her horizons. However, not only do foreign countries thrill her heart, but the inner journeys to new insights and perceptions inspire her time and again. Whether because of her work or personal inclinations, she likes to go on "expeditions" through art and culture. She listens attentively to reports by globetrotters, leafs through travel guides, attends lectures, rummages through libraries, and looks into various philosophies and religions. Although she has no problem in dealing with luxury and enjoying the amenities of life, when forced to decide, she will be glad to do without the everyday comforts and neglect all outward appearances immediately in order to go on an important journey.

Someone who wants to impress her or win her heart will be permitted to lay it on a bit thick. However, a homebody has no chance since she is truly impressed by a wide horizon, liberal-mindedness, and the unfamiliar charm of strange places and things. She loves the generous man who trusts her, the liberal spirit who she knows will support her and not limit her freedom of movement and development. On the other hand, what she really cannot put up with is dishonesty, mistrust, and someone who squares accounts like a bookkeeper.

She expects much more than just a mutual mastering of everyday life from a relationship. Philosophical talks about God and the world, contacts in many languages with many countries, and searching together for the meaning of life are important to her. She loves everything elevated, whether it is the mood, the education, the social class, or the professional position. This is why she supports and motivates her partner in his working career as well; after all, her man is a man of the world who is made for important tasks. As long as he doesn't severely disappoint her, she will believe in him and is absolutely convinced she has the best partner at her side. She has no problem at all imagining emigrating with him or pitching her tent in a completely new environment. Mutual future projects and big plans, or even just playing with possibilities for the future, keep her life-fire burning. In all of this, she treats herself in quite a generous way and allows herself a lot of freedom to spread out and develop.

She usually has a large circle of acquaintances and also maintains friendly and intellectual relationships with other men. At the same time, she voluntarily remains faithful to her partner. However, if she feels herself to be too constricted or even observed and controlled with chronic jealousy, she will quickly take to her heels. Eroticism and things exotic are related to each other for her, which is why her chosen one may easily come from another cultural group than her own. Once the erotic fire within her has been aroused, she can be very temperamental and passionate. Yet, since she considers herself to be "good" and also understands this to include moral irreproachability, there may be surprises if this attitude leads to a moral constraint that would hardly be expected in such a liberal-minded woman.

When there are difficulties in love, she will first be deeply disappointed since it is actually beneath her dignity to have something so profane in her relationship. This is why she first tries using her generosity and tolerance to overlook the problem. Only when her partner sins so much that she feels she will always have to be ashamed of him is the damage too extensive. In all other cases, the problems will be solved within the shortest amount of time thanks to her confidence and solid belief in the goodness of human beings.

In her home environment, she also needs generosity. This is expressed in her preference for spacious rooms in the upper stories with the corresponding panorama. Above all, her furnishings must be comfortable and usually display a collection of different styles and a bright mix of colors since her taste knows no boundaries. Souvenirs from everywhere are reminders of the numerous vacations and her perpetual yearning for faraway places. However, she was not born to do housework since she quickly finds routine boring and routine also limits her freedom. She can improvise well at any time. And since she travels so frequently, she doesn't even make herself too much at home.

As a mother, she passes on her basic trust and optimism to her children. She will support and motivate them in their plans and wants them to become familiar with the world at an early age. As the good soul of the family, even when situations are difficult, she doesn't lose heart, but prefers to find something positive about them. Her cheerful manner helps others see the beauty in this world. A good education for her children is very important to her. When they are growing up, she allows them a great deal of space so they can have their own experiences. Another reason for this is so that she can also gain more freedom for herself as a result.

Those who want a down-to-earth, conventional woman for hearth and home will have a hard time keeping up with her free spirit and far-ranging future projects. But someone desiring a carefree, cheerful person at his side who is easy to enthuse and knows how to build up and support her partner will hit the jackpot with this woman.

Capricorn
As the Feminine Searching-Image or Self-Image.

In the **feminine** horoscope as the self-image of the young woman;
In the **masculine** horoscope as the main symbol of the anima and the searching-image.

In the **feminine** horoscope as self-image of the mature/motherly woman; In the **masculine** horoscope as the motherly/complementary portion of the anima and searching-image.

ARCHETYPE: The sage.	ELEMENT: Earth
TYPE: The hardworking woman, the responsible individual, the iron lady.	STYLE AND TASTE: Prefers classical elegance and quality, limits herself to what is necessary, and likes the simple style of Zen.
MATURE FORM: The dignitary, the dutiful woman, the grand old dame.	NAIVE OR DISTORTED FORM: The tough lady, the conformist, the pessimist, the austere person, the embittered individual.
STRENGTH: Conscientious, honest, clear, responsible, objective, simple, has an eye for what is essential.	PROBLEM AREAS: Standoffish, intolerant, hardened, inexorable, controlling, emotionally cold.
RELATIONSHIP STRENGTHS: The reliable partner with whom one can talk at any time and develop something on a long-term basis.	RELATIONSHIP PROBLEMS: Can be severe, austere, or withdrawn, and give the partner the feeling of not measuring up to her standards.
BASIC MOOD: Tends to be sober, objective, and disciplined, seldom lets herself go emotionally, and avoids sentimentality.	EROTICISM: Deep feelings, yet very much in control. Doesn't like hearing "sweet little nothings" and needs a secure setting.

PLACES AND SITUATIONS WHERE SHE MAY BE ENCOUNTERED:
At the cross on the summit, in the desert, working for the police, on the governing board, at the internal revenue office, in silence, at the intelligence office, at the reform school, at the tea ceremony, doing gymnastics for her back, climbing mountains, doing a fasting cure, in seclusion, in Alaska.

BASIC PRINCIPLE:
First work, then play.

Capricorn

Interpreted as the feminine searching-image or self-image, the sign of Capricorn corresponds to a respectable, responsible woman with practical skills, often in the area of handicrafts. Her behavior is completely unaffected, can be quiet and business-like, but also formal, serious, and correct. Her glance is firm, and her voice is clear, with dry undertones. In her appearance, she is straightforward in every respect since she sometimes is reminiscent of an iron lady, and her actual beauty can only be recognized at second glance. In her clothing, she prefers subtle elegance with classical style and chooses timeless cuts to fast-moving, eccentric fashion trends.

Calm reserve is her basic temperament. It can take a long time for her to show feelings, and only when she feels secure does she open up emotionally. But even then, she doesn't really let herself go or lose control. Her innermost self is like private chambers into which friends are at most permitted to take a quick look and only the closest confidants are let in. A true soul, much softer than her outer hard shell would lead one to believe, is concealed behind this reservedness. Her charm has an austere fragrance to it, but surrounds her with an aura of simple honesty that invites others to trust her. She tends toward a purposive pessimism in the belief that later disappointments can be prevented in this manner. In connection with her serious approach toward life, this attitude can lead to a joyless careerism and embitterment, but also to a simple, cheerful contentment. The latter is the case particularly when she has retained her good, but individualistic, sense of humor and knows how to laugh at herself as well.

Her world is work and public life. Her nature combines ambition and a distinct sense of perfection into a mixture that frequently brings her into high professional positions. Whether in the business world, in a handicraft that she practices, or working in house and garden, wherever she applies herself, she is highly diligent, dutiful, and conscientious. Whatever she does, she does it 100 percent. Her public commitment to social tasks and obligations corresponds to her sense of responsibility and the desire to earn social affiliation and recognition. However, with all her power she can also be completely selfless in placing herself in the service of a cause without having an eye on the laurels. Her self-control is perfect, and she naturally never steps out of line in her behavior, but always knows what is proper.

The way to her heart is like climbing a mountain: the path is long, rocky, and strenuous, and requires patience and endurance. Yet, at the summit the persevering man will be met with eternal faithfulness as a reward for his tirelessness. This woman has absolutely no interest in a light and easy flirt. Love is no game for her, but meant to be serious from the start and accordingly binding. Because she expects a more mature sense of responsibility and solidified character from older people, she keeps an eye out for a man who is established and has already achieved something in terms of his profession.

Her understanding of a genuine relationship is a clear decision for a partner, and she tends to seal this decision earlier rather than later with a marriage certificate. Naturally she must thoroughly consider the candidate, and it may take some years before she has made her decision. With her strong need for security, she very much values the legal blessing, even if other people find it to be long outdated and old-fashioned. She loves things that are respectable, durable, and have developed over time, which means that love and affection—like good wine—also grow and ripen more and more through the years. A life together with her takes a steady and calm course, except if she is so professionally committed that she overworks on a regular basis. Then her private life will naturally be neglected, and her husband's needs will end up in second place. When there are mutual, work-related projects, she is the ideal partner. She will set aside personal needs for a goal that she wants to achieve and accept even longer hauls without complaint, demanding much of herself, as well as others. She can energetically pitch in and be very undemanding at the same time.

Affairs don't interest her at all since she wants clear circumstances in every respect. Faithfulness is a self-evident truth for her, and someone who has met her high standards and passed her "qualifying exam" can be certain of her absolute loyalty from that time on. Eroticism is a strange area for her. She often isn't even aware of her charm. Since playfulness is foreign to her nature, she may make an austere and reserved impression, yet experience a deep sensuality and complete enjoyment at the same time.

When there are problems in love, she is always aware of her share of the responsibility. Even in difficult times, she stands by her partner and tolerates even longer bottlenecks without questioning the relationship because of them. She is also persevering and dispassionate when striving for solutions, and expects the same from her partner. Empty promises cause her to react quite indignantly, and she doesn't think much of "dream" solutions anyway. Instead, she insists on continually working on difficulties until they have been truly cleared up. Since she knows that a relationship always means conflicts and hard work, she is willing at any time to take on her share of this. She feels at home when there is order and clarity within her four walls. Her furnishings tend toward beautiful simplicity instead of Baroque richness. So she tends to live in a correspondingly simple and practical way, but with a sure taste for forms and proportions and a preference for few but exquisite pieces of furniture. This lack of frills and cool aloofness ultimately also reflects her aversion to sentimentality, emotional dependence, and too much closeness. She doesn't even have a hard time being alone, since she learns at an early age to take care of herself. Her friends tend to be few in numbers, but they are good friends, and she usually also grows old with them.

If she has decided on the role of mother, which frequently only is the case later in life, she will take her duties seriously and be aware of her responsibility. Her reliability personifies security for her children. She offers them a solid structure in everyday life, in which they can easily find their way and orient themselves. Whenever they need her, she is there since she very well knows what she owes her children. Although she demands a lot, she is also willing to give a great deal. As a result, she imparts discipline, steadfastness, and healthy ambition as values that in her opinion are a part of coping with life. Later, as her children gradually become adults, she will discover whether her standards were too strict and conservative in the extent of their rebellion.

Those who seek passionate declarations of love, a light-footed ballerina, or a scintillating fairy-tale princess won't strike gold with this woman. Her love has nothing effusive to it, but it is deep and constant. She is an upright, highly-principled woman who can be counted on in any situation.

Aquarius
As the Feminine Searching-Image or Self-Image.

In the **feminine** horoscope as the self-image of the young woman;
In the **masculine** horoscope as the main symbol of the anima and the
searching-image.

In the **feminine** horoscope as self-image of the mature/motherly
woman; In the **masculine** horoscope as the motherly/complementary
portion of the anima and searching-image.

ARCHETYPE:
The philosopher.

ELEMENT:
Air

TYPE:
The individualist, the sharp mind, the independent woman.

STYLE AND TASTE:
Prefers original, bizarre forms and extravagant materials. Likes modern art and unusual, unique creations.

MATURE FORM:
The humanist, the reformer.

NAIVE OR DISTORTED FORM:
The rebel, the woman involved in scandals, the crank, the cool girl.

STRENGTH:
Imaginative, independent, creative, original, humorous, believes in the future, liberal.

PROBLEM AREAS:
Flighty, indifferent, cool, noncommittal, flippant, aloof.

RELATIONSHIP STRENGTHS:
The open, tolerant friend who is always good for a surprise.

RELATIONSHIP PROBLEMS:
Tends to be flighty and emotionally detached with her urge for independence.

BASIC MOOD:
Cheerful and carefree, in as far as she doesn't feel herself to be constricted.

EROTICISM:
Playful and keen on experimentation, open for something new but tends not to be very passionate. Loves surprising encounters and unusual ambience.

PLACES AND SITUATIONS WHERE SHE MAY BE ENCOUNTERED:
At the computer, in the scene, in an astrology class, on the airplane, at the synthesizer, at a demonstration, at the ad agency, in Disneyland, jumping on the trampoline, studying sociology, sharing an apartment, at the cabaret, in the Council of Europe, at the masked ball, in virtual reality, in utopia.

BASIC PRINCIPLE:
Freedom must be boundless—above the clouds!

Aquarius

Interpreted as the feminine searching-image or self-image, the sign of Aquarius corresponds to an independent, open-minded woman who may sometimes also have a somewhat curious, eccentric touch. Her behavior is casual; it may also be provocatively unusual; her glance alert, and her bright voice sounds light and vivacious. In her appearance she personifies the androgynous type of woman. Her unconventional taste and her preference for breaks in style is obvious when it comes to her clothes. With the greatest degree of naturalness, she likes to wear today what will be fashion in two years. Shrill colors, plastic, nylon, as well as bold costume jewelry, are not a question of esthetic feeling for her, but the spirit of the times by which she likes to be inspired.

Her basic mood is cheerful and carefree. She appears to have a monopoly on eternal youth, and her effervescent temperament is infectious and sometimes even a bit high-strung. Any attempt to find emotional depth or steady feelings in her will probably be in vain. Sudden outbursts, unexpected changes in mood, and a restless nervousness are more in character for her. She often appears to be a live wire, and has simply too little patience for thoroughness and depth. A familiar environment isn't necessary for her to feel well since she can also relax in the middle of a very hectic pace. What she looks for is variety and relaxed contacts that don't stand in the way of her drive for individuality. When too much commitment is demanded of her, she likes to stay well clear of the situation. It's easy for her to subordinate her inner needs to her intellectual interests. This may let her appear to be cool and untouchable, awakening the impression that she doesn't really need emotional closeness. She senses her individuality and likes to play the role of the unpredictable, willful woman.

Her world is utopia. Wherever traditional thinking in roles and the barriers of gender, age, or nationality have been eradicated, where the focus is completely on the human being, she is at home. Liberated in every sense, she loves to step out of line and looks for new ways time and again to prove her independence. She often plays the outsider who rebels against traditional lifestyles, frequently acts defiant, and resists any type of label. She steadfastly refuses to do what everyone else does and loves living out her crazy ideas because she enjoys provoking in her own way in order to wake up other people and stimulate them to think about things. This is why she has a natural talent for all activities in which original or innovative ideas are required. Binding agreements aren't to her taste. They leave her little room for spontaneous decisions and become more problematic the longer they last. On the other hand, if she can develop her creativity, she may come up with some remarkable models. However, turning her ideas into concrete plans is frequently delayed by her tendency to once again sail far past reality with her theories.

Unusual paths and conversations in which there are flashes of inspiration lead to the heart of this woman. If a man comes up with something special for her, this will interest her far more than a perfect outward appearance or the obligatory invitation to dinner. Her great tolerance and desire to try out new things may sometimes cause some unusual or crazy encounters. If she is called eccentric, she considers this a genuine compliment.

Life with her is scintillating and exciting. She is like an intellectual surprise packet and constantly produces new ideas, which are sometimes more and sometimes less ingenious. A man who gets involved with her should be uncomplicated, flexible, and tolerant enough to be able to live with her flightiness, her enjoyment of variety, and her constantly new surprises. On the other hand, continuity and security mean little to her. Well-established routines and the monotonous everyday life of a relationship are emotive terms for her. If she feels her independence threatened—and this happens more quickly than some people know—she will immediately take a step backward and create more distance. Before she has to defend herself against expectations that are all too great, she would prefer to stay unattached. However, she also has no problem imagining a marriage in which she lives separately from her partner or being involved with a man who resides somewhere far away or is frequently absent because of his work. But this certainly doesn't mean that she is alone. To the contrary: she knows people everywhere and has heaps of friends.

For her, the most important thing about a relationship is that it is voluntary and based on equality. If she is unfaithful, this will usually happen quite spontaneously. At the same time, she never has the feeling of doing something forbidden or betraying someone. Apart from this, she is rarely driven by purely sensual desire. Instead, her eroticism takes place in her thoughts and ideas, particularly since passionate entanglements could obstruct her independence. So it is easier for her to do without this area more than others, which sometimes lets what was a sensual affair at the start become a platonic friendship.

When there are problems with love, she becomes distant. Although she helps others in solving their difficulties and can come up with astonishing ideas in doing this, as soon as she is involved personally, she doesn't like digging in the depths. She is quite willing to think about everything and discuss it, shows great insight, and is also theoretically completely ready to take the consequences; however, when it comes to translating the steps recognized as necessary into practice, it often becomes too strenuous for her and she quickly bails out. Then she prefers to go her own way, and since she gets along quite well alone, she will very much enjoy the regained independence for a while.

It is difficult for her to reach a state of domestic bliss since she tends to be constantly on the go and everyday routines tend to immediately trigger her tendency to flee. Even though she hardly gets around to using them, she loves to have all the achievements of modern technology in her home. If she does happen to be at home for once, friends will find her door open all the time since she loves a lot of activity and unexpected visitors. With her enjoyment of communication and variety, she could also imagine sharing a place with others, in as far as this doesn't force her to do things with them. With her provisional or crazy furniture, she also shows in her decorating style that she doesn't want to meet any standards.

She doesn't take on the traditional role of mother rashly, and her desire for children isn't particularly strong. If she does decide to have her own family, she will develop progressive methods of raising her children. She is naturally ready to exchange roles at any time. Instead of being a caring mother, she tends to be more of an interested friend for her children. She prefers to support her children's intellectual development and encourages them to be independent at an early age, instead of coddling them or binding them too tightly by caring for them too intensively. Particularly during puberty, she provides a lot of interest and understanding for her children, because she knows how important this inner struggle for independence is, and has a very good memory of it on the basis of her own experiences.

Those who long for a warmhearted, caring/motherly partner will catch cold with this cool bird of paradise. But someone seeking an unconventional, tolerant, self-sufficient partner who is completely open-minded will find in her a humorous woman who is always good for a surprise.

Pisces
As the Feminine Searching-Image or Self-Image.

In the **feminine** horoscope as the self-image of the young woman;
In the **masculine** horoscope as the main symbol of the anima and the searching-image.

In the **feminine** horoscope as self-image of the mature/motherly woman; In the **masculine** horoscope as the motherly/complementary portion of the anima and searching-image.

ARCHETYPE:
The fairy.

ELEMENT:
Water

TYPE:
The devoted woman, the muse.

STYLE AND TASTE:
Prefers flowing transitions and blurred contours, the illusion of perfection. Loves the style of symbolism.

MATURE FORM:
The artist, the medium, the mystic.

NAIVE OR DISTORTED FORM:
The addict, the martyr, the victim, the unrealistic dreamer, the illusionist.

STRENGTH:
Inspiring, devoted, empathetic, intuitive, selfless, sensitive, contemplative, willing to sacrifice, responsive.

PROBLEM AREAS:
Dependent, prone to addiction, has a victim attitude, engages in wishful thinking, helpless, unstable, susceptible, negligent.

RELATIONSHIP STRENGTHS:
The imaginative woman who can enchant and inspire.

RELATIONSHIP PROBLEMS::
Tends toward idealized concepts of relationships, which are always followed by painful disappointment.

BASIC MOOD:
Very sensitive, empathetic, and changeable. Easily influenced by the individual environment.

EROTICISM:
Seductive sensuality, enormous ability to be devoted, and strong need for merging. Loves states of rapture in a transcendent ambience.

PLACES AND SITUATIONS WHERE SHE MAY BE ENCOUNTERED:
By the sea, at the meditation center, in the hospital, on an island, in the home for people seeking political asylum, in prison, in the convent, in the ashram, in the media, in the temple, in a state of euphoria, painting with watercolors, taking violin lessons, in the theater, in seventh heaven.

BASIC PRINCIPLE:
Live your dream!

Pisces

Interpreted as the feminine searching-image or self-image, the sign of Pisces represents the devoted, tender woman and inspiring muse. Her behavior is reserved and discreet, her glance is clear in a watery way and sometimes lost in thought. Her voice is gentle and quiet. In her fairylike appearance, she often makes a graceful and fragile effect, and her aura has something mysteriously transfigured about it at times. She prefers to dress in wide, flowing materials and loves imaginative creations in constantly changing colors.

Her mood is very dependent on her environment, and is therefore quite changeable. She appears to be connected to the world soul with an invisible umbilical cord, resonates symbiotically in the emotional states of her fellow human beings, and as a result, has difficulty in setting limits against external influences. Instinctively, she absorbs all the vibrations of her surrounding world and is thereby so influenced in part by the wishes, needs, and expectations of others that she even has a hard time in closing herself off to unspoken expectations in her environment. In her boundless empathy for others, it may happen that she is flooded by pain and suffering, and at times practically swept away by it. Then a deep *weltschmerz* overcomes her and she feels helplessly at its mercy, without even being able to explain why. Her tendency to take a spiritual path and withdraw from time to time is a healthy attempt to find herself instead of completely losing herself in the outside world.

She often appears to be not completely from this world. Instead, she seems like a wanderer between dream and reality, for whom there is undoubtedly more than one reality. According to her level of maturity, she may develop phenomenal knowledge and is well versed when it comes to the supernatural world, or becomes a sad victim of her wishful thinking time and again. The only—but very effective—protection that she has against illusion and deception is her high development of sound instinct. But when she doesn't hear her inner warnings because her longing for the dream world is even stronger, or when she surrenders herself to the seductive power of a tempting insinuation from the outside, she may crash rudely on the hard ground of reality time and again. She may have a difficult time learning from these experiences, even after many disappointments, and protecting herself.

She can selflessly dedicate herself to some type of social work and committedly look after people who need solace and help. With her mediumistic tendencies, she may not only feel others' deepest needs but can also truly help them with her subtle powers. The longing for transcendental experiences often leads her to spiritual and religious circles, and her sensitivity gives her an excellent access to art. Her emotional experiences are often the material that she magnificently expresses as a sublime mixture of longing, devotion, and sweet melancholy in music, painting, and dance, or with which she deeply touches others as an actress.

The heart of this sensitive woman can be won by inspiring her imagination and sweeping her off to a sea of dreams and images. A walk to the end of the rainbow is particularly well suited for this purpose or—somewhat simpler—a concert evening, a visit to the cinema or theater. But the most important thing is that a man touches her heartstrings with great intuitive understanding.

Life with her is wonderful and wondrous. Even after living with her for many years, her partner will still find her to be mysterious in some respects. She perceives the universal dimensions of everyday life, senses secret correlations, and knows how to open other people's eyes for invisible worlds. What she needs in a relationship is the stability that she often can't find on her own. Although she knows how to superbly support and intuitively guide her partner with love, when she feels helpless and lost herself, she will also need his comfort and his strong shoulders to lean on. Then she needs some very practical help in life because at such times her delicacy doesn't permit her to cope with the harshness of reality. Yet, a man will hardly have her all to himself, since even in the most beautiful moments of deepest emotional connection, he will feel how her love streams beyond him and gets lost somewhere in the distance. Her ability to love is so extensive that she has difficulty in focusing on one single person. So he will frequently get the impression that she encounters all other creatures on Earth with the same love and attention that she gives him. It's best for him not to be too jealous about this.

This is no reason to call her unfaithful because her overflowing love tends to seek additional containers. Her erotic fantasies are often as boundless as her entire being. Together with her strongly intuitive understanding and knowledge about other people's wishes, she becomes a master at the art of seduction. However, she may also sacrifice the physical aspect for a spiritual relationship or a secret crush that can never be fulfilled and has no place in everyday life.

When there are problems in love, when she feels too many demands placed on her by difficulties, or the everyday life of the relationship, she simply flees from the unpleasant reality. Then she either makes herself scarce emotionally and becomes hard to comprehend, or she tries to avoid painful confrontations by running to her fantasy world in order to dream of a perfectly harmonious relationship and pine for her soul mate. By the time she reappears from her fictitious reality, the problem has often solved itself or has at least disappeared for the moment—sometimes including the partner!

Since earthly things aren't really to her taste, everyday domestic life isn't all that important. Her living space may be furnished in an unusual way, and may appear to be absolute chaos or an enchanted castle from "1001 Nights." She has a distinct sense of good atmospheres, which she knows how to magically create independent of external structures. Anyone who visits her will quickly feel at home. Because of this, her home is frequently not only a shelter from the outside world but also a refuge for others. She feels best close to water, even if it's just an aquarium in her living room.

She is very receptive to motherhood. Even during the pregnancy, and particularly during the infancy of the child, she appears to sense precisely what the little, helpless being needs at the moment. In the following years as well, she cannot be fooled, yet it is easy for a child to wrap her around its finger since resoluteness isn't one of her characteristics when she deals with her offspring. Her deep understanding of her children's small and large concerns lets her be indulgent time and again. She always makes an effort to helpfully be at their side, because the happiness of the little ones is more important to her than her own needs. Even when her children become adults, she still selflessly orients herself toward their wishes.

Those seeking a practical housewife or a cool, clever business partner will despair at the fragility of this sensitive woman. But a man desiring an inspiring muse, a partner who can boundlessly love and enchantingly seduce him will wind up in seventh heaven with her.

PART IV

The TWELVE
MASCULINE TYPES

Aries
As the Masculine Searching-Image or Self-Image.

In the **masculine** horoscope as the self-image of the young man;
In the **feminine** horoscope as the main symbol of the animus and the searching-image.

In the **masculine** horoscope as self-image of the mature/fatherly man;
In the **feminine** horoscope as the fatherly/complementary portion of the animus and searching-image.

ARCHETYPE: The hero, the warrior.	**ELEMENT:** Fire
TYPE: The lively go-getter, the conqueror.	**BASIC ATTITUDE:** Loves challenges and facing them. Encounters the world directly and spontaneously.
MATURE FORM: The pioneer, the courageous man, the trailblazer.	**NAIVE OR DISTORTED FORM:** The hothead, the destroyer, the macho, the brute, the egomaniac.
STRENGTH: Assertive, willful, spontaneous, decisive, courageous, open, quick-witted, has drive and personal courage.	**PROBLEM AREAS:** Restless, egotistical, shortsighted, acts without thinking, violent-tempered, inconsiderate.
RELATIONSHIP STRENGTHS: The man who always comes up with new, animating impulses.	**RELATIONSHIP PROBLEMS:** Egotistically lives out his impulses without thinking of his partner.
TYPE OF ASSERTIVENESS: Goes at everything head first, is spontaneous and energetic, takes the offensive. TYPE: The hothead, the sprinter.	**SEXUALITY:** Hot-blooded and impatient, enjoys making conquests.

TYPICAL PROFESSIONAL AREAS:
Everywhere he can help new projects make a breakthrough, as well as dangerous or competitive situations: athlete, manager, stockmarket trader, dentist, stuntman, hunter, policeman, soldier, smith, fireman, emergency physician, surgeon, entrepreneur, politician, attorney.

BASIC PRINCIPLE:
If I'm not the right person, then who is? If not now, then when?

Aries

Interpreted as the masculine searching-image or self-image, the sign of Aries stands for a lively, aggressive man, a bold go-getter, and an adventurer willing to take risks. His appearance has something very masculine about it—an athletic figure, a muscular and fit body, or simply a certain macho attitude. His brash glance and prominent voice make sure that he is noticed immediately. He can be found anywhere something is going on, frequently in games, sports, and other competitions.

His strength is his spontaneity, his immense willpower, and his daring nature. He is the born conqueror of territory, the active and vital man who faces life intrepidly and always fights on the front line. His desire to risk even the impossible grows along with the size of the challenge. Even the smallest impulse is often enough to set him on fire. The immediate present is what interests him, and he finds spontaneous actions tempting. His refreshing impulsiveness and sometimes naive carefreeness have something loveable to them. Since he always looks straight ahead, he only perceives what takes place directly in front of his eyes. Although he hardly learns from the past, he can just as quickly forget setbacks and negative experiences. Thanks to an inexhaustible reservoir of sparkling vital energy, he has the ability to bounce back and even start from the beginning any time after a defeat.

In the distorted form, he can become a destroyer, an aggressive, undisciplined brute who ruthlessly asserts his own interests. The greatest challenge for him lies in the fact that his powers will also wane in time and cause him to hit against his limits. This is a highly unpleasant realization for him, which he tries to suppress with shows of strength, strenuous sport programs, and constant restlessness. Consistency and staying power aren't among his strong points since he is quite easily distracted, which is why longterm goals aren't for him. He can quite suddenly become enthusiastic about something, yet his interest often flags just as quickly as it started, particularly when he discovers that the goal can't be reached with power, but only with patience and perseverance. This makes him an excellent sprinter, but rather unsuited for long distances. He is so impatient that he has a hard time enduring tension. If he feels an impulse, he must immediately turn it into action or work it off in some other way, whereby he experiences difficulties in waiting for the right time to act. For this reason, he usually starts too soon, too hastily and thoughtlessly, wasting the great part of his excessive energies by jumping the

gun over and over. At the same time, he is a poor loser who can only grudg-
ingly admit his weaknesses.

Self-fulfillment is easiest for him to achieve in freelance work in which
he can apply his fiery sense of initiative and his enterprising spirit without
too many obstacles. He loves conquering new ground and helping an idea
make a breakthrough. Wherever it appears impossible for others to get
through, he is the pioneer who intrepidly leads and clears the way. He is a
lone fighter who tends to tangle just as easily with competitors as with a dis-
liked superior, and understands teamwork to mean that everyone dances to
his tune. Any type of routine takes away his momentum. What he needs is
variety, freedom of movement, and new challenges time and again. Only then
will he enjoy his work.

When a woman fascinates him, he goes all out. Any means will suit him
to conquer her. However, he understands little about the gallant way of
courting her. He will practically catch her off guard, make gestures that are
more or less adroit in a completely uninhibited manner, together with
impressive actions to catch her attention, and wins it through his refreshing
directness. With his totally unpolished approach, he is something like a big,
fresh rascal. His strength is making overtures. Afterward, his interest can
wane very quickly since he finds the actual thrill primarily in the act of conquest and the fascination of something new.

A relationship with him is very lively, and characterized by variety and
surprising actions. So that no boredom arises, he makes a lot of fuss about
nothing, and constantly creates some sort of excitement. He likes to dictate
the tempo and the direction, making it quite strenuous for his partner to constantly adapt to his arbitrary changes of direction. For this reason, it is best
not to make any longterm plans with him since he will just chuck them the
next day anyway. His impulsiveness and storming ahead don't leave him any
time to be considerate, and so he has tremendous difficulty including his
partner in his deliberations. He is hardly aware that he presses others up
against the wall and hurts them with his egotistical actions, and they seldom
occur because of any ill will on his part. He is just simply too occupied with
himself to perceive other people's needs as well. He knows stillness at best as
the calm before the storm or when he must prove to himself for once that he
can also get along without anyone else. Then he is actually a lonely cowboy
within the depths of his soul, who time and again must go his own way for a
while.

He loves reacting to every challenge and likes to face tests of courage to
prove his masculinity. However, should his partner get sick of always having
to admire his heroics, the situation can very quickly become critical. In order
to flatter his ego, he will soon look around for new conquests, because he is
basically only faithful to himself. It is his nature to play with fire, and when

the need for adventure awakens within him, then nothing can hold him back. His intensely instinctual nature can also be seen in his sexuality. He is the type of fiery lover who is driven by wild desire and only achieves his goal when the woman becomes weak at the sight of so much masculinity.

He is easily put off when someone tries to rein him in, civilize him, or make him settle down—or, even worse, when a woman contends with him for first place. Because he relates everything to himself, he quickly feels himself to be under attack and is much more sensitive than others would think him to be. His favorite motto is "attack is the best defense," and he goes directly on the course of confrontation. A fight with him is heated, loud, and impulsive. When he is rubbed the wrong way, he easily loses control and freely vents his anger. In the process, plates can fly and the neighbors become startled when he argues with banging doors. In order to make up with him, it is usually enough to stop adding fuel to the flames. As quickly as he gets worked up about things, he will also forget them again and does not hold grudges.

Although he may quickly and spontaneously decide upon having a family, the responsibility and long-term commitment of fatherhood will hit him unexpectedly hard afterward. He has difficulty with the many necessary compromises, and he doesn't like to subject himself to personal restrictions. This is why he encourages his children at an early age to act independently. He isn't fearful when they take their first steps, and even encourages them to try something new. As long as he personally has fun in the process, he will spend lots of time with them and is a good pal with whom they can compete at sports and games. However, if his children are too willful and stubborn, or if they make too much work, or if they lack in enthusiasm, he can quickly become annoyed and lose interest.

This man doesn't exactly tend toward contemplation and reliability, yet he is a dynamic and active partner and companion with whom life certainly won't be boring.

Taurus
As the Masculine Searching-Image or Self-Image.

In the **masculine** horoscope as the self-image of the young man;
In the **feminine** horoscope as the main symbol of the animus and the searching-image.

In the **masculine** horoscope as self-image of the mature/fatherly man;
In the **feminine** horoscope as the fatherly/complementary portion of the animus and searching-image.

ARCHETYPE:	ELEMENT:
The farmer, the good shepherd.	Earth

TYPE:	BASIC ATTITUDE:
The good-natured man, the down-to-earth individual.	Is seldom in a hurry, enjoys life. Encounters the world in a benevolent and cautious way.

MATURE FORM:	NAIVE OR DISTORTED FORM:
The connoisseur, the guardian.	The miser, the pighead, the Philistine, the glutton.

STRENGTHS:	PROBLEM AREAS:
Steadfast, calm, has stamina, persevering, resolute, loyal.	Excessive, indolent, defiant, materialistic, stubborn, unyielding.

RELATIONSHIP STRENGTHS:	RELATIONSHIP PROBLEMS:
The man who is always there when he is needed; he has a lot of patience.	Resists changes that disturb his peace and quiet, can be very possessive.

TYPE OF ASSERTIVENESS:	SEXUALITY:
Things that seethe for a long time ultimately turn into anger. Slowly but surely. TYPE: The weight lifter.	Pleasurable, passionate, and with enjoyment of familiar things.

TYPICAL PROFESSIONAL AREAS:
All areas where things are cared for and looked after and where developed structures set a secure framework: farmer, banker, businessman, realtor, cook, gardener, forest ranger, antique dealer, shepherd, restorer, millionaire, defense lawyer, restaurant owner, biologist, masseur.

BASIC PRINCIPLE:
A bird in the hand is worth two in the bush!

Taurus

Interpreted as the masculine searching-image or self-image, the sign of Taurus represents the good-natured, down-to-earth, strongly sensual man who knows how to enjoy life from the depths of his soul. A calm glance and firm voice lend good humor and warmth to his aura. His external appearance—depending on how much he has surrendered to the pleasures of life—may be husky, portly, or corpulent. He is encountered where there is sociability and a cheerful mood, in the circle of good friends, and in a familiar environment.

His strength is his calmness, his enormous staying power, and his steadfastness. He usually has skills at handicrafts, but is in any case a pragmatist, a practical man, and an untiring doer with a sense for useful and easy solutions. A hectic pace isn't at all to his taste, and when the world around him starts to panic, he keeps his cool. He doesn't think anything of purely speculative values. With his sure instinct for worthwhile investments, only achievable goals and solid, lasting results are of interest to him. His leisurely temperament is like that of a diesel engine that just slowly warms up. However, once he has started up and an objective appears worthwhile to him, he works toward it in a straightforward, persevering, and totally tenacious way. He knows how to carefully plan the individual steps, patiently wait for the appropriate opportunities, and also imperturbably stay on the ball where others have already long thrown in the towel. And when there is something to wait for, he proves to be better than anyone else at sitting things out.

In the distorted form, his annoyance at changes can also make him obstinate and stubborn, his clinging to traditions causes him to be too conservative, and the fear of material loss can promote his miserliness. Then he will hoard things without enjoying them, and his joy in life, which is otherwise quite sensual, becomes suffocated beneath his greed for more possessions and security. He can get completely bogged down in something and even stubbornly cling to it until the end, even if the conditions for doing this have long changed. If his sense of the familiar degenerates into a purely repetitive compulsion and he keeps turning in circles that get increasingly smaller, he can become very narrow-minded. Then he will just cultivate his prejudices and hermetically shield himself behind his garden wall against everything strange and unknown.

He finds his professional self-realization in a job that is reliable and crisis-proof, in which he can look after, care for, and multiply solid values. He prefers to apply his energy for the purpose of creating a solid basis, acquiring possessions, and setting up secure reserves. He will take the bird in the hand over the two in the bush at any time. Pragmatic values are his capital, and this is why he will only leave a sound job in order to expand his knowledge or increase his competence. He is very cautious and doesn't like to be in the front lines. This makes him the born second man who likes to do the preliminary work for those who bear the responsibility for the enterprise. He only has authority conflicts when he feels his person and his work to be underestimated.

When it comes to winning over a woman, he also tends to be deliberate and cautious. This particularly applies since he himself needs a bit more time than others to be really smitten by her. Yet, this also means that his fire is warmer and more lasting in comparison. He will win the trust of his chosen one through patience and reliability and her love through his warm hearted way of pampering her. He is a sensual seducer who doesn't rush anything and knows how to totally enjoy an erotic flirtation.

Life with him is distinguished by a sense of nature, of everything that takes time to grow and become familiar. His rich satisfaction develops increasingly with each repetition. It is the greatest pleasure for him to eat and drink in a small circle of good friends and savor life in all its facets. Someone desiring to flatter him should admire him for his reliability and endurance, as well as everything that he has achieved. One shouldn't expect any spectacular excitement around him, and he doesn't care for adventure and sudden surprises. Instead, he can always be depended upon. Once he has taken a liking to something, he doesn't understand why he should open up to something new and uncertain. It is very difficult to shake him up. He stands in life like a tower of strength, and all attempts to ruffle him bounce off the wall. Starting a relationship with him simultaneously means becoming his possession. Yet, this isn't all that tragic because he looks after everything he has with love and care. Things can become difficult when he believes that he must protect his territory against an attacker, a presumed rival. Once his jealousy is unleashed, he becomes a wild bull who sees only red.

Because he places importance on the familiar and secure rather than the excitement of something new, he is also a very faithful person. This makes marriage his ideal form of relationship, which very much meets his need for security. Only the greatest frustration can drive him out of familiar regions to a new, strange territory. He experiences being unfaithful to his wife as much too strenuous, except when a woman makes him an easy offer. His sensual nature gives him a strong, sexual energy. He is a tender and tireless lover with a deep ability to experience love, but he can get into a routine.

A woman will quickly scare him away by spoiling his enjoyment of pleasure or reprimanding and restricting him in the process. And he can't stand having his good nature taken advantage of over a longer period of time or even systematically, or when someone proves to be unreliable or attacks his possessions. If there is a conflict, he gets defensive, stubborn, and silent. He reacts to pressure with counterpressure, and the greater the resistance, the rougher he can become. His strength lies in the defense, and so he builds a defensive wall with all his might. People may find the pigheadedness with which he does this a hard nut to crack. The situation may become dangerous when he is lured out of his reserve and continually provoked until his patience wears thin. When angered, his purely defensive attitude turns into an uncontrolled, offensive force that is very destructive and mows everything down like a steamroller. The best way to reconcile with him is to first give in since, if he has totally become fixed on or stuck in his anger, his aggression will increase from day to day until he has ultimately become so trapped in it that he no longer can get out on his own, even if he really wants to. However, if the other person gives in, he is not only relieved but also immediately willing to reconcile.

He is very much suited for the role of father since family also means tradition and security for him. He wants to own his home. He enjoys the comforts of home and he also likes to make his contribution to it, especially when this concerns his physical well-being. He is patient and understanding with his children. Family life only becomes difficult when children react defiantly against his authority and go their own way. Then he can vigorously insist on long outdated rules and regulations, rejecting all the new "nonsense" of the younger generation on principle. Concealed behind this defensive attitude is his need to keep the family together, as well as his fear of the transitory nature of life.

Although he certainly isn't a "party animal" and is not particularly interested in experiments, he is a faithful, extremely good-natured *bon vivant* with whom it is possible to have a very good life.

Gemini
As the Masculine Searching-Image or Self-Image.

In the **masculine** horoscope as the self-image of the young man;
In the **feminine** horoscope as the main symbol of the animus and the searching-image.

In the **masculine** horoscope as self-image of the mature/fatherly man;
In the **feminine** horoscope as the fatherly/complementary portion of the animus and searching-image.

ARCHETYPE: The scholar.	ELEMENT: Air
TYPE: The agile individual, the cunning fellow, the bright man.	**BASIC ATTITUDE:** Is constantly in motion and interested in everything. Encounters the world with attention and curiosity.
MATURE FORM: The mediator, the intellectual.	**NAIVE OR DISTORTED FORM:** The lout, the rake, the word twister, the gossip, the windbag.
STRENGTH: Flexible, has a quick intellectual grasp, nimble, eloquent, witty, always has a snappy comeback.	**PROBLEM AREAS:** Noncommittal, overly intellectual, hectic, suffers from inner conflicts, constantly relativizing, cynical.
RELATIONSHIP STRENGTHS: The man who brings new ideas and suggestions into the relationship time and again.	**RELATIONSHIP PROBLEMS:** Remains noncommittal in terms of emotions and often doesn't abide by agreements.
TYPE OF ASSERTIVENESS: Jack-of-all-trades, quick, tactically skilled, and agile with sudden changes of direction. TYPE: The track-and-field athlete.	**SEXUALITY:** Little sex drive, enjoys diversity, prefers verbal eroticism.

TYPICAL PROFESSIONAL AREAS:
All areas in which information is exchanged and linguistic abilities are required: journalist, reporter, teacher, secretary, correspondent, writer, interpreter, bookseller, customs officer, traffic policeman, bus driver, magazine salesman, publisher, talkmaster, broker, critic, rhetorician, postman.

BASIC PRINCIPLE:
Knowledge is power!

Gemini

Interpreted as the masculine searching-image or self-image, the sign of Gemini reveals a light, agile, clever man, an intellectual who always retains something youthful about him no matter how old he is. His wide-awake glance and buoyant voice give him a look that somehow seems clever. He likes to appear casual and nonchalant and can be encountered wherever bustling activity prevails, wherever news is exchanged, or stimulating conversations are held.

His strength is the world, his quick intellectual grasp, and his mental agility. He can analyze problems in a flash, propose theoretical solutions, make contacts, and simply give very smart advice. Coupled with his charming wit, this makes him an interesting person to be around and someone with whom it is entertaining to have a conversation. He pursues his goals with playful, carefree ease and is always open for the new ideas that cross his path. When he is tired of his work, when the air becomes too heavy, or a sudden idea stimulates him, he is quickly very willing to immediately change direction. He doesn't like to be limited in his possibilities and is even less enthused about other people setting restrictions for him. His nature is so greatly diversified that he likes doing several things at once and attempts time and again to think a number of thoughts simultaneously. Like no other type, he possesses the ability to improvise when there are problems and is quickly receptive to new, changed circumstances. He is sly, verbally skilled, adept at repartee, interested in everything, and very well-read, both in the field of higher literature and pulp magazines.

Problems arise when just his addiction to novelty drives him into the negativity. Then his life becomes erratic and illogical. As a result, some of the magnificent ideas that he announced so eloquently come to nothing. This is because following up his thoughts with actions isn't particularly one of his strong points. His interest is aroused quickly, but whether or not he will stay with the matter, make something of it, or whether it "just" interests him and he will start up something new the next day cannot be predicted. With so much restlessness, it is no wonder that he frequently appears to be jumpy, superficial, and flighty, or that other, more calm individuals complain about his nervous and hectic approach. In addition, he is a notorious skeptic who questions everything and cannot be pinned down because he always keeps a back door open through his eternal relativizing. He can also withdraw in an elegant and eloquent manner whenever he is required to show commitment or really put his cards on the table. He simply cannot be pinned down.

This individual finds self-realization in his encounter with other people, wherever he can make contacts, where his knowledge, his advice, and his "brains" are in demand. He is an experienced trader, a skilled broker, and a clever expert whose differentiated opinion is well considered. His place is wherever he can satisfy his curiosity, wherever flexibility, quick reasoning, and eloquence are required, and wherever critical questions are valued. Variety is important to him, with security and continuity lagging far behind, which is why he also frequently makes changes in terms of his work and activities. He rarely runs up against authority conflicts because he is typically a freelancer, or has organized himself to be so independent as an employee that there can be little friction with superiors.

When he becomes interested in a woman, he attempts to impress her with his knowledge, his esprit, and his brilliant intellect. It is dazzling to see what he can dish up; as if he has read his way through entire libraries and memorized a multivolume encyclopedia. Yet, he is a master of the skilled bluff since in most cases he has only skimmed through the table of contents and thought up the rest. And still, it is impressive and wonderful to listen to him. But how could he come up with more endurance when he goes courting than in the other areas of life? If he doesn't make progress rapidly enough, he will lose his interest just as quickly as it arose. This is why he usually has several irons in the fire in order to switch to another, if necessary.

Life with him is quite eventful and certainly not boring. He knows how to bring a pleasant fresh breeze into any relationship. Someone who wants to flatter him should admire his quick, crystal-clear intellect, his clever advice, and his refreshing wit. His door is always open to a large circle of acquaintances; yet, he doesn't feel all that well for a longer period of time as part of an intimate couple. There are not only many stimulating conversations with him, he never appears to run out of ideas when it comes to trying things out. He also is interested in whatever concerns the person with whom he engages in conversation. Admittedly, his interest isn't particularly deep. But this is probably the accusation that he hears over and over again. However, depth, commitment, and steadfastness are not part of his light nature. At times he appears to also lack in intuitive understanding, particularly when he tries to statistically record, de-emotionalize, or simply talk away his partner's feelings, thereby overlooking her needs with his torrent of words.

He loves the excitement of something new and likes a change of pace—even within the relationship. But when he finds himself stuck in a routine or sees himself pinned down to rituals of habit, his interest may quickly subside so that he seeks new stimulation somewhere else. Yet, if he is left enough leeway, he can by all means be faithful. Companionship is actually more important to him than great passion, which he doesn't actually believe in at any rate and, with its emotional intensity, would constrict him too much. His sexuality also tends to be influenced more by a playful curiosity than deep desire. He is the archetype of the sophisticated lover who has new ideas time and again, very much enjoys experimentation, and prefers verbal eroticism.

He can be put off when someone restricts his freedom, tries to pin him down, or take him for a ride. And he also has a hard time putting up with boredom and tests of patience of any kind. Like quicksilver, he will elude every attempt to hang onto him. If he is reminded of agreements that have been made, they suddenly weren't made in this way, or were meant to be interpreted entirely differently. Like no one else, he knows how to use his intellect as a weapon and, with snappy comebacks, use his sharp tongue to simply make the person he is talking to speechless within the shortest amount of time. Someone who wants to reconcile with him is advised to leave the emotional level and ask him in all objectivity what he thinks would be the smartest solution. If his proposal isn't completely unacceptable, the partner should at least agree on a trial period in which she agrees to it as a test.

As a father, he understands his children's curiosity and is always willing to deal with their questions. He is less suited as a caring guardian for the little ones, but can handle the teenagers so much the better for it. For the children, he is a companion interested in doing things with them, an interested person to talk to, with whom they can thoroughly discuss all their problems, since he always has an open ear for new ideas coming from the younger generation. He supports their intellectual development and is concerned with making sure they get a good education. However, the family will seldom be the focus of his life since he cannot sit still long enough for domesticity and feels himself constricted by the rituals of family life. He will immediately be interested in any solution that promises relief and improvement, whether it is of a technical nature or in the person of a babysitter.

Although he is neither a dreamy romantic nor the personification of reliability, he is a versatile, witty companion and good entertainer.

Cancer
As the Masculine Searching-Image or Self-Image.

In the **masculine** horoscope as the self-image of the young man;
In the **feminine** horoscope as the main symbol of the animus and the searching-image.

In the **masculine** horoscope as self-image of the mature/fatherly man;
In the **feminine** horoscope as the fatherly/complementary portion of the animus and searching-image.

ARCHETYPE: The poet.	ELEMENT: Water
TYPE: The romantic, the sensitive man.	BASIC ATTITUDE: Reserved and shy. Encounters the world with understanding and a willingness to help.
MATURE FORM: The caring therapist, the artist.	NAIVE OR DISTORTED FORM: The gusher, the coward, the pouter, the dreamer.
STRENGTH: Has a rich emotional life, imaginative, understanding, willing to help, empathetic.	PROBLEM AREAS: Inconsistent, too willing to blame others, indolent, fearful, touchy.
RELATIONSHIP STRENGTHS: The man who is capable of deep emotional experiencing and lovingly opens up to the needs of his partner and cares for her.	RELATIONSHIP PROBLEMS: Vents his moods on the immediate surrounding world and makes others responsible for his failures.
TYPE OF ASSERTIVENESS: Confidently moves toward goals with the sidling walk of a crab, hesitant, indirect, and with many detours. TYPE: The sailor.	SEXUALITY: Intensive feelings and imaginative. Seeks tenderness and closeness.

TYPICAL PROFESSIONAL AREAS:
All areas in nursing and social work and the area of art: director of a home, social worker, nurse, preserver of regional traditions, historian, psychologist, musician, interior decorator, author, pediatrician.

BASIC PRINCIPLE:
Why roam afield when good things are so close at hand?

Cancer

Interpreted as the masculine searching-image or self-image, the sign of Cancer reveals a romantic, an empathetic, and a sensitive man with a big heart. His appearance tends to be calm and reserved, and the sensitivity of his being can be perceived in his shy glance and gentle voice. He avoids anonymous situations and can be encountered where the intimacy of a family setting prevails and a personal ambience allows a sense of security to be created. His strength is his emotional depth, which gives him an intuitive understanding and an extraordinary sense of empathy, as well as an extremely vivid imagination. Driven by a deep longing for love and security, he is at home in the world of romanticism, where poetry and music let his soul resonate. He values stillness and seclusion, is a good listener and imaginative storyteller who inwardly participates in everything related to his immediate environment. People feel like they are understood when they are close to him. Anyone seeking his solace has the feeling of never being a burden to him in the process. He shows decisive commitment wherever he can help others and his protective instinct is required. Using his power in his own interests may not be one of his strengths, but his courageous commitment on the part of people close to him gives him the strength of an ox at any time. He seldom takes action on his own, but waits for an impulse from the outside. But even then, he doesn't develop very much initiative of his own. He is no go-getter, but will usually tend to carefully take meandering paths, frequently changing the direction and pace, taking detours time and again, letting himself be guided by his feelings and sure instincts. This is how he directly reaches his goal in an indirect way.

In the distorted form, his problem lies in the refusal to become an adult and assume responsibility. Instead of doing this, he shifts the blame for insults suffered onto his surrounding world and makes the entire world responsible for his inability to assert himself. Although he may have many ideas because of his powerful imagination, and his wishful thinking is quite pronounced, he may lack the strength to turn his dreams into reality. Straightforwardness and decisiveness are simply foreign words to him. His tendency to dwell on memories and get lost in the familiar past also reflects a reluctance to confront the hard facts of the present. He prefers to hide away and declare himself to generally not be responsible at the start. When it comes to making concrete demands, he has a variety of completely amazing defense mechanisms.

His self-realization is found in the development of his creativity and wherever his deep empathy, his great ability to care, and his knowledge about the human soul is required. He has difficulty in asserting himself in the professional world, which he often experiences as hostile. Hierarchies and authorities are often hard for him to deal with, and success on the career ladder is much less important to him than the feeling of being a part of things and belonging. He prefers to work in a family business or a small, clearly organized team. In order to protect himself from injuries and rejection, he doesn't like to put himself in the front row but prefers to act from the background. There he is valued above all as an understanding helper and adviser because of his warm, caring nature. He has a problem with the masculine role of conqueror, and not just when it comes to the woman of his dreams. Even when it comes to flirting, his indecisive way of waiting for an outside impulse can lead to all types of misunderstandings because it is hard to know what he actually wants. This hesitant back-and-forth practically invites the female sex to lure him out of his reserve and even take the initiative. His shyness is appealing on its own, and once he begins to trust someone, he develops his enchanting charm and his romantic side.

Life with him is characterized by intimate togetherness as a couple in a warm, comfortable nest. He needs to be close to a beloved person as much as he needs air to breathe and therefore wants to be together all the time. This is why he wants to have a place together with his beloved and start a family, which he likes to look after in a caring way, as soon as possible. A person close to him can confidently let go and be certain that he will catch her. When he is admired for his intuitive grasp and his great sense of understanding, he is deeply flattered. Time and again he will seek a sense of security within the relationship, not needing any personal freedom. He contributes toward a close life with his partner since he enjoys cooking and also lovingly looks after everything. Seen in this light, life together with him is idyllic—if it wouldn't be for the other side of the coin. He naturally doesn't want to permit his partner any freedom, whereby life at his side may be limited to domestic seclusion. His avoiding the harshness of life on the outside can also let him become moody and dissatisfied at home, particularly when he feels that he isn't doing justice to his role as a man. These fluctuations in mood must then be endured by the people who are otherwise so important to him. He is a thoroughly loyal and devoted mate, at least as long as he senses exactly where he belongs and experiences the same commitment from his partner. However, if he gets lost in his fantasies and memories, or dwells too much on his longings, the dream of fulfilling his desires can let him become fickle. His sexuality is also very dependent upon his moods and emotions, and determined above all by the need for togetherness. He is a sensitive, tender lover who doesn't push and demand but likes to hug and cuddle a lot. He feels the wishes of his beloved and fulfills them.

He can be put off quickly when his partner is too logical, wants to precisely analyze his nature and his dreams, but above all, when his feelings are made fun of and his tenderness is ridiculed. And he naturally feels utterly misunderstood when toughness in life is demanded of him and he is subject to a strong pressure to perform. He will only engage in conflict with quite a bit of hesitation. As soon as there are problems, he withdraws in disappointment and hurt, and pouts. A great deal must take place before he will risk coming out of this protective fortress and confront an open conflict. However, if he should fight with total passion, the deep injuries to his soul can be sensed; and he will never forget these wounds. He is extremely resentful and often shows his reactions only when no one expects them anymore. And this is precisely his tactic because he starts his pursuit at the moment when the other person thinks he has long reached safety. Someone who wants to reconcile with him must help him lick his wounds. Doing this requires quite a bit of good will and patience because every pain will once again quickly remind him how much injustice he has suffered. Someone who is truly interested in reconciliation will also succeed in showing him how wonderful everything was before, and thereby once again return to the original idyl.

Family means a great deal to him, both the one that he originated from and his own. He is a clan person and very interested in maintaining family bonds. Even if he is quite committed to his professional life, his private life will always take first place. Children are a natural part of things for him. He likes to spend a great deal of time with them and makes sure that family traditions and rituals are cultivated. The role of the tender, caring, loving father virtually suits him to a tee. But when the young ones slowly stand on their own and start to go their own way, he tries to tie those escaping the nest to the family. This is why he celebrates all the holidays in his religious tradition.

He certainly isn't a courageous hero, a grim performance-oriented individual, or even an eloquent charmer, but instead he is a sensitive and caring friend who is always there when he is needed. He has a great deal of understanding for those he cares for, and is there when others are experiencing the dark night of the soul.

Leo
As the Masculine Searching-Image or Self-Image.

In the **masculine** horoscope as the self-image of the young man;
In the **feminine** horoscope as the main symbol of the animus and the searching-image.

In the **masculine** horoscope as self-image of the mature/fatherly man;
In the **feminine** horoscope as the fatherly/complementary portion of the animus and searching-image.

ARCHETYPE: The king.	**ELEMENT:** Fire
TYPE: The victor, the "golden" boy.	**BASIC ATTITUDE:** Likes to take over leadership. Encounters the world with self-confidence and hearty charisma.
MATURE FORM: The shining example, the master of the art of living, the prudent man.	**NAIVE OR DISTORTED FORM:** The show-off, the stag, the big kid, the braggart.
STRENGTH: Very kindhearted, has ability to lead others, cheerful, brave, has creative genius.	**PROBLEM AREAS:** Pompous, presumptuous, arrogant, wasteful, egocentric, overbearing, thoughtless.
RELATIONSHIP STRENGTHS: The man who is generous and pampers his partner.	**RELATIONSHIP PROBLEMS:** Likes to be waited on and constantly needs admiration.
TYPE OF ASSERTIVENESS: He came, he saw, and he conquered! Courageous and brave, with a loud roar and imposing gestures of victory. TYPE: The bodybuilder.	**SEXUALITY:** Self-assured, ranging from lustfully playful to powerfully dominating.

TYPICAL PROFESSIONAL AREAS:
All areas in which strength of leadership and personality are required, as well as in artistically creative fields: manager, goldsmith, consul, showmaster, circus director, film/stage/television director, tennis instructor, animal tamer, barkeeper, opera singer, entrepreneur, business manager, jeweler, politician, organizer, representative.

BASIC PRINCIPLE:
Life is short—make the most of it!

Leo

Interpreted as the masculine searching-image or self-image, the sign of Leo corresponds to the playful "golden" boy, the radiant victor. With a winning glance and a loud voice, he appears supremely confident and sparkles with a joy in life and vitality. No matter whether he shows up in casual, sporting, or elegant attire, his outer appearance displays his preference for brand names. He can be encountered any where social activity dominates, where people go to be seen, and where fun and games are on the agenda.

His strength is his self-assurance, his confident initiative, and his natural magnanimity. The sidelines and background aren't for him. He is driven to constantly be in the foreground on stage, in the limelight, at the center of attention. There he knows how to magnificently put himself in the spotlight and rake in the admiration for which he is willing to do so much. Whatever he organizes or plans is a big hit. On the other hand, he lets the little fish get away. He often achieves his goals through his unshakeable belief in himself. It is part of his nature to take over the leadership and he prefers to pass on the detail work to others. His courageous commitment and apparent joy in doing this are so contagious that he can also get other people enthused about his cause. He loves taking risks and is interested in testing his powers time and again. In doing this, he is skillful and sure of victory, as he goes all out in order to overtake his opponents with loud volume and an impressive pose.

Self-doubt isn't part of his vocabulary. While other people try to be modest, he suns himself in the bright light. However, if he is blinded by his own significance, he may lose sight of what is truly important in life. In the distorted form, or when he lacks in maturity, he may sometimes seem like a boisterous child with primadonna airs, which may even express as compulsive, narcissistic showmanship. Because of his dependency on attention and admiration, he then relies so much on an audience that he hardly finds the time to perceive himself as independent. In the process, he risks overestimating his powers, denying any type of weakness, and thereby burning out.

His professional self-realization rarely takes place in the back room. Even at an early age, he looks for his place in the sun. Since he likes to take on responsibility for others and set the tone, he can best develop his abilities in a managing or self-employed position. He is accustomed to always taking the initiative and needs enough freedom for his decisions. If he is forced to extensively subject himself or adapt to others, conflicts with authority can quickly arise. However, if he is permitted to hold the scepter, he can be a level-head-ed, generous boss who represents an integrating power with his honest com-mitment and heartiness; he manages his employees in a responsible way, and knows the best way to motivate them.

He wins the woman of his heart through his irresistible smiles and abil-ity to always show his better profile when flirting. He envelops the chosen one with an aura of luxury and gives her the feeling of being unique and extremely desirable. He doesn't recognize rejections as such but considers them to be errors. Anyone who doesn't like his wooing and doesn't give him any attention is clearly not worthy of him and must therefore do without his favor.

Life at his side is correspondingly magnificent. He loves everything beautiful, expensive, and luxurious, enjoying it when the people close to him can participate in this. So he pampers his sweetheart, adorns her like a princess, and likes to take her out in order to be seen with her. Being togeth-er just with her in the intimate environment of the home is less to his liking than being surrounded by crowds of people and a diversity of social contacts. To the same extent, he also loves any type of amusement and likes to make hay while the sun shines. As a born socialite and zestful man, he clearly feels attracted to the external joy of life.

However, no matter how loveable he is, the woman at his side may at times feel like she is in a gilded cage. This may happen because the role of the representative partner isn't made for her, or because he frequently has too little sense of equality within the relationship. He is the king with all the special privileges, which he takes advantage of at any time in a self-evident manner and lets no one dispute his right to them. However, a woman who understands how to allow him the leadership role in the formal sense, praise him for successes, and tell him often enough how wonderful he is will not only be rewarded with his benevolence but pampered by him over and over again in every way. As long as he receives his partner's undivided attention, his love will be constant. But if his pride is wounded because he feels neglect-ed, he will feel compelled to prove to her how attractive other women find him. Since he is a master at flirting, he will naturally receive the desired attention very quickly. Yet, at the bottom of his heart he is actually faithful and simply likes to flirt with opportunities to confirm his attractiveness. In the area of sexuality, he is also a playful, lusty lover with strong erotic ener-gy, capable of stimulating his partner greatly when he is receives the appro-priate admiration.

He is put off when he is given the cold shoulder, criticized, or when his generosity is responded to with ingratitude. He sees this to be an insult that he punishes with royal wrath. When there is a conflict, he can become very imperious and—provided there is enough of an audience—he will loudly and dramatically set the clash into the limelight. A conflict initiated by others is the same as a rebellion to him, which he attempts to suppress with all means available. There is no point in coming to him with logical arguments because he is basically always right, and anyone who fails to see this immediately still has a lot to learn. Someone who wants to reconcile with him must make a full apology, show regret, and appeal to his magnanimity. This will cause his annoyance to vanish immediately, and with his conciliatory manner, he will quickly forget all the offenses committed; he isn't at all resentful and long quarrels don't fit in with his cheerful nature.

He is a proud and self-assured father who likes to show himself everywhere with his children. Whenever his time permits it, he can also become enthused about games and fun. He naturally also pampers his offspring with his generosity. All that he expects in return is respect and good behavior. He isn't strict, but because of his innate authority his children know precisely what they must do. He obviously has high expectations for their future. Although he likes to use his own ideas as the standard for everything, he is willing to support their interests and talents. It isn't always easy to grow up next to him, but he is a committed, strong father.

Although he isn't a profound thinker, and certainly is not a placid homebody, he is a generous man. He is accustomed to success and enjoys the beautiful aspects of life from the depths of his heart.

Virgo
As the Masculine Searching-Image or Self-Image.

In the **masculine** horoscope as the self-image of the young man;
In the **feminine** horoscope as the main symbol of the animus and the searching-image.

In the **masculine** horoscope as self-image of the mature/fatherly man;
In the **feminine** horoscope as the fatherly/complementary portion of the animus and searching-image.

ARCHETYPE: The scientist.	ELEMENT: Earth
TYPE: The realist, the practical man.	BASIC ATTITUDE: Wants to be useful. Encounters the world with caution, a critical eye, and without any great illusions.
MATURE FORM: The pragmatist, the man able to cope with life.	NAIVE OR DISTORTED FORM: The complainer, the spoilsport, the perfectionist, the small-minded individual.
STRENGTH: Diligent, hardworking, has a sense of reality, is precise, careful, objective, reasonable, modest, skilled.	PROBLEM AREAS: Narrow-minded, hair-splitter, petty, overly cautious, mistrusting, lacks a sense of humor.
RELATIONSHIP STRENGTHS: The man who reliably keeps promises and is made happy by the little things in life.	RELATIONSHIP PROBLEMS: Leaves little leeway for experiments and frequently closes up emotionally.
TYPE OF ASSERTIVENESS: Step-by-step; well planned, methodical, and with enormous meticulousness. TYPE: The orientational runner.	SEXUALITY: Earthy and well-controlled, considerate with tact and sensitivity.

TYPICAL PROFESSIONAL AREAS:
All areas in which work is done scientifically, where accuracy, precision, and exact powers of discernment are demanded: pharmacist, editor, clockmaker, precision mechanic, bookkeeper, auditor, analyst, economist, mathematician, tax advisor, archivist, notary public, probation officer, nutritional consultant, educator, craftsman, computer techno-wiz.

BASIC PRINCIPLE:
Don't torment yourself! Organize!

Virgo

Interpreted as the masculine searching-image or self-image, the Virgo character corresponds to the sober, practical realist whose reliable nature can even been seen from a distance. His no frills appearance, his wide-awake and attentive glance, and his lively voice show his directedness. Or he may be inconspicuous. He can be encountered where work is done in a concentrated and diligent way. His strength lies in his practical reasonableness, his sense of what is useful, and his love of details. The desire for perfection is a driving force within him. His way of doing things is systematic and oriented toward sober facts, since risky speculations aren't his style. As an experienced energy economist, he knows how to be thrifty in every respect and only applies his energies where they can achieve the greatest benefits. No one is as good as he is when it comes to separating the wheat from the chaff. His quick intellect allows him to immediately perceive whether something is useful or worthless, appropriate or futile, harmful or helpful. This talent, which he likes to put to use as often as possible, allows him to become an excellent critic. He also likes to look at and plan his own objectives step-by-step. There is something rather dry about his earthy manner, which, in combination with a good sense of humor, makes him very likeable. However, the humorless Virgo may be quite boring.

In the distorted form, this disposition can let him become finicky with a very petty, stereotyped standard deeply irritated by even small deviations from the rules. Then he sticks to the naked facts with nerve-racking grimness and mistrusts everything that his intellect cannot comprehend. Behind his constant bustling activities and his emphatically sober manner is often the attempt to conceal his great insecurity and his vulnerability. Then the enormous and unpredictable variety of life appears to him like a chaos that threatens everything and must absolutely be battled with reason. This not only makes him extremely petty and inflexible in many respects but also causes him, in an increasingly desperate way, to attempt to force his everyday life and surrounding world into a narrow framework. Through absolute planning and categorization, he hopes to be able to perceive, control, and prevent unpredictable events. Because of this urge for the predictability of all eventualities, he may possibly sacrifice his spontaneity and joy in life.

He seeks self-fulfillment through useful contribution to the good of the community. With his consciousness of social responsibility and enjoyment of systems for creating order, he is gratified to experience himself as a part of the organization. If this also demands his scientific mind and zeal for research, then he knows he is completely in the right place. It doesn't matter to him whether or not other people consider this to be the profession that they have always dreamed of as long as he is aware of the importance of his function. He tends to feel best in the second row and likes to let others take the chances. He knows quite well that he will very quickly make himself indispensable at his place of work through his careful and reliable approach. He particularly enjoys making something good even better, whereby he may sometimes appear to be pedantic or compulsive. Yet, it is his joy in details and his inexhaustible way of working that gives him a deep sense of satisfaction. However, inactivity provokes his complaining, cynical side.

In terms of his conquests, he certainly cannot be accused of rashness, either! When a woman interests him, he will carefully and unobtrusively approach her. He has usually known his chosen one for a long time and has precisely observed and scrutinized whether or not she is right for him, and thought about how good his chances are with her. If he decides that it's worth it, he will start "working" with his usual diligence. Bluffs, big gestures, and superficial flattery aren't his style. Instead, he will win her heart gradually with his sense of humor and, above all, by making himself useful and proving to be a dependable, skillful, and capable friend until he becomes indispensable.

He is a conscientious partner who is reliable, and who proves his practical abilities particularly in everyday life. Whenever he becomes involved with something, his care and love of detail is obvious. This also applies to his approach to his partner since he is capable of great tact and sensitivity, as well as comforting clarity, in difficult situations. Someone who wants to flatter him should admire him for this quality and tell him how much his competence and pragmatism is appreciated. Although life at his side may not always be exciting and scintillating, he guarantees a high degree of stability since he naturally stands by anything once he has made a positive decision in its favor. In addition, he is willing to make compromises, is able to adapt without difficulty, and can practice being frugal once he has perceived the necessity for this. He doesn't have exaggerated demands and doesn't expect the impossible to become possible, which allows him to be pleasantly content when living with another person. He knows how to use small gestures and a few words to give his partner the feeling that he deeply appreciates her.

It is a self-evident truth for him to adhere to agreements, and since he also isn't very daring and not particularly spontaneous, he will hardly come up with the idea of being unfaithful on his own. His sexual energy is moderate but constant. His way of living it out is frequently described as not very exciting, and even prudish, which does injustice to him. In this respect, he certainly isn't an adventurer and is no friend of erotic curiosities, but he has a gentle manner and knows how to enjoy his earthy sensuality in a pleasurable and regular way with his beloved. However, he is also good at controlling himself and can do without when it is pointless to try.

He is put off when someone disturbs his order, whether in his home or in the office. It doesn't please him either when the other person disregards agreements or neglects responsibilities. The same also applies when someone labels him as unimaginative and makes fun of his nit-picking. If a quarrel arises, he becomes very tough and then lets loose all the critical, sometimes bitter accusations that he had previously held in check. As a crafty tactician, he knows exactly how to present his criticisms so they have maximum effect. His weapon is the meticulousness with which he quick-wittedly picks his opponent's arguments to pieces and defuses them. At the same time, he is so nimble-minded and skilled that it is difficult for the other person to catch him. When someone wants to make up with him, it is best to be reasonable and not get carried away by any further emotional accusations or threadbare arguments. In any case, this means leaving the scene of the battle, making an effort to reconcile the fronts in an intelligent conversation, and looking for solid and lasting solutions to the problem.

As a father, he takes his obligations seriously and is interested in giving his children the necessary qualifications on their path in life. He is a conscientious, practical, and responsible father who only establishes a family when he is certain that he can also feed it, that the relationship is suitable for everyday life, and that he can later make it possible for his children to get a good education. He may sometimes make a brittle and strict impression in how he raises his children because he establishes rules that leave little leeway for exceptions. On the other hand, he will himself reliably adhere to any agreements that have been made and will stand by his children in word and deed whenever they need him.

He certainly isn't an overly optimistic person, and also won't be enthusiastic about things that are irrational and inexplicable. Instead, he is a considerate, upright, and reliable partner with whom it is easy to share the days of your life.

Libra
As the Masculine Searching-Image or Self-Image.

In the **masculine** horoscope as the self-image of the young man;
In the **feminine** horoscope as the main symbol of the animus and the searching-image.

In the **masculine** horoscope as self-image of the mature/fatherly man;
In the **feminine** horoscope as the fatherly/complementary portion of the animus and searching-image.

ARCHETYPE: The artist.	ELEMENT: Air
TYPE: The cavalier, the gentleman, the Bohemian.	BASIC ATTITUDE: Has the need to communicate. Encounters the world with friendliness and charm.
MATURE FORM: The diplomat, the esthete.	NAIVE OR DISTORTED FORM: The beau, the drab fellow, the shirker, the wryneck.
STRENGTH: Confident of his good taste, amiable, charming, has a sense of justice, balanced, fair.	PROBLEM AREAS: Halfheartedness, inhibited in expressing aggressive feelings, uses evading maneuvers, noncommittal, fickle.
RELATIONSHIP STRENGTHS: Courteous and considerate, attempts to create a pleasant atmosphere.	RELATIONSHIP PROBLEMS: Lack of depth in emotional area and denial of problems.
TYPE OF ASSERTIVENESS: Discretion is the better part of valor! Uses well-planned strategies and diplomatic skill. TYPE: The dancer.	SEXUALITY: Cultivated, loving, charming, with a preference for erotic mental games.

TYPICAL PROFESSIONAL AREAS:
Wherever communication is important, where compromises are negotiated, in the areas of leisure and fashion as well as in art and design: fashion designer, hairdresser, designer, decorator, entertainer, pop singer, dancer, diplomat, justice of the peace, graphic artist, respiratory therapist, cosmetic surgeon, owner of an art gallery, negotiator, mediator, art expert, theater director, marriage broker.

BASIC PRINCIPLE:
I will give you a clear "maybe"!

Libra

Interpreted as the masculine searching-image or self-image, the sign of Libra corresponds to the man who is a charming cavalier. His behavior is polite, cultivated, and his well-groomed appearance is evidence of good taste and fashion consciousness. With his friendly glance and pleasant-sounding voice, he quickly wins other people's sympathies. He loves social life and can be encountered at a great variety of cultural events, wherever people gather to communicate and enjoy themselves.

His strength lies in his ability to make friends easily, his diplomatic talent, his sense of form and formalities, and a very fine feeling for esthetics and equilibrium. As a sociable, entertaining person who is never at a loss for friendly words, he always knows what topics are best to discuss with whom. He loves harmony, whether this is in music or the other arts, and naturally in the interpersonal area. What he cannot stand is discord, breaks in style, and rudeness of any kind. He is driven to bring peace and beauty into the world, and he is skilled at mediating conflicts or at least negotiating a truce. In the process, he proves to be a clever strategist who, with his very good sense of balanced proportions, understands how to weigh the relative strengths of those involved. Since he is always concerned with fairness, he not only suffers because of the injustice in this world but also may be very hesitant in making the decisions involved in his everyday life. He simply needs a great deal of time to compare both sides with each other so that an optimal judgment can be made—one that does as much justice to both sides as possible.

However, in the distorted form this can also make him incapable of taking any action. Because of pure avoidance of conflicts, he may become a spineless position-changer who simply trims his sails to the wind. Then even truly clever and balanced decisions stay up in the air, particularly if their realization will probably meet with a great deal of resistance. Instead of turning his ideas into reality, he prefers to leave it up to others to take the initiative and create a distinctive image. So that he isn't forced to make a move, he conceals his inconstancy behind a cloud of charming empty phrases and a pleasant-sounding but windy way of saying yes to everything. Even if he has absolutely no rough edges, he is still not easy to deal with, because he avoids everything in such a polished, politely obliging manner that the other person is just left holding hot air.

His self-fulfillment takes place wherever he can work on a team, but above all in the area of interpersonal relationships, where there are contacts to be made, conflicts to arbitrate, and opposites to balance. Wherever solutions must be found and strategies worked out, he proves his mental agility. This is why he is well suited for advisory activities. However, with his diplomatic skill he is also an outstanding canvasser, a talented negotiator, and a good mediator. The entire area of culture and art is naturally suitable for him since he can develop in ways that are both theoretical and related to art and design. Authority problems with superiors are just as rare with him as those with his colleagues.

If he falls in love with a woman, he is in his element and sparkles with charm. The ability to flirt appears to be a natural-born quality. Like no other character type, he understands how to stylishly court the lady of his heart, take her out to elegant and cultivated events, and entertain her anywhere and at any time in a skillful, relaxed, and charming manner—without ever becoming too pushy. Yet, he will sometimes hesitate indecisively until he receives a clear sign from her, since he doesn't like to take the risk of being rejected.

Life with him has style. It is distinguished by a sense of the fine art of living and is always full of encounters with new people at a great variety of social occasions, exhibitions, or in the theater. These contacts usually aren't very deep. Instead, like everything else about him, they tend to be easy and happy-go-lucky. A life with him also leaves enough space for both partners to develop on their own. In place of territorial battles, there are well-contrived rules that he, as a peace-loving person, likes to polish to the point that—at least theoretically—there can no longer be any conflicts. His uppermost concern in this process is fairness, equality, and consideration. However, he likes to overlook the fact that some conflicts are only half-suppressed and become bombs beneath the relationship. He usually gallantly gets himself out of things before there is a big explosion and also keeps his ideal world intact even in difficult times through the policy of burying his head in the sand. Apparently quite willing to make compromises, he sometimes neglects giving concrete answers and the lightness with which he at times appears to float above emotional needs can also be hurtful. A partnership with him is certainly pleasant and friendly, but sometimes lacks depth and intensity. Someone who wants to flatter him should admire him for his charm, his cultivated agility, and his taste, which is both good and confident.

He will hardly be unfaithful as a result of his own impulses, but he may be easy to seduce since he doesn't like disappointing other people's expectations and has difficulty in saying no. His sexual energy tends to be moderate, and he certainly isn't love-starved and hot-blooded. Instead of sweaty passion, he prefers graceful playfulness, an erotic charge, and the art of skillful seduction. The intellectual and esthetic level of a relationship is usually more important to him than physical eroticism.

He is easily put off when someone insults his taste, steps all over his artfully designed models, and, above all, when someone pressures him to make quick decisions and wants to tie him down in some way. As long as possible, he will attempt to avoid conflict. But when it does happen, he will react cooly and become aloof so that he won't be tempted to forget his good upbringing. As a clever strategist, he will initially attempt to diffuse the other person's arguments before he—in his mental agility—seeks to win the fight with well-considered, objective reasons. Like an experienced chess player, he always tries to keep a clear head and will hardly be carried away by thoughtless reactions. It is easy to reconcile with him; he usually initiates the process. Since he suffers greatly when there is domestic strife, he will usually quickly accept a peace offer since harmony is much more important than winning or being right.

A family and children is something he can well imagine for himself in the theoretical sense, and he sees himself as the ideal father. But in reality, he doesn't always have an easy time with the concrete demands on his authority in raising children. Here as well, he has a hard time saying "no" and, as a result, his children have little difficulty in wrapping him around their little finger. He is a good friend to them and an attentive listener, making an effort to do justice to them in addition to all his other interests. Yet, in contrast to his partner, children will rarely occupy the most important position in his life. He likes doing things with his mate so that the relationship doesn't get monotonous, and he is careful to see that a healthy measure of mutual respect is maintained.

He is neither a striking matador or a sensitive consoler, but he is a likeable, courteous man with a distinct sense of fairness and the cultivated aspects of life.

Scorpio
As the Masculine Searching-Image or Self-Image.

In the **masculine** horoscope as the self-image of the young man;
In the **feminine** horoscope as the main symbol of the animus and the searching-image.

In the **masculine** horoscope as self-image of the mature/fatherly man;
In the **feminine** horoscope as the fatherly/complementary portion of the animus and searching-image.

ARCHETYPE: The magician.	ELEMENT: Water
TYPE: The fearless individual, the irresistible man, the black knight.	BASIC ATTITUDE: Doesn't let anyone look at his cards. Encounters the world in an unwavering, emphatic, and powerful way.
MATURE FORM: The healer, the researcher, the alchemist.	NAIVE OR DISTORTED FORM: The extremist, the destroyer, the dictator, the sadist.
STRENGTH: Committed, passionate, thorough, willing to take risks, intense, has fortitude, charismatic.	PROBLEM AREAS: Unscrupulous, manipulative, dominant, thirsty for power, brutal, merciless, sarcastic.
RELATIONSHIP STRENGTHS: The man who doesn't throw in the towel, not even in times of crisis.	RELATIONSHIP PROBLEMS: Tends toward power games and fervent jealousy.
TYPE OF ASSERTIVENESS: No matter what it costs! Manipulative and tough to the point of self-destruction. TYPE: The extreme athlete.	SEXUALITY: Passionate, without taboos, demanding, with a strong sex drive.

TYPICAL PROFESSIONAL AREAS:
Wherever things deep and concealed are focused on, or wherever absolute dedication is required, above all in the social taboo zones and in the therapeutic/medical area: surgeon, gynecologist, detective, undertaker, inspector, watchman, miner, garbageman, tunnel builder, spelunker, atomic physicist, hypnotist, depth psychologist, canal digger, occultist, researcher, chemist, tax advisor.

BASIC PRINCIPLE:
If it doesn't kill me, it will make me stronger.

Scorpio

Interpreted as the masculine searching-image or self-image, the sign of Scorpio reveals the black knight, a man with a charismatic aura and great powers of attraction. His behavior is silent, his penetrating glance probing, sometimes even piercing, and his voice is suggestive. There is something irresistible in his outer appearance, which tends to make a lasting impression because it is usually striking and extreme. He will either be very attractive or have something repulsive about him, but he is never inconspicuous. He can be encountered wherever intrinsic things are important, the exciting and enigmatic aspects of life.

His strength is his inner force, which gives him his power, as well as his almost uncanny sense for weakness of any kind. He likes to be invisible and therefore prefers to stay in the background. From there, he influences events. A Faustian urge drives him into the depths. Whatever is concealed or forbidden attracts him just as magically as all the shadow and borderline areas. Above all, taboos hold a particular fascination for him. Transgressing them is often an irresistible thrill. Whenever his mistrust tells him there is rotting ground beneath an inconspicuous or even beautifully designed surface, he is driven to expose it. So he deliberately puts his finger on the weak spots of society and unmasks the hypocritically puffed-up posturer by unerringly sinking his stinger into the place where this person can be deflated. That he doesn't always make friends as a result is of little concern to him since his drive for effectiveness is usually greater than his sense of tact.

In the distorted form he will—in a completely self-tormenting manner—be driven by the compulsion to control everything and even bore deeper when the threshold of pain has long been crossed. His commitment will then go to the point of giving himself up for lost and grows with every danger and every form of resistance. Once he fixates on a goal, he will follow it with an undaunted decisiveness that can even take on traits of obsession. A person who attempts to stop him from doing this, or even gets in his way, will meet with merciless severity. His thirst for power and his unwillingness to compromise have something threatening for others and often turn him into a loner. He relies only on himself and maintains a high degree of mistrust against the world. He ultimately sees his greatest enemy to be his own weaknesses, which causes him to be immensely self-controlled. In his entire nature, he is uncompromising, unscrupulous, fearless, immoderate, but never harmless.

His self-realization primarily takes place in borderline areas that attract little in the foreground and are seldom suitable for putting him in the spotlight. He is interested in everything that the society has prohibited and suppressed because things only become exciting for him in these areas and he presumes that precisely in these areas the actual, essential values are to be found. The "mental garbage" of others fascinates him as much as anything else that people carelessly throw away and suppress. And it's only natural for him to be a mystery-monger who prefers to crack taboos and air hushed-up scandals. In all of this, he is a tough, lone fighter who is used to making his decisions for himself. Teamwork means little to him. He would much rather hold all the strings in his hand himself since he desires power and also knows how to exercise it. In this process, he is driven to take over the most decisive position and not the highest position. If his influence is taken away from him or his privileges are restricted, he will defend himself with all the means available—and it is certain that these will not always be fair.

If he wants to win a woman for himself, he will put his hopes in his irresistibility. Yet, she must be difficult to win over since the hunt is more exciting than the booty. Once he has found the woman who is difficult to conquer, he will develop an impressive repertoire of magical arts in order to enchant her. He appears to be spinning a net of invisible threads in an enticing place in order to force her into it with his magical powers. There he will hypnotize her with his mysterious glance until she has fallen head over heels in love with him.

Life with him is exciting and intense since nothing else interests him. Things are rarely straightforward and harmonious since he finds danger much too fascinating. But since he usually has the situation under control despite any adversities, the person at his side isn't very likely to go under. Despite this, his partner shouldn't be overly sensitive, and should be able to live with his unpredictability. His feelings are deep but—as everything else related to him—extreme. This means he can love tremendously but also hate abysmally. In critical phases he will not only prove to be crisis-proof but also willing to do much for the relationship and work together with his partner on the solution to the problem. Wherever something is rotten, he is bound to stumble over it and then do his best to remove the obstacle. His seriousness in the everyday life of the relationship is the way he expresses deep attachment and love to his companion. Someone who wants to flatter him must admire his dauntlessness, his irresistibility, and his inner strength. But he will mercilessly expose every compliment that isn't totally honest. The other person can also wait in vain for spontaneous expressions of emotion. He only has a hard time concealing his extreme jealousy. These are the moments when others sense that his outer harshness is only a protective mask behind which his great emotional vulnerability is concealed.

Faithfulness is a thorny topic for him. He naturally demands that his partner be unconditionally faithful. But the uncanny attraction that everything clandestine has for him means that she will never really be certain of what he does in secrecy. Sexuality is his domain and his masculine energy is immense. He is a passionate and demanding lover who naturally seeks the intensive experiences beyond all taboos in this area as well, carrying his partner away into the lusty realm of the senses in the process.

He can be put off with platitudes and beer-happy brotherliness but also when someone capitulates to him. Life with him is sometimes like a permanent power struggle. The special thing about it is that the relationship is indissoluble for him as long as the battle lasts. But if his partner surrenders or even turns herself into his victim, he will quickly lose interest and look for another person who is a harder nut to crack. A fight with him is no picnic. He is a dangerous opponent who doesn't show his cards and always shoots his unerring arrow when no one reckons with it. To win him over is nearly impossible because he cannot be pinned down. The only way to conquer him is by completely turning away from him and refusing any continuation of the conflict. When he feels that his stinger no longer reaches the opponent and his arrows have no effect, he will point his weapons at himself. It will take time for him to be able to reconcile since he is slow in forgiving and has difficulty in forgetting. If the other person wants to iron out the conflict, she should make a gesture of submission. But do this with great care! It must always be possible for him to sense an unyielding pride in it because if it is made in a way that is too unconditional and devoted, he will lose all respect and turn away.

His attitude toward life can also be seen when he plays the role of father. He will totally adore his children, but lets there be no doubt that his authority is sacrosanct. Even when they are quite young, he will teach them how to cope in life and never give up, even in difficult situations. On the basis of his convictions, he will raise them to be self-disciplined and may sometimes also ask too much of them with his harshness and unyieldingness. This can make him a strict, emotionally unapproachable "superdad." There will hardly be a trace of the fact that he does all this because he loves his children. At the same time, he is the one who suffers the most from his inability to permit weakness and closeness. Yet, he would ultimately truly do everything for them.

Although he isn't a playful teddy bear, a superficial wisecrack, or a harmless charmer, he is a fascinating man capable of the deepest feelings who proves his inner strength particularly in times of crisis.

Sagittarius
As the Masculine Searching-Image or Self-Image.

In the **masculine** horoscope as the self-image of the young man;
In the **feminine** horoscope as the main symbol of the animus and the searching-image.

In the **masculine** horoscope as self-image of the mature/fatherly man;
In the **feminine** horoscope as the fatherly/complementary portion of the animus and searching-image.

ARCHETYPE: The high priest, the missionary.	**ELEMENT:** Fire
TYPE: The globetrotter, the explorer, the optimist.	**BASIC ATTITUDE:** Believes in the good within all human beings. Encounters the world with openness and confidence.
MATURE FORM: The benefactor, the cosmopolitan, the nobleman.	**NAIVE OR DISTORTED FORM:** The wise guy, the conceited man, the inquisitor, the braggart, the patronizer.
STRENGTH: Farsighted, perceptive, tolerant, generous, optimistic, open, benevolent, has power of conviction.	**PROBLEM AREAS:** Tends to exaggerate, preaches to others, fanatic, arrogant, condescending, opinionated, not open to advice.
RELATIONSHIP STRENGTHS: The man who supports and promotes his partner in word and deed.	**RELATIONSHIP PROBLEMS:** Is frequently too good for the daily necessities.
TYPE OF ASSERTIVENESS: Faith moves mountains! Full of confidence and self-assurance. TYPE: The high jumper.	**SEXUALITY:** Freedom-loving, virtuous, and easily stimulated by exotic thrills.

TYPICAL PROFESSIONAL AREAS:
All areas in which long-term projects and a strong effect must be achieved, such as in the fields of education and law: judge, attorney, speculator, adman, traveling salesman, foreign correspondent, geographer, ethnologist, Peace Corps volunteer, philosophy professor, preacher, missionary, orchestra conductor, travel guide.

BASIC PRINCIPLE:
If you show what you are, you'll get more out of life!

Sagittarius

Interpreted as the masculine searching-image or self-image, the sign of Sagittarius stands for a noble man with wide horizons, a higher level of education, and aristocratic manners. His behavior is distinguished, his glance always confident and cosmopolitan, and his voice has the true ring of conviction to it. There is something exalted in his outward appearance that may sometimes also have a presumptuousness to it. He makes a physically imposing impression since he is typically tall. He can be encountered wherever big projects and visions are developed, in educated circles, or traveling through distant lands.

His strength lies in his strong faith, his farsightedness, and his power of conviction. Since he loves proclaiming the truth that he has found, his place is wherever he finds that people like to listen to him. He is drawn to far-off shores and new horizons. This makes him a citizen of the world who maintains friendships and contacts on all the continents, as well as an inner traveler who constantly attempts to expand his mental horizons. He is a wholehearted optimist who considers even the impossible as feasible and can motivate and inspire others with his enthusiasm. Because he never loses hope and believes so intensely in himself and the victory of "the good," he is successful in many ways.

Although he enjoys promoting good in the world, even in the distorted form of his character type, he may be so euphoric because of his magnanimity that he will allow himself some types of encroachments or overstepping of his competence "for good reasons." If he is criticized because of this, he reacts in a shocked and highly indignant manner, especially if he is reproached for self-righteousness, presumptuousness, or even vanity. When he sweeps aside all reservations in his flashy manner and simply ignores concrete facts, he makes a very self-conceited and extremely arrogant impression. His presumptuously feigned education then reveals itself to be boundless self-importance, his jovial attitude deteriorates into a hollow, patronizing gesture, and his tendency to gloss over things, his purposive optimism, and immense way of exaggerating becomes obvious. With dramatic gestures, he will then try to depict even the simplest of acts as brilliant feats. However, if his convictions about himself are actually shaken for once, he can also plunge into the deepest hopelessness with the same degree of enthusiasm.

His self-realization lies in his enormous sense of a mission, whether this is as a public proclaimer of great truths in politics and culture, or as a traveler who establishes and maintains international contacts. In any case, he feels that he has a higher calling and doesn't like to struggle with the trivial matters of everyday life. He knows what possibilities he has and would like to achieve a corresponding occupational position. Thanks to his unshakeable belief in his abilities, his nose for the right moment, and his sure touch, he usually succeeds without having to get involved in unpleasant power struggles. In order to pursue his need for expansion and his enterprising spirit without any hindrances, he will sooner or later feel the urge to become self-employed.

When it comes to winning the woman of his heart, he becomes the noble knight for whom the role of the conqueror has been written. He shows no lack of confidence, charm, and self-assurance in the process. With cosmopolitan flair, he will court her, impress her with his extensive education and generosity, and let her know that the future at his side is promising in every way. At the same time, he is not only skilled at flirting but also knows how to motivate his beloved. He is a master at flattering her self-confidence by showering her with compliments and telling her how wonderful she is.

Life with him is very eventful. He naturally has to show his loved ones all the places in the world in which he feels at home. And this not only includes all corners of the globe but the areas in which he is intellectually knowledgeable. This means that the entire cultural program, as well as short and long trips, may be part of the relationship. In addition, he supports his partner in her own plans and projects. He doesn't expect her to adapt to him, yet he must sense how much she values the fact that he is a genuine stroke of luck for her. It is easier to flatter him since it is possible to simply admire him for everything, but, more than anything else, he wants to know that his far-sightedness, his high ideals, and his noble-mindedness are recognized and appreciated. When things are seen in this way, his partner will very much enjoy life at his side. Even in the difficult situations of everyday life, he will know how to always make the best of things and look for generous solutions. Yet, there isn't just sunshine with him every day. His self-complacency can take on obtrusively snooty traits, and in his self-righteousness, he may permit himself liberties that he isn't willing to grant his partner. He will attempt to justify these differing rights with moral arguments that usually just sound convincing to his own ears.

When it comes to faithfulness, he has a liberal attitude. Since he cannot tolerate any constriction, he also cannot approve of any agreements that appear to be totally materialistic. Trust is the basis of every relationship for him, while mistrust gnaws at its roots. His sexual energy is easily aroused, particularly by exotic thrills. If he hasn't become stuck between hypocritical transfiguration or moral constriction, he will share it with his partner in a very lustful and lively way.

If his noble intentions are questioned, or when a person is mistrustful of him over a long period of time, he will be put off. Then he will react with indignation and contempt. When there is a conflict, he can get all worked up about things. The more vehement he becomes, the more he will turn into an opinionated know-it-all and fanatic. From his perspective, he will always ultimately have the better and more convincing arguments. His weapon is the moral thunder with which he can beat down his opponent in a way that is tantamount to civic degradation. That he sets himself up to be the standard of right and virtue goes without saying. Someone who wants to reconcile with him must at least show a minimum of insight, since he actually— at least from his perspective—is always 100 percent right. In order for his preaching to not have been in vain, he must have the feeling that at least a spark of his message has hit home. He isn't resentful, and prefers to return to his basic positive, optimistic attitude as soon as possible.

He will often be open to starting a family, as long as he doesn't have to restrict himself too much in his larger plans. Domesticity doesn't really appeal to him, yet he has faith in the idea that a satisfactory solution can ultimately be found for every problem. As a father, he passes his basic positive attitude on to his children and encourages them to always strive for the optimum results in whatever they do. This can naturally also lead to unrealistic expectations when it comes to his children's future. From his viewpoint, he is fundamentally tolerant and can easily forgive foolishness, except when he sees someone has taken advantage of his generosity or not valued it. Yet, his good-naturedness is almost boundless as long as he feels himself to be respected as a role model. With his liberal spirit, he is a good companion for his children and likes to show them "his" big, wide world—particularly during the years of their youth.

He certainly isn't a practically predisposed ordinary person and is also not a sensitive listener. However, he is a liberal-minded partner with vast visions and an unshakeable belief that everything has its meaning and will end well.

Capricorn
As the Masculine Searching-Image or Self-Image.

In the **masculine** horoscope as the self-image of the young man;
In the **feminine** horoscope as the main symbol of the animus and the searching-image.

In the **masculine** horoscope as self-image of the mature/fatherly man;
In the **feminine** horoscope as the fatherly/complementary portion of the animus and searching-image.

ARCHETYPE: The patriarch.	**ELEMENT:** Earth
TYPE: The doer, the ascetic, the man of action, the reliable individual.	**BASIC ATTITUDE:** Adheres to rules and duties. Encounters the world with seriousness and responsibility.
MATURE FORM: The natural authority, the bearer of great responsibility.	**NAIVE OR DISTORTED FORM:** The embittered man, the slave driver, the grouch, the recluse.
STRENGTH: Disciplined, willing to take action, ambitious, concentrated, has endurance, willing to be responsible, has a sense of duty, reliable.	**PROBLEM AREAS:** Grim, inflexible, lacks humor, stickler for principles, excessively demanding, tense, extremely reserved.
RELATIONSHIP STRENGTHS: The man who keeps his promises.	**RELATIONSHIP PROBLEMS:** Often difficult to reach emotionally and tolerates no deviations from the rules.
TYPE OF ASSERTIVENESS: With the sweat of his brow, straight-forward, goal oriented, and with tough endurance. TYPE: The marathon runner.	**SEXUALITY:** Tireless and deeply capable of intensive experiences if he isn't put under pressure to perform.

TYPICAL PROFESSIONAL AREAS:
Anywhere that requires endurance and discipline, but above all in politics, and as a bearer of responsibility in public life: statesman, mayor, soldier, policeman, district attorney, teacher, sculptor, mountain guide, trustee, architect, master builder, mason, miner, geologist, officer.

BASIC PRINCIPLE:
If you try hard enough you can reach the stars!

Capricorn

Interpreted as the masculine searching-image or self-image, the sign of Capricorn represents the prime mover, the ambitious and conscientious man of action. His behavior is correct and occasionally somewhat stiff. His glance is concentrated, his voice powerful and clear, and sometimes a bit growling. His distinct profile allows his strong will to be seen, as well as his sense of reality and his persistence. He can either be encountered all alone or in places where important decisions are made, such as in business life or on the political parquet.

His strength lies in his discipline, his immense perseverance, and a will to assert himself that becomes even stronger in keeping with how difficult things are. Whenever a top performance is demanded, he feels called upon. There is no peak too high, no task too difficult, no challenge too great to truly deter him. He may take things into thorough consideration and examine them closely at the start, only warming up to a project very slowly, but once he has made a decision, it is very difficult to dissuade him. In this respect, he can be compared to a marathon runner who tries to rise above himself and fights tenaciously for his success alone with the sweat of his brow. He will often go to the limits of his psychological and physical powers of endurance, and experiences his deepest satisfaction when he has finally achieved his goal.

In the distorted form, he becomes quite inflexible. Then he makes the obsessive effort to always do everything right and feels extremely insecure when there are errors or deviations from the norm. It is difficult for him to accept help in this case, and with each arising difficulty he will retire further into his shell, or plunge deeper into his work. This causes him to visibly harden and make a very tense and strict impression in an overly-controlled unemotional manner. As a result, he will preach pedantically about what is proper and what is prohibited. With his exaggerated sense of duty, he may tyrannize his surrounding world and punish with his disdain those who allow themselves the liberties that he considers inadmissible. In this way, he ultimately turns himself into a slave of his rigorous sense of duty and his narrow-minded model for explaining the world without noticing that he has built a wall of loneliness around himself.

Like any other human being, he naturally enjoys social acceptance. However, his self-realization takes place when he knows that he has fulfilled his duties and met his responsibilities, even if he doesn't receive much of a response. His professional career takes a straightforward path without any shortcuts. This career is based on his well-considered plans, and he is willing to defer his private interests in favor of his occupational position. He is virtually predestined for responsible tasks and long-term projects. If he decides to participate on a team, he will be a highly reliable teammate who may think about what he consents to do, but then will give his very best to make a punctual and perfect contribution. In the process, he distinguishes himself time and again through his inexhaustible effort and clear, proper decision making. He has no patience with personal animosities and is therefore able to make compromises when it comes to deferring his own interests. But he is uncompromisingly tough when it comes to the business at hand since the result must satisfy the very highest of standards—namely his own.

The same applies to finding a woman as his companion in life: he is a tough suitor who is capable of wearing down rivals with his staying power. Yet, before he even starts, he will quite soberly examine what his prospects are. He isn't a good loser—not so much because he fears rejection, but because he regrets the lost time. For this reason, he first must figure that he has good chances and meet with the right opportunity before he goes to work. Flirting isn't exactly his strong point since there is nothing playful about his brittle charm. He is as he is: direct, unvarnished, honest, and sometimes rather dry.

Life with him is serious; not solemn, but still pervaded by a sobriety that leaves little time for fun and games. His everyday life is clearly structured and uncomplicated. He doesn't like to improvise and tolerates neither chaos nor surprises that confuse his plans. This is why he finds it so important to be able to depend on his partner. Because of this, his concepts of a relationship are rarely unrealistic. Since he doesn't surrender to any great illusions, he also doesn't experience any disappointments that are worth mentioning.

If there are difficulties in the relationship, he is immediately willing to engage in a realistic confrontation. Admitting errors is never a matter of pride for him. He is actually quite concerned with doing everything right and this also means doing them correctly and in accordance with agreements that have been made. However, if he is additionally confronted with emotional expectations that cannot be organized, structured, or regulated, things will get difficult for him. The problem isn't that he cannot feel them in a deep and upright way, but that displaying these emotions truly isn't his strength. If someone flatters him, he will smile in an embarrassed sort of way because he doesn't quite know how to deal with compliments. Yet, above all it does him good to have his enormous capacity for work, his iron will, and his high degree of responsibility recognized and admired. Even if he sometimes appears to be gruff, one should know that an honest soul and a good heart is concealed behind the rough outer shell. Seen in this light, he is a truly good person to grow old with, especially when his great ambition gives way to a mature, humorous serenity with the years.

Faithfulness is a matter of course for him, as well as being binding for both partners like any other agreement. Once he has made a decision, he will seldom keep an eye out for other possibilities. This makes marriage the ideal form of relationship for him. His sexual energy is enormous, yet he can control it like no other character type. As long as he isn't put under pressure, he is a tireless lover who is capable of deep experiences.

He is put off when someone proves to be unreliable. Constantly changing moods, prima donna airs, or swaggering and boasting are intolerable to him. When he notices that a freeloader has come to make herself at home, she will quickly be thrown out the door. When there is a conflict, he turns into a tough customer. However, even in the most vehement of confrontations, he will always remain so disciplined that he never loses his self-control. His weapons are his toughness and perseverance, and whenever the conflict appears to be futile and insoluble, he can curtly turn away without ever turning around again. Someone who wants to reconcile with him must make him an offer of peace that contains realistic suggestions as to how the contentious topic can be solved, avoided, or dealt with in a better way in the future. If the suggestions seem suitable to him, he will accept them and is willing to also make his contribution. But the confrontation won't be forgotten, particularly not before the new agreements have proved their worth.

Establishing a family is a decision that he must first thoroughly consider. He is completely aware of the responsibility related to this step. If he feels no need to have children, he won't make a secret of this sentiment. However, if he does decide to begin a family, he will be a conscientious father who is concerned with always being a good role model. He gives them a solid framework within which they can freely develop. In return, he expects that they will adhere to any rules and agreements to which he sees himself bound. In this way, he will already treat them like little personalities, even at a very young age. He takes his children seriously. He is seldom a daddy to cuddle with, but he is a just father with whom the children always know where they stand. Puberty is difficult for him to deal with. If he lacks benevolent tolerance and humorous serenity, his authority may easily become a target for adolescent rebellion.

He certainly isn't a big charmer or a dreamy romanticist, and no one has ever accused him of sparkling spontaneity. Instead, he is a sure-footed companion with an intense sense of integrity with whom a woman can climb many peaks.

Aquarius
As the Masculine Searching-Image or Self-Image.

In the **masculine** horoscope as the self-image of the young man;
In the **feminine** horoscope as the main symbol of the animus and the searching-image.

In the **masculine** horoscope as self-image of the mature/fatherly man;
In the **feminine** horoscope as the fatherly/complementary portion of the animus and searching-image.

ARCHETYPE:
The humanist.

ELEMENT:
Air

TYPE:
The individualist, the eccentric, the revolutionary.

BASIC ATTITUDE:
Loves to have it his way and be surprising. Encounters the world with tolerance, but is very individualistic.

MATURE FORM:
The philosopher, the free-thinker, the inventor.

NAIVE OR DISTORTED FORM:
The anarchist, the rebel, the oddball, the exception, the snob, the crank.

STRENGTH:
Richly imaginative, original, humorous, has good powers of deduction, is a free spirit, understands theory.

PROBLEM AREAS:
Flighty, unreliable, unpredictable, nervous, has kinks, faddish, putting things into practice.

RELATIONSHIP STRENGTHS:
The man who is a good friend because of his openness and tolerance.

RELATIONSHIP PROBLEMS:
Doesn't really get involved and avoids responsibility.

TYPE OF ASSERTIVENESS:
With cunning and deceit! Theoretic, noncommittal, and with surprise effects.
TYPE: The skydiver.

SEXUALITY:
Not much drive, enjoys the unusual, prefers mental pleasures.

TYPICAL PROFESSIONAL AREAS:
Wherever new ideas and innovative thoughts, technical understanding, and flexibility are required and wherever freelance work and part-time work are possible: computer wiz, programmer, ecologist, sociologist, inventor, head of marketing, adman, pilot, electrical engineer, futurologist, doctor for alternative medicine or healing practitioner, supervisor, choreographer, astrologer, technician.

BASIC PRINCIPLE:
I am an original and not a copy!

Aquarius

Interpreted as the masculine searching-image or self-image, the sign of Aquarius represents an individualist, an original, unique, and sometimes rather quirky man. His behavior is casual and unconventional, his glance is restless, and is voice bright and animated. It is easy to see that he is a colorful character, and something conspicuous and crazy can always be discovered in his appearance. He can be encountered wherever the spirit of the times prevails and, because of his unpredictability, also in places where one would least expect to see him.

His strength lies in his wealth of ideas and his surprise effects. With his cheerful nature, his openness and tolerance, he is a popular person to be around and a good friend. His place isn't always at the center but rather "excentric"—in the fringes and outskirts—or simply outside the framework of things. He doesn't like to conform, and also dislikes meeting outside expectations. He is the born rebel who has a difficult time with norms and therefore prefers to be in a no-man's-land or in free spaces where he can live his own rules and laws. At the same time, he can also make a completely inflexible and cranky impression and be everything but open for what is new. He is driven by the search for things that are unusual and special, for utopia. He loves to hatch ideas, to experiment, to think up new models and solutions to problems that make it easier for human beings to be together. His astonishing powers of imagination support him in doing these activities, as well as his split-second deductive skill. Some of his ideas are truly ingenious, others just sound like they are, and many are simply way ahead of their time.

In the distorted form, his individuality can become a problem—at least for other people. Then his desire for it will become so obsessive that he must basically act differently than he is expected to, and he will do this at every opportunity. To be an original at any price then becomes a merciless mandatory dictate, with which he frequently makes a silly and ludicrous impression because his approach is so obviously artificial and transparent. Together with a very snobbish conceit, this drives him increasingly into isolation. He will personally explain this outsider position by saying that the others simply aren't as intellectually advanced as he is. Even if he happens to be right about this, this path leads him into a naive pseudo-reality that exists and is valid for him alone. Then he will maintain his image as an unappreciated genius in proud resignation.

He sees his self-fulfillment wherever he can break open structures that have become stuck in a rut; he wants to be the intellectual father of new developments. A strong urge to experiment and a constant need for change drive him to new shores. This means that the path of his career is rarely straightforward, but characterized by taking a side door, abruptly changing direction, and meeting with unexpected coincidences. He is actually the typical freelancer since he immediately runs into trouble with the norms and his superiors as an employee. His ability lies in voluntarily working together in a network in which he can contribute his ideas, inventions, and unconventional solutions. In terms of his career, he rarely has great ambitions, especially not in the customary sense. Only when he can take his own path and do things in his own way is he truly content. His ingenious ideas can just remain wild notions, or he can also have a great deal of success with them.

When it comes to attracting a woman's attention, he is quite unique. His art of conquest is wonderfully crazy or has something bizarre or even loutish about it. His chosen one certainly won't be bored with well-worn standard lines or the obligatory invitation to dinner followed by a look at his stamp collection. But if he does do this, he may be so far out, so complicated and awkward, that he once again makes an original and loveable impression.

Life with him is seldom normal and certainly not monotonous. He is a strange character, eccentric, witty, and full of humor, defending himself against any type of daily routine. As a result, he either travels a great deal because of his profession, or he makes sure that life has enough diversity through activities and friends. If he doesn't invent something new on his own, he will drag home the newest of novelties because he is either convinced that this object is absolutely necessary these days, or because he simply likes to be up-to-date. If something doesn't function at some point, he naturally is well informed about the tricks of technology. And when the damage really cannot be repaired, he is still capable of eloquently philosophizing for hours on the theoretical solution to the problem. Someone who wants to flatter him should admire his originality, his quirks, kinks, and fads, since he is—at least secretly—quite proud of them.

He is naturally a complete bachelor, for whom bonds and commitment are disturbing notions. "Free love for everyone" is his motto, and he means it literally. It is obvious that he also allows his partner all the freedom she needs, yet things may become difficult if she doesn't permit him to enjoy it as well. His sexual energy isn't particularly pronounced. Masculinity is something that he understands less as muscle power or potency but much more as a sharp intellect and an agile mind. He isn't driven as much by his physical urges as by curiosity and the joy of unusual experiences with interesting people. As a lover, he is keen on experimenting. As in other areas, the norms of society don't interest him, and he doesn't permit anyone to dictate his behavior when it comes to sexuality. In the world of his imagination, he isn't bound to one gender, age group, or two as a number. His sensuality blossoms in an environment of freedom, tolerance, and openness. Purely platonic relationships also attract him, particularly since an intellectual "orgasm" is often more exciting for him than pure physical desire.

He can be chased off by trying to force him into a stereotype or a uniform, by trying to restrict his freedom and independence, or by pointing a moral finger at his libertine ways. When a conflict arises and he doesn't immediately withdraw from the situation, he will fight in an ice-cold manner and be unpredictable. His sharp intellect is the weapon with which he achieves some surprising effects. Seen in precise terms, he only wants to engage in conflicts that can be decided by something like a check move in chess. A direct confrontation, particularly when it occurs in a loud manner, is repulsive to him. Someone who wants to reconcile with him must show understanding for his abstract theories and once again allow him freedom. Above all, the other person must be willing to redefine the rules of the game together with him since he hopes that the next conflict can be avoided by doing so.

Marriage as a traditional institute is actually out of the question for him. This is why he will only agree to a family and children when he doesn't have to force himself into the conventional structures of everyday life. It is easy for him to imagine being a househusband, particularly since he will once again be out of the ordinary in this position. His family is never limited to just blood relations, but is wherever like-minded people get together and affinities develop. Since he knows how important his friends are, he will also be very supportive of his children's contacts in terms of friendships. He is tolerant and grants them much freedom. Letting them go off on their own some day is no big problem for him since by then he will have long become more of a good friend than a father.

Although he has a hard time with binding agreements and a great deal of passion isn't to his taste, a woman who likes his crazy whims and mental utopian games, as well as his yellow overalls, will have an enjoyable life with this eccentric man.

Pisces
As the Masculine Searching-Image or Self-Image.

In the **masculine** horoscope as the self-image of the young man;
In the **feminine** horoscope as the main symbol of the animus and the searching-image.

In the **masculine** horoscope as self-image of the mature/fatherly man;
In the **feminine** horoscope as the fatherly/complementary portion of the animus and searching-image.

ARCHETYPE: The prophet.	ELEMENT: Water
TYPE: The artist, the helpful man, the dreamy individual.	BASIC ATTITUDE: Seeks transcendental experiences. Encounters the world imaginatively and with deep empathy.
MATURE FORM: The spiritual advisor, the mystic.	NAIVE OR DISTORTED FORM: The chaotic person, schemer, freeloader, outsider, addict, swindler.
STRENGTH: Intuitive, spiritual, mediumistic, sensitive, willing to help, empathetic, understanding, devoted, inspired, imaginative, creative.	PROBLEM AREAS: Lacking in willpower, spineless, unstable, complicated, fainthearted, dependent on others, unable to lay down limits.
RELATIONSHIP STRENGTHS: The man who opens up emotionally and can love selflessly.	RELATIONSHIP PROBLEMS: Lack of willingness to face difficulties and assume responsibility.
TYPE OF ASSERTIVENESS: Let me out of here! Acts on the basis of sure instincts, frequently by refusing or withdrawing. TYPE: The diver.	SEXUALITY: Very easily seduced, devoted, and capable of the ecstasies of tantric love.

TYPICAL PROFESSIONAL AREAS:
All areas in which empathy and intuition are required, as well as in the areas of social services and therapies, and the art of illusion: first-aid volunteer, spiritual advisor, prison guard, nurse, musician, painter, photographer, filmmaker, magician, fisherman, medium, chemist, distiller, esotericist, yoga instructor.

BASIC PRINCIPLE:
We only see well with our hearts; the essential things are invisible to the eye!

Pisces

Interpreted as the masculine searching-image or self-image, the sign of Pisces represents a sensitive, imaginative, and musically talented artistic character who often also has a deep spiritual vein. His behavior is subdued, sometimes even shy, his glance is soft and understanding, occasionally also insecure, and his voice tends to be quiet but melodious. He will often adapt his appearance to his surrounding world to the extent that he seems to be invisible at times. He can be encountered in quiet, secluded places, in artistic circles, in spiritual communities, or in the world of film.

His strength is his empathy, his ability to dedicate himself, and his astonishing sureness of instinct, on which he can very well depend. Like a highly sensitive seismograph, he registers external impressions and thereby gains an inner knowledge about the right point in time. He will often only recognize his goals for what they are long after he has reached them through many detours and winding paths. His sensitivity lets him not only do the right thing time and again, but also helps him clear dangerous obstacles with an uncanny sureness, and without harm to himself.

His powers of imagination are immense and his responsiveness makes him a channel for all kinds of vibrations, whether these are of a subtle or an emotional nature. With a great deal of empathy, he will participate in other people's concerns and troubles. In addition, he is an extremely sympathetic listener who makes others feel deeply accepted. Since he shows an understanding for everything and neither sits in judgment nor evaluates others, he often becomes a person who can comfort fellow human beings who trustingly pour out their hearts to him. His sympathy is so upright and agreeable that sometimes a person who has cried her heart out to him and gotten rid of her "emotional garbage" with him will go home with a deep sense of relief.

In the distorted form, his boundless empathy leads him to an involuntary but absolute act of self-sacrifice. Then his responsiveness has become so extreme that he no longer can differentiate between other people's problems and his own needs, directly experiencing every emotional pain in his environment as his own suffering. As a result, he will be less and less capable of distinguishing between himself and others. He may then lose himself and have increasing difficulty in coping with life. He may evade reality, dream up pseudo-solutions, and insist so naively on believing in the good in every individual that he lets himself be shamelessly taken advantage of and ultimately becomes a slave to the pitiful role of victim. If he doesn't succeed in coming back to reality and finding the ground beneath his feet, he will gradually sink into chaos and become a pitiable image of the eternal loser who is only concerned with proving to the world that he can no longer be helped. Then he has usually already taken the step toward a flight into intoxication or other addictions. The result of this is that he, who longs for unity from the bottom of his soul, will be pushed to the edges and become an outsider in society.

His self-realization usually takes place after a long search in areas where he can approach his idea and desire for a better, more intact world. This often leads him into the world of art, to theater, film, or music, where the desired ideal can at least be created as an illusion. His willingness to help and his empathy naturally often let him become involved in the field of social work. The healing, spiritual-advising professions and anything concerned with the subtle or spiritual energies are all areas where he can develop his abilities. However, he rarely makes a conscious effort to find a profession. Instead, he tends to be found by it. Having a career in the customary sense means little to him, and he therefore likes to also leave the classical leadership roles to others. Yet, even though it may hardly be perceptible to the outsider, he does like to influence events in a subtle manner. And when the entire situation and all the participants are doing well, he experiences the highest satisfaction because he feels that he has made an essential contribution to this state.

When it comes to enchanting the lady of his heart, he is in his own element. His gentle, yearning glance, imbued with a touch of lascivious sensuality, brings out the weak side of certain women. Like no one else, he knows how to stimulate her fantasies and her secret desires, showing her the face that he instinctively knows reflects her fantasy image. This not only makes him a perfect seducer but also lets him play the role of the fairy-tale prince who had been given up for dead.

Life with him has many facets and can certainly be chaotic from time to time. He is an artistic character who knows how to fade out everyday life and let his muse participate in the wonderful images of his fantasy world. He would actually like nothing better than to live for the moment and fully devote himself to his dreams and longings. It is very easy to flatter him since he naturally likes being admired for his empathetic abilities, his inspiring ways, and his willingness to help and to make sacrifices. As long as no one tries to force him into constricting structures or demands too much in the way of resolute actions, he is deeply content. However, if his partner reminds him from time to time of the everyday chores and necessities, or even accuses him of lacking a sense of reality, he will feel unjustly treated and intensely misunderstood. He is actually willing at any time to immediately skip his own interests for the sake of others, and drop everything to look after them with love and enormous devotion. On the other hand, his partner may sometimes have difficulty accepting the fact that when it comes to his own concerns he is not decisive.

Faithfulness is a very broadly defined, highly imprecise, and completely flexible concept. His emotions encompass everything, and he has a universal feeling when it comes to matters of love. So this romantic fairy-tale prince can occasionally reveal himself to be a rogue who knows all the tricks. As in everything else, his sexual energy depends on the mood of the moment. He tends to be rather suspicious of masculinity and potency in the customary sense, and an aggressive approach isn't his strong point. Instead, his desire develops in sexual fantasies or through an exchange with his muse, by whom he likes to be kissed and seduced. He is capable of the greatest devotion and ecstatic experiences in the realm of the senses.

He is put off when someone jokes about his feelings, has no appreciation of his artistic sides, constantly confronts him with sober facts, or wants to educate him about competence in everyday life. Because he is aware of his great vulnerability, he likes to withdraw from any type of conflict and prefers to evade confrontations. Like an octopus, he shrouds himself in impenetrable streaks of fog and dives into the depths. However, if the other person catches him, hangs onto him, and attempts in this way to force a confrontation, he will either play the role of victim or imperceptibly wrest himself from the grip with the help of defensive games that are meant to confuse. If the other person wants to reconcile with him, the best way is to just let him go. Since he will only initiate conflicts in cases where he must defend himself against being treated like a child, being subjected to educational measures, or other types of discipline, this is also resolved in the moment that he is permitted to swim on in peace.

In the role of father, he also shows his great sensitivity in the loving and tender care of his children. It is easy for him to feel his way into their world of fantasy, and he promotes their musical and artistic abilities at an early age. In addition, he is a patient listener and understanding advisor. He also prefers to let himself be guided more by his intuition than clear rules in his way of raising his children, usually giving his dependents a very good start in life. However, if he feels that the desires and demands of his family have become too much for him, he may completely withdraw for a time by being physically present but mentally unreachable.

He isn't a skillful tactician, and his world is certainly something other than sober reality. Instead, he is a sensitive and helpful partner with whom a woman can experience fantastic moments time and again.

PART V

KNOWING
the HOROSCOPE

Adjusting the Searching-Image and Self-Image

The inner persons, or archetypes, of father, mother, son, and daughter that have been described in the previous sections are usually not initially predisposed within us in an equal, harmonious, and identical way. There are configurations through which they are valuated more positively or more negatively, and these let us see one as superior and another as inferior, as well as first-class or second-rate, desirable, or even disdainful. These valuations can primarily be derived from the aspects that the more slowly moving planets reflect on the respective planets of the searching-image or self-image. The most important statements to this effect are made by the planets Jupiter (♃) and Saturn (♄), and Neptune (♆) and Pluto (♇) in the broader sense. On the other hand, instead of upgrading or downgrading, the aspects of Uranus (♅) create a split, which will be discussed in the next section.

We experience everything that Jupiter (♃) touches in our horoscope as good, noble, desirable, valuable, and outstanding. These are the sides of our being that we are proud of, that we like to show off, and where we feel rich and gifted. Exactly the opposite is true, at least at the beginning, with the aspects of Saturn (♄). We feel impoverished, inhibited, fearful, or neglected in the areas that it critically touches. These are the themes of which we are ashamed, that are connected with effort and exertion, where there are disappointments and hardships, and which we often experience to be inferior. Growing in Saturnine areas in order to overcome the initial constriction is one of the most essential tasks in life that can be read from the horoscope. This doesn't change the fact that we often initially feel ourselves to be weak or even worthless and devalue these areas.

Whatever Neptune (♆) touches in the horoscope we experience as idealized and transfigured, whereby this glorification can go so far that this respective theme completely becomes removed from reality and is experienced as incomprehensible in every respect. As a contrast, a dark fascination is exuded by Pluto (♇), which often creates an obsession and lets the corresponding areas appear to be subject to a taboo, objectionable, indecent, forbidden, or even demonic.

If several of these planets throw an aspect on a searching-image or self-image planet, messages may arise that are initially irritating in their conflicting nature, but prove to be quite an outstanding mirror of the inner contradictoriness when they are examined more closely. Yet, particularly when there are accumulations of aspects it is helpful to differentiate the individual aspects from each other. There are three criteria for doing this:

1. *The exactness of the aspects.* The more precise the aspect, the stronger its effect will be. The less precise, which means the larger its orb is, the more subordinate its effect will be.

2. *The type of aspects.* Conjunctions (☌), oppositions (☍), and squares (□) have the strongest effects, followed by trines (△) and sextiles (✳); the quincunx (⚻) and the sesquisquare (⚼) have a lesser effect. The significance of the remaining secondary aspects is so weak that it can be neglected in this regard.

3. *The position of the planet forming the aspect.* If, despite both of the above-mentioned criteria, two planets appear to be equally strong, then their placement in the house and sign will be decisive. Whether they rule, are in exaltation, fall, or detriment, this position decides which one of the two is weightier.

However, the type of valuation depends not only on the respective planet but also on the type of aspect that it forms. To do this, a differentiation should be made between the harmonious aspects of trine (△) and sextile (✳), as well as the tension aspects of opposition (☍), square (□), quincunx (⚻), and sesquisquare (⚼), and—in this case—also interpret the conjunction (☌) in the sense of the tension aspects. The individual aspects have the meanings shown in Table 11.

With this way of considering things, it becomes clear how the individual archetypes of the inner relationship quartet are ranked. This means that a young woman may not be valued because Saturn is conjunct Venus, whereby a Jupiter aspect to the Moon glorifies the mature or motherly woman, while a Pluto-Sun aspect throws a obsessive shadow on the father, and a friendly Neptune aspect to Mars idealizes the youthful hero.

In addition, aspects can also be used to read how a person values the masculine and the feminine in general: whether he ranks one gender to be better, more important, more significant, superior, or if he looks down on the other in a contemptuous way, or even demonizes and despises it. We should naturally always keep in mind when looking at the horoscope that it only shows the predisposition, but not what an individual has done with it, or will do with it, in the course of his or her life.

Two very contrary examples can illustrate these valuations. The strong Jupiter aspects on the feminine planets in Oswald Kolle's horoscope (Chart 3, page 180) show his unmitigated esteem for the feminine sex, which he expressed during the 60s and 70s in his activities as the head of a public information campaign in Germany in the book and film "Die Frau, das

PLANET	HARMONIOUS ASPECT	TENSION ASPECT
♃ Jupiter	Positive valuation, high esteem	Overvaluation, uncritical overestimation
♄ Saturn	Sober valuation, slight devaluation	Negative valuation, appraisal
♆ Neptune	Idealization, transfiguration	Overidealiation, vagueness
♇ Pluto	Fascination, slight devaluation	Obsession, contemptuousness

Table 11. Upgrading and Downgrading by Aspects.*

*It is obvious that these valuations aren't binding. Like all other themes of the horoscope, these aspects show our disposition. Whether things remain like this, or we become mature and develop this disposition into something higher cannot be read from the horoscope.

unbekannte Wesen ["The Woman as the Unknown Being"]. On the other hand, the horoscope of the underground writer Charles Bukowski (Chart 4, page 181), who can probably openly be called a pornographer and a highly questionable Don Juan, displays a Saturnine devaluation of the feminine planets of Venus and the Moon in contrast to a jovial glorification of the masculine. This attitude is reflected in his books (such as *Notes of a Dirty Old Man*), in which he describes his sexual excesses of using women and degrading them to a commodity, in pornographic detail.

The effects of these inner relationships are extremely diversified and cannot be reduced to a simple formula. It would therefore be an extremely unproductive Sisyphean task to try to describe all the possible combinations. This applies even more since we cannot discern on which level an individual lives out this predisposition.

A strong Plutonic emphasis on the opposite sex, for example, can lead to a corresponding demonization. Whether this means disparaging disdain, to fearfully turning away from it, to devoted subjection, or an enormous urge to control the opposite sex, depends on the extent to which a person's own gender is experienced as good and strong. However, if an individual's own gender is occupied by Pluto and the opposite sex is transfigured in a Neptunian way, this person either may not risk approaching the pure, idealized image of

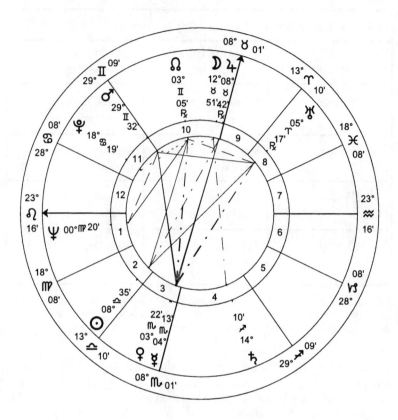

Chart 3. Oswald Kolle. Born October 2, 1928, 2:00:00 CET, Kiel, Germany (010:08:00W 54:20:00N, 01:00:00 GMT). Koch houses. Birth data from U. Waack. During the 60s and 70s, Oswald Kolle expressed his high esteem for women as the head of a public information campaign. His horoscope shows this valuation through the strong Jupiter aspects with the feminine planets (♀☌♃ and ☽☍♃).

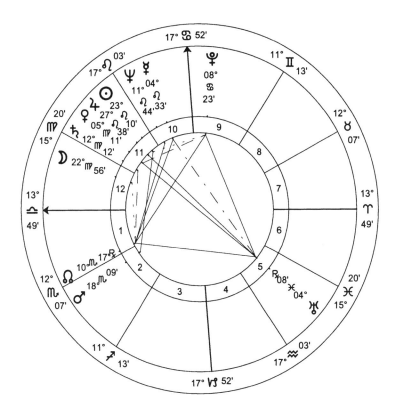

Chart 4. Charles Bukowski. Born August 16, 1920, 10:100:00 CET, Andernach, Germany (007:24:00E 50:26:00N, 09:00:00 GMT). Koch houses. Birth data from birth register. The horoscope of the underground writer Charles Bukowski reflects his glorification of the masculine in the conjunction of Jupiter and the Sun (☉♂♃) and the (rather remote) square with Mars (♂□♃), whereby the Saturn conjunction with Venus and the Moon (☽♂♄ and ☉♂♄) indicates his contempt for women.

the other because of his or her own sordidness, or may accept and identify with the demonic role and force the Neptunian partner into the role of victim.

Yet, this upgrading and downgrading doesn't in any way exhaust the significance of the slowly moving planets. It additionally gives the respective self-image or searching-image a special coloration, shading, or even overlapping. Only in this correlation will the great variety of effects of our inner values scale be understandable.

How the Searching-Image and Self-Image Are Influenced by Aspects

As they have been described in the previous section, the searching-images and self-images are just sketches that only assume individual form when we also consider the influences from aspects to other planets. Since the Sun and Moon are just seen as aspect-receiving bodies here, only the planets from Mercury (☿) to Pluto (♇) are significant for this survey. The intensity of their coloration grows according to the following criteria:

1. *With the preciseness of the aspects.* The more precise an aspect is, the stronger its influence. The less precise it is, meaning the size of its orb, the intensity of its influence diminishes.

2. *With the slowness of the planets that form the aspect.* The slower a planet moves, the stronger its effect will be. (In the following description, the planets are listed in the order of their speed.)

3. *The type of aspect.* The conjunction (☌), opposition (☍), and square (□) have the strongest effects, followed by the trine (△) and sextile (✶), while the quincunx (⚻) and the sesquisquare (⚼) have the least effects. The remainder of the secondary aspects can be omitted here.

In addition, the harmonious aspects and the tension aspects should be differentiated, as in the previous section (see page 177).

When considering the individual aspects, we can differentiate between whether these themes were originally related to the father (Sun ☉) or the mother (Moon ☽), or if they are experienced as distinctly separate from the parents. The latter is something that newly enters the person's life and is initially experienced with one's own or the opposite gender, the masculine (Mars ♂) or the feminine (Venus ♀) sex.

In the following section, we discuss the planets again. We use a heading called "Inner Message," behind which the early-childhood imprints are usually concealed. We encounter all our aspect themes in the first years of life, and draw our early "conclusions," which then become inner messages. An inner message is a conviction that is not always conscious, yet it is unshakeable, of how this world is structured. If this is an exaggerated positive message, life itself will make sure that our image of reality is adjusted. On the other hand, the negative messages for which we constantly find new evidence supporting their justified existence, are much more stubborn. They originate from a distorted picture that has been created from a helpless, childlike perspective. The way in which we react to this false picture is found under "Compensation." It is obviously just as false for the adult individual as the message that is stored from the earliest days of childhood. If we don't become aware of this fact and insist upon our childhood perceptions instead of finding new answers appropriate to our age, these negative messages will radiate considerable, lasting disorders for our relationship life. The individual fields in the following section are explained below:

SELF-IMAGE +   The positively colored image that a person has of himself or herself.

SELF-IMAGE -   The negatively colored image that a person has of himself or herself.

SEARCHING-IMAGE +   The type of character that the person reacts to in a positive way.

SEARCHING-IMAGE -   The problematic variation of this type of the foe image.

PARENTAL IMAGE +   The inner image of the father (Sun aspects) or Mother (Moon aspects) in its positive form.

PARENTAL IMAGE -   The inner image of the father (Sun aspects) or mother (Moon aspects) in its negative form.

INNER MESSAGE +   The positive message from childhood that corresponds to this aspect.

INNER MESSAGE -   The negative message from childhood that corresponds to this aspect.

COMPENSATION   The obvious but false answer to the negative message.

☿ Mercury gives the respective image an intellectually accented coloration. It represents mental agility, analytical and logical thinking, tactics and verbal fluency, a clever, well-informed, and usually well-read person who has an answer for everything. Mercury problems let the person appear to be coldly calculating, untruthful, and wily, a cunning bluffer, a fake, cheater, a profiteer who knows all the tricks.

SELF-IMAGE +	I am wide-awake, clever, skilled. I am informed.
SELF-IMAGE -	I am sly, shrewd, and tricky.
SEARCHING-IMAGE +	The clever person who is eloquent and well-read.
SEARCHING-IMAGE -	The braggart who lies through his teeth.
PARENTAL IMAGE +	Father/Mother is intelligent, talkative, astute, and well versed.
PARENTAL IMAGE -	Father/Mother cannot be beat with words.
INNER MESSAGE +	Men/Women are interesting, bright, and entertaining.
INNER MESSAGE -	Men/Women are calculating, dull, and cold.
COMPENSATION	Don't believe anything that men/women say!

Venus gives the respective image a kind influence. It represents grace, charm, the striving for peace and harmony, for pleasure and enjoyment in life, for an individual with good taste, for someone who opens the other person's eyes for the beauty in this world. Venus problems often result in the image of a vain, shallow, and purely superficial person for whom appearances are more important than value.

SELF-IMAGE +	I am beautiful, charming, and simply lovable.
SELF-IMAGE -	I can't stand conflicts and am too conforming.
SEARCHING-IMAGE +	The peaceful person with a likeable aura.
SEARCHING-IMAGE -	The person whose beauty is only skin deep.
PARENTAL IMAGE +	Father/Mother is very kind.
PARENTAL IMAGE -	Father/Mother is my competitor.
INNER MESSAGE +	Men/Women are highly attractive and loveable.
INNER MESSAGE -	Men/Women are superficial, vain, and phony.
COMPENSATION	Men/Women can be enticed but not let in.

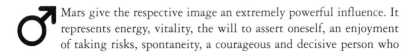

Mars give the respective image an extremely powerful influence. It represents energy, vitality, the will to assert oneself, an enjoyment of taking risks, spontaneity, a courageous and decisive person who represents views and interests in an assertive way—someone who stands in life with full power. On the other hand, Mars problems let a person appear to be dangerous, hot-tempered, violent, instinctive, brutal, sadistic, or as egoists who inconsiderately live out their own interests.

SELF-IMAGE +	I am powerful, spontaneous, courageous, and manly.
SELF-IMAGE -	I am egotistical, unpredictable, and violent.
SEARCHING-IMAGE +	The brave individual with whom other people feel secure.
SEARCHING-IMAGE -	The dangerous person who is experienced as a threat.
PARENTAL IMAGE+	Father/Mother is vital, strong, and assertive.
PARENTAL IMAGE-	Father/Mother is threatening, violent, and choleric.
INNER MESSAGE +	Men/Women are good sports!
INNER MESSAGE -	Men/Women are dangerous!
COMPENSATION	Men/Women must be fought against!

♃ Jupiter colors the image in a noble and dignified way. It stands for generosity, justice, for an optimistic, benevolent person who gives others trust and wins their trust, for a truly good, exemplary, totally proud person who receives and earns respect and admiration. Jupiter problems lead to an uncritical attitude toward other people, who are seen as positive, who are admired. The result of this is that even self-complacency, hypocrisy, and thick-skinned laziness are overlooked.

SELF-IMAGE +	I am great, popular, and terrific.
SELF-IMAGE -	I am overbearing.
SEARCHING-IMAGE +	The good, trustworthy person who one can be proud of.
SEARCHING-IMAGE -	The conceited, condescending person, the con-man.
PARENTAL IMAGE+	Father/Mother supports me, is generous and exemplary.

PARENTAL IMAGE-	Father/Mother is the standard for all things and unequaled.
INNER MESSAGE +	Men/Women are wonderful and mean well with me.
INNER MESSAGE -	Men/Women are always right and are permitted everything.
COMPENSATION	I must be on good terms with men/women.

♄ Saturn gives the respective image something unassuming and lends it a serious color or influence. It stands for clarity, stability, consistency, and a responsible, reliable, patient individual who, in mature modesty, is capable of cutting back his or her own interests without resentment. Saturn problems allow the person to appear to be inaccessible, hard, ungracious, unjust, withdrawn, embittered, strict, mean, or even evil. In addition, they can mean pessimism, inhibitions, feelings of inferiority, and can lead to a person seeing himself as not having a chance, as a stepchild of life, and developing dogged ambition based on the feeling of not being good enough and sufficing nowhere.

SELF-IMAGE +	I am responsible, disciplined, and serious.
SELF-IMAGE -	I am difficult, unpopular, and not worth anything.
SEARCHING-IMAGE +	The person who can be depended upon.
SEARCHING-IMAGE -	The strict person who confines himself or herself, is cold and disapproving.
PARENTAL IMAGE+	Father/Mother is dependable, predictable, gives support and security.
PARENTAL IMAGE-	Father/Mother can't be pleased, is severe, demands respect, is inaccessible.
INNER MESSAGE +	Men/Women can be depended on.
INNER MESSAGE -	Men/Women are difficult, unfriendly, reserved, and cold.
COMPENSATION	Men/Women must be treated in an ice-cold way, must have a tight rein and iron grip kept on them.

♅ Uranus brings an original, unique, completely shrill color into the picture. It stands for freedom and independence; for everything modern; for a person who is special, an individualist who rebels against mental narrowness, outdated ways of living, and encrusted structures; for a free-thinker who is open to all kinds of innovations. Uranus problems mean exaggerated extravagances and stand for a person who cannot be relied upon, who is eccentric, who may be crazy, who feels himself or herself to be something very special, and whose love of freedom is always greater than the sense of responsibility; who gives himself the right to do anything and, as a result, is unpredictable and impossible to control in every respect.

Above all, difficult Uranus aspects can also polarize the respective picture and lead to special forms of sexual relationships. This includes the platonic love that exists next to physical passions, as well as something like a bisexual relationship. And this naturally also includes the polarization into good and bad, particularly in the "classic" variation as the loving relationship to the good wife combined with a love-hate relationship to the evil mother-in-law.

SELF-IMAGE +	I am original, inventive, and unattached.
SELF-IMAGE -	I am high-strung, complicated, trying, eccentric, and noncommittal.
SEARCHING-IMAGE +	The scintillating, extraordinary person, the colorful character.
SEARCHING-IMAGE -	The unreliable person who tends to disappear sooner than later.
PARENTAL IMAGE+	Father/Mother is my friend, original, modern, and open.
PARENTAL IMAGE -	Father/Mother is crotchety, unpredictable, crazy, unreliable.
INNER MESSAGE +	Men/Women are exciting.
INNER MESSAGE -	Men/Women cannot be depended on.
COMPENSATION	I must always maintain an inner distance to men/women!

♆ Neptune transfigures the picture and gives it an idealized influence. It stands for the highest degree of empathy, for mediumistic abilities and spiritual striving, for a very sensitive and spiritual person who develops a genuine willingness to help based on deep sympathy, and who doesn't hesitate to make great self-sacrifices. Neptune problems often make the person incomprehensible and give such an overly idealized coloration that this image becomes nebulous and gets carried away into the unattainable. However, it may also represent Neptunian lapsing from virtue into vice; an unstable, constantly intoxicated person who is unsteady and addicted; a weak, helpless victim ripped back and forth by all the currents; and the tendency to become inaccessible and wriggle out of everything.

SELF-IMAGE +	I am empathetic, mediumistic, devoted, very sensitive, understanding.
SELF-IMAGE -	I am weak, helpless, oversensitive, chaotic, confused.
SEARCHING-IMAGE +	The person with whom one can merge, the kindred spirit.
SEARCHING-IMAGE -	The heartthrob who inspires dreams and longings but has disappeared when one awakes.
PARENTAL IMAGE+	Father/Mother is willing to help, tender, loving.
PARENTAL IMAGE -	Father/Mother is weak, sick, nebulous, spiritually transfigured or inaccessible because of constant intoxication.
INNER MESSAGE +	Men/Women are fantastic.
INNER MESSAGE -	Men/Women are scintillating swindlers who always disappoint.
COMPENSATION	It is better to sacrifice longing and do without men/women!

♇ Pluto gives the respective picture a dark, intensive, fascinating coloration. It stands for power and profound transformation; for a charismatic person of enormous emotional powers of influence who may heal others and can help them because he or she has lived through deep abysses, emerging from crises both strengthened and transformed. Pluto problems let the image appear dark, dangerous, or even merciless. They represent an individual who is experienced as power-hungry, obsessive, despotic, sadistic, fanatic, or deeply evil, from whose influence it is hardly possible to free oneself because in either an open or concealed way he or she knows how to manipulate, control, and make others dependent; but also someone who doesn't really admit a lust for power, who is ashamed of his or her strong domination by physical urges, or one who lives out these physical urges in an inhibited and totally sadistic way.

SELF-IMAGE +	I am fascinating, influential, powerful, and irresistible.
SELF-IMAGE -	I am power-hungry, threatening, dominated by my physical urges, and evil.
SEARCHING-IMAGE +	The captivating person who has a magnetic aura.
SEARCHING-IMAGE -	The manipulative person with whom one falls head over heels in love.
PARENTAL IMAGE+	Father/Mother is omnipotent.
PARENTAL IMAGE-	Father/Mother is so overly powerful that one cannot escape his/her influence.
INNER MESSAGE +	Men/Women are irresistible, desirable, and intensive.
INNER MESSAGE	Men/Women are dominating, ice-cold, demonic, and evil.
COMPENSATION	Men/Women must be controlled, suppressed, and subjugated.

Venus and Mars in the horoscope also stand for eroticism and sexuality. The attitudes toward these areas are described under the respective character types and are colored and influenced by the aspects. The following table gives an overview of the specific coloration of the slower moving planets for this area of partnership.

Table 12. Eroticism (♀) and Sexuality (♂) Influenced by Aspects to the Slower Planets.

PLANET	HARMONIOUS ASPECTS TO ♀ AND ♂	TENSION ASPECTS TO ♀ AND ♂
♃	Has great enjoyment in this area and completely accepts sensuality.	The same—but with a tendency toward exaggeration and immoderation.
♄	Somewhat reserved, sometimes standoffish. Is good at controlling and maintaining set limits.	Self-conscious, inhibited, frustrated, and stiff. Considers these themes to be forbidden, unattainable for himself, or as sinful, which often creates a bad conscience.
♅	Enjoys experimenting and is quite casual. Provides surprising encounters and unusual experiences.	Blasts all norms and loves the thrill of unusual relationships. Demands freedom for the drives or strives for freedom from the drives.
♆	Imaginative and devoted. Spiritualizes the area of sensuality from tantra to platonic relationships.	Lets every interest die; or flees into the impersonal, intoxicated willingness to be seduced, feels like a victim, and lapses from virtue into vice.
♇	Fascination and magnetism, irresistible powers of attraction, lust-filled intensity.	Strong domination by physical urges, wicked lasciviousness, lack of taboos, dependence, and sexual bondage.

The Inner Relationship

If these inner persons are now seen in relation to each other, interesting perceptions can naturally be derived just on the basis of how their respective
themes tolerate each other. The way in which they relate to each other, how
much they like each other, are at enmity, attract, and contradict each other is
a mirror that makes some of the inconsistencies in the external relationship
life visible and easier to understand. Up to now, we have primarily dealt with
the aspects that the other planets form. Now we will explore the positions
and aspects of the searching-image and self-image planets with each other.
Not even a true aspect is required to trigger corresponding dynamics in many
cases. Often, just a tense sign positioning is adequate, as illustrated by the
following example.

For example, if the Moon and Mars are located in opposite signs, the
motherly feminine (☽) will experience the youthful masculine (♂) as a
provocative challenge. The reverse situation also applies—the hothead (♂)
will feel uneasy about the motherly woman (☽). A genuine conflict between
the two is only indicated when they are positioned so that an opposition is
formed (☽☍♂). Then the youth (♂) fears being swallowed up by the feminine (☽); then the woman (☽) experiences masculine directness, sexuality, or
aggression (♂). A great variety of themes can result from this opposition,
depending on the placement of the Moon or Mars. The following images can
easily be derived from it.[1]

The mother (☽) who controls the son (♂).
The youth (♂) who rebels against the mother (☽).
The woman (☽) who fears being raped (♂).
The young man (♂) who distances himself from the mother (☽).
The woman (☽) who looks for a man (♂) hostile (☍) toward
    motherhood (☽).

Since a rousing provocative thrill is found particularly in oppositions, other
images may also result such as: the woman (☽) who loves trying her strength

---

[1]The spectrum of interpretations for this configuration naturally ranges from sudden rage to
family rows, acts committed in the heat of passion, and swallowed anger up to the point of
stomach disorders. However, we are only concerned with describing the persons of the inner
relationship here.

out on a macho male (♂), or the woman (☽) who loves the excitement of challenging sexuality (♂), which means the opposite of cuddly sex.

This section is based on aspects. The most significant ties will come from direct aspects, but even aspects that are formed by sign will have some effect. The aspects can be read as described below. Aspects are exciting for they explain why you are different from other people born in the same sun sign that you are.

1. ✱ SEXTILE (60°)—SIGN AFTER THE NEXT and;
   △ TRINE (120°)—FOUR SIGNS APART
   These harmonious aspects give the inner relationship harmony and peace. They also show how much the connected inner persons like and support each other.

2. ☌ CONJUNCTION (0°)—SAME SIGN
   The conjunction basically means that the participating planets form a union. In most cases, they will be experienced harmoniously. However, there is also the possibility that the planetary powers have a rivalry with each other.

3. ☍ OPPOSITION (180°)—SIGNS LOCATED OPPOSITE EACH OTHER
   The opposition between two planets indicates a fundamental polarization. It is often experienced as a challenge, yet also has a very attractive side, for opposites are known to attract each other.

4. □ SQUARE (90°)—THREE SIGNS APART FROM EACH OTHER
   This aspect links two themes that appear to exclude one another. Seen in this way, the square is the most difficult aspect, and the great troublemaker of the inner relationship.

5. NO ASPECT
   No aspect between two planets simply means no message in this consideration.

Beyond pure tolerance between the planets, the following themes can also be perceived in these aspects:

Sun–Moon

Aspects that the Sun and Moon form with each other show the relationship between the parents; in more precise terms: how the parents' relationship was or is experienced from the child's viewpoint.

Conjunction (☌):	As a unity, possibly rivaling with each other
Sextile (✶) and Trine (△):	As a harmonious couple
Opposition (☍):	As a polarity, probably rivaling each other
Square (□):	Candidates for divorce

Moon–Venus

The aspects of the feminine planets with each other show how the young woman (♀) regards the motherly woman (☽).

In the feminine horoscope, this makes it possible to read how the early self-image of the woman (♀) relates to the motherly role model (☽).

Conjunction (☌):	Mother and daughter are similar and close; possible rivalry.
Sextile (✶) and Trine (△):	Mother and daughter get along well; the mother is the role model for the daughter.
Opposition (☍):	The daughter experiences herself as the counterpole of the mother.
Square (△):	Mother and daughter compete or have enmity with each other; under no circumstances does the daughter want to become like the mother.

These aspects are naturally valid for the next generation as well. When the woman becomes a mother herself, they will be the mirror of her relationship to her own daughter. In addition, these aspects naturally show how the transition to the role of mother may be: without any problems (☌✶△), full of tension (☍), or problematic (□).

In the masculine horoscope, the aspects of the Moon and Venus show how much the anima (♀) of the man is imprinted by the motherly role model (☽), how much he orients himself toward his mother in his searching-image.

Conjunction (☌):	Very close.
Sextile (✶) and Trine (△):	Harmonious. The mother is a positive role model.
Opposition (☍) and Square (□):	His wife should be completely different from his mother.

Moreover, these aspects permit us to recognize how he experiences the transition when his own wife becomes a mother.

Sun–Mars

The aspects of the masculine planets between each other show how the youth (♂) relates to the father (☉). The other way around, their significance corresponds precisely to what has been said about the Moon and Venus.

In the masculine horoscope, this makes it possible to read how the early self-image of the youth (♂) relates to the fatherly role model (☉).

Conjunction (☌):	Father and son are similar to each other and close; possible rivalry.
Sextile (✶) and Trine (△):	Father and son get along well; the father is a role model for the son.
Opposition (☍):	The son experiences himself as the opposite of the father.
Square (△):	The father and son have enmity with each other; under no circumstances does the son want to become like his father.

These aspects are naturally valid for the next generation as well. When the man becomes a father himself, they will be the mirror of his relationship to his own son. In addition, these aspects naturally show, as well, how the transition to the role of father may be: without any problems (♂✶△), full of tension (☍), or problematic (□).

In the feminine horoscope, the aspects of the Sun and Mars show how much the woman's animus (♂) is imprinted by the fatherly role model (☉), how much her searching-image is oriented toward her father.

Conjunction (☌):	Very closely.
Sextile (✶) and Trine (△):	Harmonious; the father is a positive role model.
Opposition (☍) and Square (□):	Her husband should be completely different from her father.

Moon–Mars and Sun–Venus

These two pairs of aspects primarily express generational issues: how the son (♂) relates to the mother (☽) and the father (☉) to the daughter (♀). The various levels of expression have been illustrated in the example at the beginning of this section (page 192).

Venus–Mars

The way in which the young woman (♀) relates to the young man (♂) says much about passion, eroticism, and sexuality, and to what extent these themes are a supportive pillar of the inner relationship (☌△✱), an area of tension (☍), or a problem field (□).

For example: A very conflict-ridden inner relationship, in which the feminine planets are suppressed, can be seen in the horoscope of the Marquis de Sade, whose name has been used to define violent contacts with the opposite sex.

The horoscope of Donatien Alphonse Francois Marquis de Sade shows a war between the sexes, for the masculine is favored and the feminine is downgraded. This is the well-known Marquis de Sade, from whom the word "sadism" originates. The Sun (☉) and the Moon (☽) form a square (□) with each other, as well as Mars (♂) and Venus (♀). The Sun (☉) is clearly upgraded through the conjunction (☌) with Jupiter (♃). Mars (♂), as the second masculine planet, is also strongly placed in its own sign, its own house, and in conjunction to the Ascendent. On the other hand, the feminine planets, which are experienced with enmity, are downgraded. The Moon (☽) is in aspect to Pluto (♇). Although this is a sextile (✱), which actually is considered harmonious, when the Moon is in aspect to Pluto, Pluto is a "heavy" here, especially when considered with the aspects to the Sun.[2] Venus is downgraded, de-emotionalized, and oppressed by the conjunction (☌) with Saturn (♄) and tormented by the strongly positioned Mars (♂). (The objection may be made that Saturn square Mars (♄□♂) actually devalues the masculine side. This is also true in a certain sense and it may be assumed that the Marquis' masculine self-image was split between his Jupiter-like Sun side and his aggressive, but devalued, dominating physical urges (♂). But since, because of its position in its own sign and own house, Mars is clearly stronger than Saturn, which stands in detriment with its house and sign, Mars doesn't "put up" with this devaluation and reacts even more irritably to it.)

As we can see, our relationship conflicts—fortunately, the sunny sides as well—initially occur within ourselves. If we take a look at our "inner persons," with all their characteristics and the way they deal with each other, we will find many phenomena that are familiar because of our relationship life. However, in our everyday experience, we may have the impression that most problems and solutions come from the outside world. This lets us believe over and over again, or at least hope in secret, that everything will turn out all

---

[2]In mythology, Jupiter-Zeus is considered to be the ruler on Olympia, while Pluto-Hades dominates the underworld. Here, the masculine—the Sun (☉)—looks smugly down from the Olympian heights (♃) on the feminine—the Moon (☽)—which finds itself in the abysses of the underworld.

right if the right person would finally come along. If we actually recognize our own inner battles in our problems, we may just have taken the most important step toward truly changing our situation.

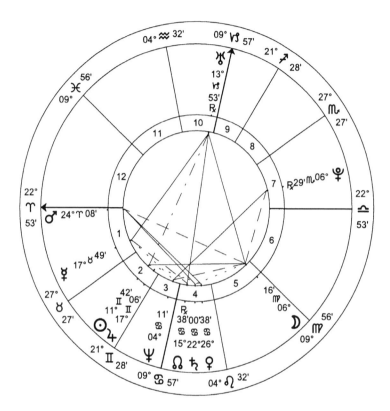

Chart 5. Marquis de Sade. Born June 2, 1740, 02:00:00 LMT, Paris, France (002:20:00E, 48:52:00N, 01:50:40 GMT). Koch houses. Source: time is speculative. For our purposes we can gain the information we need even though we are not sure of the hour, as we are dealing with planets here.

What Now?—Insight is the
First Step to Improvement

As wonderful as it might be to offer some magic formulas, instant solutions, and quick methods to solve everyone's conflicts in love and partnership, it isn't that easy. In our lives, and particularly in our relationships, the goal isn't to live without problems, but to understand them, learn from them, resolve them as much as possible, and grow as a result of having them. Without problematic configurations and tense aspects, life would lack suspense. This is why we see that the horoscopes of great personalities are frequently full of difficult configurations. Difficult aspects don't guarantee maturity, but the constant confrontation with apparently irreconcilable contradictions provides considerable support for the process of emotional growth. C. G. Jung has also said: "The serious problems in life, however, are never fully resolved. If ever they should appear to be so it is a sure sign that something has been lost. The meaning and purpose of a problem seem to lie not in its solution but in our working on it constantly. This alone preserves us from stultification and petrifaction."[1]

Working on conflicts means staying alive, consciously looking at our problems in order to gradually cope with them instead of unconsciously being a victim. "Insight is the first step to improvement." Not much would happen without insight, but insight alone doesn't effect any transformations. However, it is the unrenounceable first step. When analyzed more closely, this step can be divided into three phases:

1. The insight of who I am.

2. The insight as to what I lack.

3. The insight as to why I have had a certain experience.

The "who I am" tells us how we are predisposed and where we stand at the moment. The "what I lack" shows what our potential is, what still must be understood in order to become what we could be. The insight as to why we have had a certain experience can prevent us from running away from diffi-

---

[1] C. G. Jung, *The Structure and Dynamics of the Psyche,* vol. 8 of *The Collected Works of C. G. Jung,* Bollingen Series XX, R. F. C. Hull, trans. (Princeton: Princeton University Press, 1960), ¶771.

cult situations before we have learned what they want to teach us. "There is no problem that doesn't also carry a gift for you in its hands," said Richard Bach. "You seek problems because you need their gifts."[2]

It isn't always easy to recognize this, and we don't always feel capable of mustering up enough stability in acute crisis situations. Therapeutic help may be helpful or even comforting in one case or another. It primarily offers a protected framework so that new patterns of behavior can be considered after we have gained insights. However, therapy sessions can also wind up being merely cover-up exercises or surrogate events, for while we work hard in therapy, we may not do this anywhere else. Things that function wonderfully in laboratory situations may prove to be inappropriate in real life.

In the age of self-realization and noncommittalism, the idea of grappling with another person's peculiarities and emotional problems and struggling together for solutions, appears to be outdated. Instead of working together, many people expect a kind of happiness from love and relationships that is really a fantasy. The idea that we just have to press the right button to be in bliss with our loved one may be wonderful, but it is only a fairy-tale. A meaningful and real relationship is often a complicated, painful process that demands downright hard, sometimes even frustrating, work.

Last but not least, the people with whom we have relationships are also often a mirror of our inner relationship dynamics, making them an essential aid on our path to becoming whole. If we don't look in the mirror, our efforts for self-realization remain self-indulgent introspection. We need the other person as a companion on the path to finding ourselves. Recognizing and valuing our partner as such, even if this doesn't always seem easy, changes our attitude toward problems in partnership. If, with this insight, during the next crisis we take a step in order to better perceive what has just happened, we may possibly notice that we have once again shifted our inner relationship dynamics from inside ourselves to the outside world. Perhaps we always do this in order to take a better look at it? It will hardly become more appealing to us for this reason, but perhaps in this way we can learn to resolve something where we can truly resolve it—namely within ourselves.

Astrology is a tool we can use to open our eyes to our inner being. It can help us achieve the insights mentioned earlier. The horoscope makes visible the tension that develops between our individual predisposition and wholeness. It shows how we are predisposed and lets us recognize what we lack, what we must develop in order to become whole. But once we have understood where we come from and where we are going, then it will also be much easier for us to comprehend what the experiences that we have every day

---

[2]Richard Bach, *Illusions: The Adventures of a Religious Messiah* (New York: Delacort, 1977), p. 46.

want to teach us. Recognizing their meaning, not evading them, not talking them to death or just theoretically solving them in surrogate venues, but only going further when we have actually experienced them, when we have understood and integrated them—here lies the truly decisive step toward improvement.

It is also important to remember that the horoscope makes no direct statements as to how far a person has gone on his or her path, whether the path is even recognized, or whether he or she simply drifts along. However, the respective place in life can be read in the encounters and experiences that a person has at the moment and, above all, from the degree of maturity with which he or she reacts to these.

If you would like to use this book to have an overview of the various aspects of a partnership theme, we recommend the following survey. It isn't a questionnaire that will give you a high score, but it will let you reflect on the situation and take a critical look at where you stand in life. This is meant as an objective inventory; the message is neither good nor bad. It simply describes the momentary status quo and perhaps clarifies what your next step could be. If you have little or no knowledge of astrology, don't let this stop you from filling out the questionnaire. You can give your answers using the knowledge that you have gained from this book.

For the sake of simplicity, the following summary speaks of the partner (male or female) and the current relationship. If you don't have a solid relationship at the moment, refer back to your last significant relationship.

Questions on the Distribution of the Four Elements	
What element do I lack the most?	Fire ❏ Earth ❏ Air ❏ Water ❏
How strong is this in my partner?	Very ❏ Average ❏ Weak ❏
How much do I value his or her qualities?	Very ❏ Somewhat ❏ Not very ❏ Not at all ❏
How much do I clash with him or her about this, get worked up, or feel threatened?	Very ❏ Somewhat ❏ Not very ❏ Not at all ❏
How much do I leave the associated area in life up to my partner?	Totally ❏ Somewhat ❏ Not very ❏ Not at all ❏

Questions on the Distribution of the Four Elements, cont.	
How much do I attempt to learn from my partner in this area?	Constantly ❑ Often ❑ Seldom ❑ Not at all ❑
In which elements are my searching planets?* (Man: ♀/☽—Woman: ♂/☉)	♂/♀ Fire ❑ Earth ❑ Air ❑ Water ❑ ☽/☉ Fire ❑ Earth ❑ Air ❑ Water ❑
Which element does my partner have least or not at all?	Fire ❑ Earth ❑ Air ❑ Water ❑
How often do I miss these qualities in him/her?	Often ❑ Sometimes ❑ Not at all ❑
Which element isn't found in my searching-image but is strongly represented by my partner?	Fire ❑ Earth ❑ Air ❑ Water ❑
How much do I recognize and value the related characteristics as qualities of the opposite sex?	Very ❑ Somewhat ❑ Not very ❑ Not at all ❑
Which element is represented by my searching-image but hardly or not at all by my partner?	Fire ❑ Earth ❑ Air ❑ Water ❑
How much do I miss these related qualities in him/her?	Very ❑ Somewhat ❑ Not very ❑ Not at all ❑

*If you want to do this very thoroughly, then also include the strong aspects (♂◻☍) of the slowly moving planets with the searching-image and self-image planets. They result in the following coloration: ♃—fiery, ♄—earthy, ♅—airy, ♆—watery. (♇ cannot be clearly classified here.)

Questions about the Inner Relationship	
How familiar am I with the four inner persons of my relationship quartet; how clearly can I see them?	☉ Well ❑ Quite a Bit ❑ Little ❑ Not at All ❑ ☽ Well ❑ Quite a Bit ❑ Little ❑ Not at All ❑ ♀ Well ❑ Quite a Bit ❑ Little ❑ Not at All ❑ ♂ Well ❑ Quite a Bit ❑ Little ❑ Not at All ❑
Which upgrading and downgrading of the sexes do I have in me because of the aspects (of ♃, ♄, ♆, ♇)?	☉ Up ❑ Neutral ❑ Down ❑ ☽ Up ❑ Neutral ❑ Down ❑ ♀ Up ❑ Neutral ❑ Down ❑ ♂ Up ❑ Neutral ❑ Down ❑
Which influence does my searching-image and self-image receive through all aspects with other planets? Write the influence (planet) next to the respective planet, such as for ☉□♆ (☉ idealized, vague, incomprehensible), or for ♀☌♇ (♀ fascinating, dangerous).	☉ ☽ ♀ ♂
How do my inner persons get along with each other? Write the significance of the aspects that these four planets form with each other next to the respective planets, such as: ☽□♀ (☽ in conflict with ♀) or ☉△♂ (☉ friendly with ♂).	☉ ☽ ♀ ♂

POSITIONS *of* *the* PLANETS

Example Chart

How individual relationship dynamics can be read from the horoscope is shown using Salvador Dali's chart.

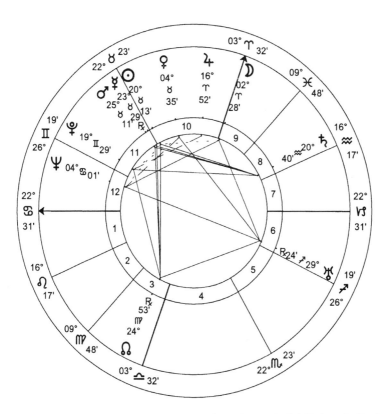

Chart A. Salvador Dali. Born May 11, 1904, 08:45:00 GMT, Cadaqués, Spain (003:17:00E, 42:17:00N). Koch houses. Birth data from birth register.

1. WEAKEST ELEMENT AND ACHILLES' HEEL

There are no personal planets in air signs. Note that neither the Ascendent nor Midheaven are located in air signs either. We can therefore consider it to be the element that Dali lacks; this would complement him, but it is simultaneously his Achilles' heel.

2. SEARCHING-IMAGE AND SELF-IMAGE CONFLICT

The two feminine planets are in earth and fire: namely Venus (♀) in the earth sign Taurus (♉), and the Moon (☽) in the fire sign Aries (♈). This means that while air is the element that complements Dali, his inner femininity persuades him that women should be fiery or earthy. This creates a searching-image conflict in any case. He will either find a fiery and/or earthy woman, who doesn't complement his missing element, or he will find this complement in an airy partner, who doesn't correspond to this fiery-earthy searching-image.

3. SELF-IMAGE

His self-image as a man is totally earthy. The two masculine planets—Mars (♂) and the Sun (☉)—are located in the earth sign of Taurus (♉).

4. UPGRADING AND DOWNGRADING—SELF-IMAGE

The two masculine planets Mars (♂) and the Sun (☉) are vehemently downgraded by the Saturn square (♂□♄ and ☉□♄). The inner message of this could be: "Masculinity is bad, forbidden, offensive, shameful, dirty."

5. UPGRADING AND DOWNGRADING—SEARCHING-IMAGE

On the other hand, femininity is clearly upgraded. While Venus (the young woman) is idealized through a Neptune sextile (♀✳♆), the Moon (the motherly feminine) stands at the Midheaven (MC) as the ruler of the Cancer Ascendent (AC♋), where it is overly idealized and becomes unattainable through a Neptune square (☽□♆).

6. COLORATION OF THE SELF-IMAGE THROUGH THE ASPECTS

In addition to the valuations already mentioned, the Saturn squares to both the masculine planets (♂□♄ and ☉□♄) mean there is a problem with the masculine self-image. The inner message of this could be: "I am difficult, unpopular. I am never good enough. I am inadequate as a man. I am too much." A little compensation is offered by Mercury, which gives the masculine self-image a smart, agile coloration through its conjunction with Mars and the Sun (☿♂♂ and ☿♂☉). This shows a man who is never at a loss for words.

7. COLORATION OF THE SEARCHING-IMAGE THROUGH THE ASPECTS

The anima, which through Neptune's influence (♀△♆ and ☽□♆) becomes nebulously transfigured in its fiery/earthy mixture (☽/♈ = fire and ♀/♉ = earth), receives an additional touch through the aspects of Uranus (♀△♅ and ☽□♅) that allows the searching image of a scintillating woman or a colorful character to emerge. However, it also contains the message that women cannot be depended upon and that they will be unfaithful sooner or later and then disappear. This Uranian influence can also lead to the division of the feminine searching-image—a polarization between a mother image transformed into an omnipresent goddess and a rather earthy, real woman.

8. THE INNER RELATIONSHIP

For the inner relationship, in addition to an obvious problem with faithfulness, this results above all in an eternal thirsting by the masculine nature, which is experienced as inferior, for redemption through the transfigured feminine, a hope for that famous "The eternal feminine draws us upward."[1] However, there is no doubt that the greatest tension lies between the self-image as a thoroughly sensual (☉/♉ and ♂/♉) but inferior, perhaps even unworthy (♂□♄ and ☉□♄) man who has Taurian claims of possession to everything (and this also includes his woman). Yet, at the same time he experiences her as someone he cannot hold onto (♆) and transfigured into the incomprehensible (♅). The spectrum shown in the staging of these inner relationship dynamics is certainly very broad. It extends from the jealous, pinched house tyrant to the Great Goddess's devoted servant of love. How much Dali worshiped this latter aspect was not only expressed in his many pictures but also in his remarkable tarot that shows his highly revered Gala as "The Empress."

Unfortunately, Gala's time of birth is unknown so that we only know the positions of the planets on the day of her birth for purposes of comparison. The Moon changed in the late morning of this day from the sign of Gemini to the sign of Cancer, so we don't know the position of this important self-image planet. For this reason, we will not do a mirror-image interpretation of the relationship from her perspective, but will point out some analogies with Dali's inner relationship.

---

[1] Johann Wolfgang von Goethe, to whom this quote is attributed, had a somewhat similar inner relationship: a Pluto square darkened his Sun (♇□☉ in ♍) while ascribing redemptive qualities to both his Venus through a Neptune sextile (♆✶♀ in ♍) and to his Moon through its position in the sign of Pisces and a sesquisquare of Neptune (♆⚼☽ in ♓).

In the Tarot by Salvador Dali, his wife and muse Gala is "The Empress." Used by kind permission of Negsa-Naipes Comas.

To what extent she was able to compensate at least in part for Dali's missing air element cannot be determined since the position of her Moon is uncertain. On the other hand, the aspects of Jupiter indicate that she placed a more benevolent and positive value on the masculine ($\odot \ast \, 4$ and $\sigma \ast \, 4$) than Dali himself, and that her earthy searching-image (σ in $\, \aleph$ and $\odot$ in $\, \mathrm{I\!I\!P}$) corresponded with his self-image, even including the Mercury influence ($\odot \sigma \, \xi$). His intense worship wouldn't have been a problem for her since she had a very healthy self-image as a woman with a Jupiter-Moon conjunction[2] ($\mathcal{D} \sigma \, 4$) and a Leo Venus ($\mathcal{Q}$ in $\, \Omega$). She would have corresponded to the transfiguration of his image had she been born in the first hours of the day, during which the Moon still formed a wide conjunction with Neptune. In any case, her self-image as an independent woman ($\mathcal{Q} \square \, \mathcal{H}$) had a clear analogy and projection surface for Dali's inner message, for he felt that women are impossible to hold, eccentric, and unpredictable.

---

[2]This conjunction existed for the entire day and can therefore be assumed despite the missing birth time.

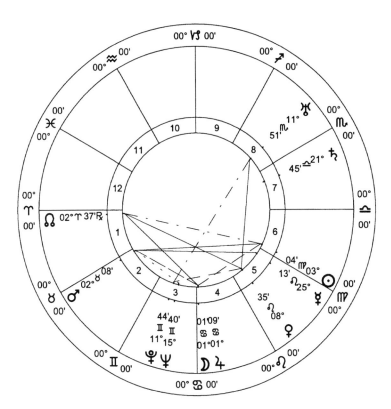

Chart B. Elena Ivanova Djakonova, called Gala, can be seen in many of Dali's pictures. Born August 26, 1894. Her birth time is unknown so we have created a solar chart for 12:00:00 LMT in Kazan, Russia (049E08, 55N49, 08:43:28 GMT). Koch houses. Birth data: only her birth day, month, and year are known.

How to Find the Searching-Image and Self-Image Planets

Planetary Positions from 1920–2000

IMPORTANT NOTE

The sign positions of the searching-image and self-image planets Sun (☉), Moon (☽), Venus (♀), and Mars (♂) can be looked up with the help of the following tables. In doing so, please consider the fact that the planets don't change the signs at midnight according to our time but during the course of the respectively listed day.

BACKGROUND

Seen from Earth, all the planets appear to circle around Earth on a common path at their own speeds. Since ancient times this has been called the ecliptic or the zodiac. We call the time that the Sun requires for this orbit one year. The Moon covers the same stretch in the shortest amount of time. Its orbit time of about 27 days is the basis for our month. Venus requires 225 days and Mars 687 days in order to circle Earth once.

The 360 degrees of this orbital path is divided into twelve equally long sections of 30 degrees each. These are named after constellations, which we commonly call the twelve signs of the zodiac. The Sun has the most even course in this orbit. Because of this, its position is the easiest to calculate of all the planetary positions. It is based on the birth date and almost everyone knows it as their "sign." However, the course of the Sun isn't always exactly identical with the course of the year, which is why a leap year comes every four years. The minor shift that results from this explains the apparent inaccuracy with which the time sectors for the individual signs of the zodiac are given in various books and magazines.

HOW TO USE THE TABLES

If you don't happen to find a transition date for the **Sun**, **Venus**, or **Mars**, meaning the first or last day of the specified period, then the stated sign position will be clear. In all these cases, you can consider the established sign positions as certain.

However, if in the **Sun**, **Venus**, or **Mars** tables you find the first day of the time sector listed, it may be that the planet is still in the sign before it, particularly if the person was born in the morning of the day. If this is the last day of the stated phase, then it is possible that the planet has already changed into the next sign; this applies even more if the person was born in the second half of the day.

The **Moon** sign is more difficult to ascertain. Since it changes sign every two days or so, it would go beyond the scope of this book to list all its sign positions for 80 years in the tables. Instead, we have used a Moon formula that has a very high probability of resulting in the right Moon position and lists the two possible signs when there is a borderline case.

Readers who are interested in having a chart calculated can have this done in many metaphysical bookshops. If there are no such bookshops in your area, you may want to go to a professional astrologer or contact:

Astro Communications Service
5521 Ruffin Rd.
San Diego, CA 92123-1314
1-800-888-9983
1-619-492-9919
fax: 1-619-492-9917
website: www.astrocom.com

The Sun ☉

TIME	SIGN
3/21–4/20	Aries
4/21–5/20	Taurus
5/21–6/21	Gemini
6/22–7/22	Cancer
7/23–8/22	Leo
8/23–9/22	Virgo
9/23–10/22	Libra
10/23–11/21	Scorpio
11/22–12/21	Sagittarius
12/22–1/20	Capricorn
1/21–2/19	Aquarius
2/20–3/20	Pisces

The Moon ☽

You can discover the position of the Moon with the following four steps:

1. Use Table A to look up the number corresponding to the month of your birth date and write it down.

2. Look for the number of the birth day in Table B. Add this number to your answer in number 1 above.

3. If you know the exact time of birth, find the number for the birth hour in Table C. If you don't know the birth time, then skip this point.

4. Add up all the numbers. If they are greater than 360, then subtract 360 from the result. You can find the sign position of the Moon in Table D by using your answer.

Table A. Finding the Number for Your Birth Date.

Year	Jan	Feb	Mar	Apr	May	Jun	Jul	Aug	Sep	Oct	Nov	Dec
1910	167	212	220	263	297	347	25	79	131	166	212	244
1911	289	336	345	37	75	128	165	213	258	298	333	6
1912	55	109	133	165	222	268	301	346	31	66	119	158
1913	211	259	269	314	346	30	63	113	166	205	256	292
1914	337	21	29	74	108	158	197	250	301	336	22	55
1915	100	147	156	207	247	299	336	23	67	99	145	176
1916	227	280	305	356	31	78	111	155	202	239	291	331
1917	23	70	79	124	156	200	234	283	336	15	67	103
1918	147	191	199	239	275	329	9	57	113	147	193	225
1919	270	318	326	18	57	109	145	192	236	268	313	347
1920	38	91	115	167	202	248	281	326	14	50	104	153
1921	194	241	249	294	325	10	44	94	148	186	237	271
1922	317	1	10	55	91	153	182	234	284	318	3	35
1923	80	128	138	188	227	280	316	1	46	78	123	159
1924	210	263	288	339	13	59	91	137	185	222	270	314
1925	4	51	59	103	129	179	214	265	319	357	48	81
1926	126	172	180	226	262	315	354	46	95	128	172	204
1927	250	299	306	359	38	90	126	172	216	248	294	330
1928	22	76	100	150	184	229	261	307	356	34	87	125
1929	175	221	229	273	304	350	25	76	130	168	218	252
1930	296	341	350	37	74	127	166	218	265	298	342	14
1931	59	109	117	170	208	261	295	341	26	58	105	142
1932	194	248	272	321	355	38	71	117	167	205	258	296
1933	345	31	38	82	114	160	196	248	302	340	29	63
1934	107	152	161	208	245	299	337	29	76	108	152	184
1935	230	280	288	341	20	72	106	151	196	229	277	314
1936	7	60	84	132	165	209	241	287	237	15	69	106
1937	155	200	208	252	285	331	8	60	114	151	200	233
1938	277	322	331	19	56	110	148	199	246	278	321	353
1939	40	90	99	153	191	242	276	322	6	39	88	126

Table A. Finding the Number for Your Birth Date (cont.)

Year	Jan	Feb	Mar	Apr	May	Jun	Jul	Aug	Sep	Oct	Nov	Dec
1940	180	232	255	302	335	19	51	97	148	188	240	277
1941	325	10	18	61	95	142	180	232	286	323	10	43
1942	87	133	141	190	227	281	319	9	55	88	131	163
1943	211	262	272	325	3	53	87	132	176	210	260	298
1944	351	43	65	112	145	188	221	268	318	357	50	87
1945	135	180	188	232	266	314	352	45	97	134	181	214
1946	258	303	311	1	38	91	130	179	225	257	301	334
1947	22	73	84	136	175	224	258	302	347	22	71	116
1948	163	215	236	282	314	358	30	77	129	168	221	257
1949	305	350	358	45	76	126	164	216	269	305	351	24
1950	67	114	121	171	209	263	300	350	35	67	111	144
1951	193	245	256	309	347	35	68	112	157	192	243	281
1952	335	25	46	92	124	167	200	248	300	339	31	68
1953	115	159	168	213	247	297	336	30	81	116	161	193
1954	237	283	291	341	29	73	111	160	205	237	281	315
1955	5	58	69	121	158	205	238	282	328	357	54	92
1956	145	196	214	262	293	337	11	60	112	151	203	239
1957	285	330	339	24	58	109	148	201	252	287	331	3
1958	47	93	101	142	190	244	281	330	15	47	92	126
1959	177	230	241	293	330	16	48	92	126	173	225	263
1960	316	6	26	71	103	147	181	231	284	323	14	50
1961	95	140	149	194	229	280	319	13	32	97	141	172
1962	216	264	272	323	2	55	92	140	184	217	263	298
1963	349	43	53	105	140	186	218	262	308	343	36	74
1964	126	176	196	241	273	317	353	43	96	135	186	221
1965	266	310	319	5	40	92	130	184	233	267	311	342
1966	27	74	83	135	174	227	263	310	355	28	74	110
1967	161	215	225	276	311	356	28	72	118	157	208	245
1968	297	346	6	51	83	129	164	215	268	307	357	31
1969	76	121	129	175	210	263	302	354	43	76	120	152
1970	197	245	255	307	347	38	74	121	165	198	245	281

Table A. Finding the Number for Your Birth Date (cont.)

Year	Jan	Feb	Mar	Apr	May	Jun	Jul	Aug	Sep	Oct	Nov	Dec
1971	334	27	36	87	121	156	197	241	288	324	17	56
1972	107	156	176	221	254	300	335	27	81	119	168	202
1973	246	290	298	345	21	74	114	165	213	246	290	322
1974	7	57	66	120	158	210	245	291	325	8	55	92
1975	145	199	207	257	290	335	7	52	98	137	188	227
1976	278	326	347	32	63	110	147	200	253	291	339	12
1977	56	100	118	155	191	245	283	335	23	56	100	132
1978	178	227	238	292	331	22	56	101	145	178	226	263
1979	317	9	18	67	100	145	176	221	269	307	1	38
1980	89	136	157	201	234	282	319	11	65	102	150	182
1981	226	270	278	325	2	55	94	145	193	226	270	303
1982	349	40	51	104	142	192	226	271	315	348	37	74
1983	127	181	188	237	270	314	346	31	80	118	171	210
1984	260	306	327	12	45	93	130	184	236	273	320	353
1985	36	80	88	136	173	226	266	316	353	36	80	113
1986	161	212	223	276	315	4	37	81	125	159	207	239
1987	296	351	359	46	80	124	156	203	253	291	344	23
1988	71	117	138	182	216	264	301	355	42	84	130	161
1989	205	250	258	306	344	38	77	127	173	206	250	284
1990	333	24	34	88	126	174	206	251	295	328	18	56
1991	109	161	168	217	250	294	327	14	64	103	156	194
1992	242	287	307	352	26	75	112	166	219	254	300	331
1993	15	60	69	118	156	210	248	297	343	16	61	95
1994	144	197	207	260	297	344	17	61	105	139	189	226
1995	280	331	340	27	60	104	138	185	236	275	329	6
1996	53	97	118	162	195	245	283	337	29	64	109	141
1997	185	230	240	290	328	22	60	108	154	186	231	266
1998	316	9	18	71	107	154	186	230	275	309	359	37
1999	91	142	151	197	230	275	308	357	49	88	140	177
2000	223	268	287	332	5	56	94	148	199	234	279	311

Table B. Day of Birth.

Look for the number that corresponds to the birth date and add this to the number from Table A.

Day	Number	Day	Number
1st	0	17th	212
2nd	13	18th	225
3rd	26	19th	238
4th	40	20th	252
5th	53	21st	265
6th	66	22nd	278
7th	79	23rd	291
8th	93	24th	305
9th	106	25th	318
10th	119	26th	331
11th	132	27th	344
12th	146	28th	358
13th	159	29th	11
14th	172	30th	24
15th	185	31st	37
16th	199		

Table C. Birth Time Adjustment.

If you know the hour of birth, look up the time in the table below. You may add or subtract a number from your total.

TIME	MIDNIGHT-6 A.M.	6 A.M-NOON	NOON-6 P.M.	6 P.M.-MIDNIGHT
VALUE	-6	-3	+3	+6

Table D. The Sign Position of the Moon.

If your number falls between	the Moon is in this sign
355–4	Pisces/Aries
5–24	Aries
25–34	Aries/Taurus
35–54	Taurus
55–64	Taurus/Gemini
65–84	Gemini
85–94	Gemini/Cancer
95–114	Cancer
115–124	Cancer/Leo
125–144	Leo
145–154	Leo/Virgo
155–174	Virgo
175–184	Virgo/Libra
185–204	Libra
205–214	Libra/Scorpio
215–234	Scorpio
235–244	Scorpio/Sagittarius
245–264	Sagittarius
265–274	Sagittarius/Capricorn
275–294	Capricorn
295–304	Capricorn/Aquarius
305–324	Aquarius
325–334	Aquarius/Pisces
335–354	Pisces

Example

Number from Table A (Finding the Number for Your Birth Date, p. 213)
Number from Table B (Day of Birth, p. 216)
Number from Table C (Birth Time Adjustment, p. 217)
Total
Minus 360, if necessary
Moon number (see Table D, p. 217)
Moon position from Table D

Bill Clinton, born August 19, 1946 at 8:51 A.M.	Hillary Clinton, born October 26, 1947 at 8 P.M.
179	22
238	331
-3	+6
414	359
-360	-
54	359
Taurus	Pisces/Aries

Bill Clinton clearly has a Taurus Moon, while the Moon changes from the sign of Pisces to Aries in Hillary Clinton's horoscope, which means you don't know the Moon sign and need to explore further. In Hillary Clinton's case, her Moon is in Pisces.

Venus ♀

In order to locate Venus, look up your year of birth in the Venus table (pp. 219–232). If you were born in 1920 between April 13 and May 6, your Venus is in Aries.

Mars ♂

In order to locate Mars, look up your year of birth in the Mars table (pp. 233–240). If you were born in 1920 between February 1 and April 23, your Mars would be in Scorpio.

Table E. Venus Placements 1920–2000.

Year	Aries	Taurus	Gemini	Cancer	Leo	Virgo	Libra	Scorpio	Sagittarius	Capricorn	Aquarius	Pisces
1920	4/13– 5/6	5/7– 5/30	5/31– 6/24	6/25– 7/18	7/19– 8/12	8/13– 9/5	9/6– 9/29	1/1– 1/4 9/30– 10/24	1/5– 1/29 10/25– 11/17	1/30– 2/23 11/18– 12/12	2/24– 3/18 12/13– 12/31	3/19– 4/12
1921	2/3– 3/7 4/27– 6/2	3/8– 4/26 6/3– 7/8	7/9– 8/5	8/6– 8/31	9/1– 9/26	9/27– 10/20	10/21– 11/13	11/14– 12/7	12/8– 12/31		1/1– 1/6	1/7– 2/2
1922	3/14– 4/6	4/7– 5/1	5/2– 5/25	5/26– 6/19	6/20– 7/15	7/16– 8/10	8/11– 9/7	9/8– 10/10 11/29– 12/31	10/11– 11/28	1/1– 1/24	1/25– 2/17	2/18– 3/13
1923	4/27– 5/21	5/22– 6/15	6/16– 7/10	7/11– 8/3	8/4– 8/27	8/28– 9/21	9/22– 10/15	1/1– 1/2 10/16– 11/8	1/3– 2/6 11/9– 12/2	2/7– 3/6 12/3– 12/26	3/7– 4/1 12/27– 12/31	4/2– 4/26
1924	2/14– 3/9	3/10– 4/5	4/6– 5/6	5/7– 9/8	9/9– 10/7	10/8– 11/2	11/3– 11/27	11/28– 12/21	12/22– 12/31		1/1– 1/19	1/20– 2/13
1925	3/29– 4/21	4/22– 5/15	5/16– 6/9	6/10– 7/3	7/4– 7/28	7/29– 8/22	8/23– 9/16	9/17– 10/11	1/1– 1/14 10/12– 11/6	1/15– 2/7 11/7– 12/5	2/8– 3/4 12/6– 12/31	3/5– 3/28

Table E. Venus Placements 1920–2000 (cont.).

Year	Aries	Taurus	Gemini	Cancer	Leo	Virgo	Libra	Scorpio	Sagittarius	Capricorn	Aquarius	Pisces
1926	5/7–6/2	6/3–6/28	6/29–7/24	7/25–8/18	8/19–9/11	9/12–10/5	10/6–10/29	10/30–11/22	11/23–12/16.	12/17–12/31	1/1–4/6	4/7–5/6
1927	2/27–3/22	3/23–4/16	4/17–5/12	5/13–6/8	6/9–7/7	7/8–11/9	11/10–12/8	12/9–12/31		1/1–1/9	1/10–2/2	2/3–2/26
1928	4/12–5/5	5/6–5/30	5/31–6/23	6/24–7/18	7/19–8/11	8/12–9/4	9/5–9/29	1/1–1/3 9/30–10/23	1/4–1/29 10/24–11/17	1/30–2/22 11/18–12/12	2/23–3/18 12/13–12/31	3/19–4/11
1929	2/3–3/8 4/21–6/3	3/9–4/20 6/4–7/8	7/9–8/5	8/6–8/31	9/1–9/25	9/26–10/20	10/21–11/13	11/14–12/7	12/8–12/31		1/1–1/6	1/7–2/2
1930	3/13–4/6	4/7–4/30	5/1–5/25	5/26–6/19	6/20–7/14	7/15–8/10	8/11–9/7	9/8–10/12 11/23–12/31	10/13–11/22	1/1–1/24	1/25–2/16	2/17–3/12
1931	4/27–5/21	5/22–6/14	6/15–7/9	7/10–8/3	8/4–8/27	8/28–9/20	9/21–10/14	1/1–1/3 10/15–11/7	1/4–2/6 11/8–12/1	2/7–3/5 12/2–12/25	3/6–3/31 12/26–12/31	4/1–4/26

Table E. Venus Placements 1920–2000 (cont.).

Year	Aries	Taurus	Gemini	Cancer	Leo	Virgo	Libra	Scorpio	Sagittarius	Capricorn	Aquarius	Pisces
1932	2/13–3/9	3/10–4/5	4/6–5/6 7/14–7/28	5/7–7/13 7/29–9/8	9/9–10/7	10/8–11/2	11/3–11/26	11/27–12/21	12/22–12/31		1/1–1/19	1/20–2/12
1933	3/28–4/20	4/21–5/15	5/16–6/8	6/9–7/3	7/4–7/27	7/28–8/21	8/22–9/15	9/16–10/11	1/1–1/14 10/12–11/6	1/15–2/7 11/7–12/5	2/8–3/3 12/6–12/31	3/4–3/27
1934	5/7–6/2	6/3–6/28	6/29–7/23	7/24–8/17	8/18–9/11	9/12–10/5	10/6–10/29	10/30–11/22	11/23–12/16	12/17–12/31	1/1–4/6	4/7–5/6
1935	2/27–3/22	3/23–4/16	4/17–5/11	5/12–6/7	6/8–7/7	7/8–11/9	11/10–12/8	12/9–12/31		1/1–1/8	1/9–2/1	2/2–2/26
1936	4/12–5/5	5/6–5/29	5/30–6/23	6/24–7/17	7/18–8/11	8/12–9/4	9/5–9/28	1/1–1/3 9/29–10/23	1/4–1/28 10/24–11/16	1/29–2/22 11/17–12/11	2/23–3/17 12/12–12/31	3/18–4/11
1937	2/3–3/9 4/15–6/4	3/10–4/14 6/5–7/7	7/8–8/4	8/5–8/30	8/31–9/25	9/26–10/19	10/20–11/12	11/13–12/6	12/7–12/30	12/31	1/1–1/6	1/7–2/2

Table E. Venus Placements 1920–2000 (cont.).

Year	Aries	Taurus	Gemini	Cancer	Leo	Virgo	Libra	Scorpio	Sagittarius	Capricorn	Aquarius	Pisces
1938	3/13–4/5	4/6–4/29	4/30–5/24	5/25–6/18	6/19–7/14	7/15–8/9	8/10–9/7	9/8–10/13 11/16–12/31	10/14–11/15	1/1–1/23	1/24–2/16	2/17–3/12
1939	4/26–5/20	5/21–6/14	6/15–7/9	7/10–8/2	8/3–8/26	8/27–9/20	9/21–10/14	1/1–1/4 10/15–11/7	1/5–2/6 11/8–12/1	2/7–3/5 12/2–12/25	3/6–3/31 12/26–12/31	4/1–4/25
1940	2/13–3/8	3/9–4/4	4/5–5/6 7/6–8/1	5/7–7/5 8/2–9/8	9/9–10/6	10/7–11/1	11/2–11/26	11/27–12/20	12/21–12/31		1/1–1/18	1/19–2/12
1941	3/28–4/20	4/21–5/14	5/15–6/7	6/8–7/2	7/3–7/27	7/28–8/21	8/22–9/15	9/16–10/10	1/1–1/13 10/11–11/6	1/14–2/6 11/7–12/5	2/7–3/2 12/6–12/31	3/3–3/27
1942	5/7–6/2	6/3–6/27	6/28–7/23	7/24–8/17	8/18–9/10	9/11–10/4	10/5–10/28	10/29–11/21	11/22–12/15	12/16–12/31	1/1–4/6	4/7–5/6
1943	2/26–3/21	3/22–4/15	4/16–5/11	5/12–6/7	6/8–7/7	7/8–11/9	11/10–12/8	12/9–12/31		1/1–1/8	1/9–2/1	2/2–2/25

Table E. Venus Placements 1920–2000 (cont.).

Year	Aries	Taurus	Gemini	Cancer	Leo	Virgo	Libra	Scorpio	Sagittarius	Capricorn	Aquarius	Pisces
1944	4/11–5/4	5/5–5/29	5/30–6/22	6/23–7/17	7/18–8/10	8/11–9/3	9/4–9/28	1/1–1/3 9/29–10/22	1/4–1/28 10/23–11/16	1/29–2/21 11/17–12/11	2/22–3/17 12/12–12/31	3/18–4/10
1945	2/3–3/11 4/8–6/4	3/12–4/7 6/5–7/7	7/8–8/4	8/5–8/30	8/31–9/24	9/25–10/19	10/20–11/12	11/13–12/6	12/7–12/30	12/31	1/1–1/5	1/6–2/2
1946	3/12–4/5	4/6–4/29	4/30–5/24	5/25–6/18	6/19–7/13	7/14–8/9	8/10–9/7	9/8–10/16 11/9–12/31	10/17–11/8	1/1–1/22	1/23–2/15	2/16–3/11
1947	4/26–5/20	5/21–6/13	6/14–7/8	7/9–8/2	8/3–8/26	8/27–9/19	9/20–10/13	1/1–1/5 10/14–11/6	1/6–2/6 11/7–11/30	2/7–3/5 12/1–12/24	3/6–3/30 12/25–12/31	3/31–4/25
1948	2/12–3/8	3/9–4/4	4/5–5/7 6/30–8/3	5/8–6/29 8/4–9/8	9/9–10/6	10/7–11/1	11/2–11/26	11/27–12/20	12/21–12/31		1/1–1/18	1/19–2/11
1949	3/27–4/19	4/20–5/14	5/15–6/7	6/7–7/1	7/2–7/26	7/27–8/20	8/21–9/14	9/15–10/10	1/1–1/13 10/11–11/6	1/14–2/6 11/7–12/6	2/7–3/2 12/7–12/31	3/3–3/26

Table E. Venus Placements 1920–2000 (cont.).

Year	Aries	Taurus	Gemini	Cancer	Leo	Virgo	Libra	Scorpio	Sagittarius	Capricorn	Aquarius	Pisces
1950	5/6–6/1	6/2–6/27	6/28–7/22	7/23–8/16	8/17–9/10	9/11–10/4	10/5–10/28	10/29–11/21	11/22–12/14	12/15–12/31	1/1–4/6	4/7–5/5
1951	2/25–3/21	3/22–4/15	4/16–5/11	5/12–6/7	6/8–7/8	7/9–11/9	11/10–12/8	12/9–12/31		1/1–1/7	1/8–1/31	2/1–2/24
1952	4/10–5/4	5/5–5/28	5/29–6/22	6/23–7/16	7/17–8/9	8/10–9/3	9/4–9/27	1/1–1/2 9/28–10/22	1/3–1/27 10/23–11/15	1/28–2/21 11/16–12/10	2/22–3/16 12/11–12/31	3/17–4/9
1953	2/3–3/14 4/1–6/5	3/15–3/31 6/6–7/7	7/8–8/4	8/5–8/30	8/31–9/24	9/25–10/18	10/19–11/11	11/12–12/5	12/6–12/29	12/30–12/31	1/1–1/5	1/6–2/2
1954	3/12–4/4	4/5–4/28	4/29–5/23	5/24–6/17	6/18–7/13	7/14–8/9	8/10–9/6	9/7–10/23 10/28–12/31	10/24–10/27	1/1–1/22	1/23–2/15	2/16–3/11
1955	4/25–5/19	5/20–6/13	6/14–7/8	7/9–8/1	8/2–8/25	8/26–9/18	9/19–10/13	1/1–1/6 10/14–11/6	1/7–2/6 11/7–11/30	2/7–3/4 12/1–12/24	3/5–3/30 12/25–12/31	3/31–4/24

Table E. Venus Placements 1920–2000 (cont.).

Year	Aries	Taurus	Gemini	Cancer	Leo	Virgo	Libra	Scorpio	Sagittarius	Capricorn	Aquarius	Pisces
1956	2/12–3/7	3/8–4/4	4/5–5/8 6/24–8/4	5/9–6/23 8/5–9/8	9/9–10/6	10/7–10/31	11/1–11/25	11/26–12/19	12/20–12/31		1/1–1/17	1/18–2/11
1957	3/26–4/19	4/20–5/13	5/14–6/6	6/7–7/1	7/2–7/26	7/27–8/20	8/21–9/14	9/15–10/10	1/1–1/12 10/11–11/5	1/13–2/5 11/6–12/6	2/6–3/1 12/7–12/31	3/2–3/25
1958	5/6–6/1	6/2–6/26	6/27–7/22	7/23–8/16	8/17–9/9	9/10–10/3	10/4–10/27	10/28–11/20	11/21–12/14	12/15–12/31	1/1–4/6	4/7–5/5
1959	2/25–3/20	3/21–4/14	4/15–5/10	5/11–6/6	6/7–7/8 9/20–9/25	7/9–9/19 9/26–11/9	11/10–12/7	12/8–12/31		1/1–1/7	1/8–1/31	2/1–2/24
1960	4/10–5/3	5/4–5/28	5/29–6/21	6/22–7/16	7/17–8/9	8/10–9/2	9/3–9/27	1/1–1/2 9/28–10/21	1/3–1/27 10/22–11/15	1/28–2/20 11/16–12/10	2/21–3/16 12/11–12/31	3/17–4/9
1961	2/3–6/5	6/6–7/7	7/8–8/3	8/4–8/29	8/30–9/23	9/24–10/18	10/19–11/11	11/12–12/5	12/6–12/28	12/29–12/31	1/1–1/5	1/6–2/2

Table E. Venus Placements 1920–2000 (cont.).

Year	Aries	Taurus	Gemini	Cancer	Leo	Virgo	Libra	Scorpio	Sagittarius	Capricorn	Aquarius	Pisces
1962	3/11–4/3	4/4–4/28	4/29–5/23	5/24–6/17	6/18–7/12	7/13–8/8	8/9–9/6	9/7–12/31		1/1–1/21	1/22–2/14	2/15–3/10
1963	4/25–5/19	5/20–6/12	6/13–7/7	7/8–7/31	8/1–8/25	8/26–9/18	9/19–10/12	1/1–1/6 10/13–11/5	1/7–2/5 11/6–11/29	2/6–3/4 11/30–12/23	3/5–3/30 12/24–12/31	3/31–4/24
1964	2/11–3/7	3/8–4/4	4/5–5/9 6/18–8/5	5/10–6/17 8/6–9/8	9/9–10/5	10/6–10/31	11/1–11/25	11/26–12/19	12/20–12/31		1/1–1/17	1/18–2/10
1965	3/26–4/18	4/19–5/12	5/13–6/6	6/7–6/30	7/1–7/25	7/26–8/19	8/20–9/13	9/14–10/9	1/1–1/12 10/10–11/5	1/13–2/5 11/6–12/7	2/6–3/1 12/8–12/31	3/2–3/25
1966	5/6–5/31	6/1–6/26	6/27–7/21	7/22–8/15	8/16–9/8	9/9–10/3	10/4–10/27	10/28–11/20	11/21–12/13	2/7–2/25 12/14–12/31	1/1–2/6 2/26–4/6	4/7–5/5
1967	2/24–3/20	3/21–4/14	4/15–5/10	5/11–6/6	6/7–7/8 9/10–10/1	7/9–9/9 10/2–11/9	11/10–12/7	12/8–12/31		1/1–1/6	1/7–1/30	1/31–2/23

Table E. Venus Placements 1920–2000 (cont.).

Year	Aries	Taurus	Gemini	Cancer	Leo	Virgo	Libra	Scorpio	Sagittarius	Capricorn	Aquarius	Pisces
1968	4/9–5/3	5/4–5/27	5/28–6/21	6/22–7/15	7/16–8/8	8/9–9/2	9/3–9/26	1/1 9/27–10/21	1/2–1/26 10/22–11/14	1/27–2/20 11/15–12/9	2/21–3/15 12/10–12/31	3/16–4/8
1969	2/3–6/6	6/7–7/6	7/7–8/3	8/4–8/29	8/30–9/23	9/24–10/17	10/18–11/10	11/11–12/4	12/5–12/28	12/29–12/31	1/1–1/4	1/5–2/2
1970	3/11–4/3	4/4–4/27	4/28–5/22	5/23–6/16	6/17–7/12	7/13–8/8	8/9–9/7	9/8–12/31		1/1–1/21	1/22–2/14	2/15–3/10
1971	4/24–5/18	5/19–6/12	6/13–7/6	7/7–7/31	8/1–8/24	8/25–9/17	9/18–10/11	1/1–1/7 10/12–11/5	1/8–2/5 11/6–11/29	2/6–3/4 11/30–12/23	3/5–3/29 12/24–12/31	3/30–4/23
1972	2/11–3/7	3/8–4/3	4/4–5/10 6/12–8/6	5/11–6/11 8/7–9/7	9/8–10/5	10/6–10/30	10/31–11/24	11/25–12/18	12/19–12/31		1/1–1/16	1/17–2/10
1973	3/25–4/18	4/19–5/12	5/13–6/5	6/6–6/30	7/1–7/25	7/26–8/19	8/20–9/13	9/14–10/9	1/1–1/11 10/10–11/5	1/12–2/4 11/6–12/7	2/5–2/28 12/8–12/31	3/1–3/24

Table E. Venus Placements 1920–2000 (cont.).

Year	Aries	Taurus	Gemini	Cancer	Leo	Virgo	Libra	Scorpio	Sagittarius	Capricorn	Aquarius	Pisces
1974	5/5–5/31	6/1–6/25	6/26–7/21	7/22–8/14	8/15–9/8	9/9–10/2	10/3–10/26	10/27–11/19	11/20–12/13	1/30–2/28 12/14–12/31	1/1–1/29 3/1–4/6	4/7–5/4
1975	2/24–3/19	3/20–4/13	4/14–5/9	5/10–6/6	6/7–7/9 9/3–10/4	7/10–9/2 10/5–11/9	11/10–12/7	12/8–12/31		1/1–1/6	1/7–1/30	1/31–2/23
1976	4/9–5/2	5/3–5/27	5/28–6/20	6/21–7/14	7/15–8/8	8/9–9/1	9/2–9/26	1/1 9/27–10/20	1/2–1/26 10/21–11/14	1/27–2/19 11/15–12/9	2/20–3/15 12/10–12/31	3/16–4/8
1977	2/3–6/6	6/7–7/6	7/7–8/2	8/3–8/28	8/29–9/22	9/23–10/17	10/18–11/10	11/11–12/4	12/5–12/27	12/28–12/31	1/1–1/4	1/5–2/2
1978	3/10–4/2	4/3–4/27	4/28–5/22	5/23–6/16	6/17–7/12	7/13–8/8	8/9–9/7	9/8–12/31		1/1–1/20	1/21–2/13	2/14–3/9
1979	4/24–5/18	5/19–6/11	6/12–7/6	7/7–7/30	7/31–8/24	8/25–9/17	9/18–10/11	1/1–1/7 10/12–11/4	1/8–2/5 11/5–11/28	2/6–3/3 11/29–12/22	3/4–3/29 12/23–12/31	3/30–4/23

Table E. Venus Placements 1920–2000 (cont.).

Year	Aries	Taurus	Gemini	Cancer	Leo	Virgo	Libra	Scorpio	Sagittarius	Capricorn	Aquarius	Pisces
1980	2/10–3/6	3/7–4/3	4/4–5/12 6/6–8/6	5/13–6/5 8/7–9/7	9/8–10/4	10/5–10/30	10/31–11/24	11/25–12/18	12/19–12/31		1/1–1/16	1/17–2/9
1981	3/25–4/17	4/18–5/11	5/12–6/5	6/6–6/29	6/30–7/24	7/25–8/18	8/19–9/12	9/13–10/8	1/1–1/11 10/9–11/5	1/12–2/4 11/6–12/8	2/5–2/28 12/9–12/31	3/1–3/24
1982	5/5–5/30	5/31–6/25	6/26–7/20	7/21–8/14	8/15–9/7	9/8–10/2	10/3–10/26	10/27–11/18	11/19–12/12	1/24–3/2 12/13–12/31	1/1–1/23 3/3–4/6	4/7–5/4
1983	2/23–3/19	3/20–4/13	4/14–5/9	5/10–6/6	6/7–7/10 8/28–10/5	7/11–8/27 10/6–11/9	11/10–12/6	12/7–12/31		1/1–1/5	1/6–1/29	1/30–2/22
1984	4/8–5/2	5/3–5/26	5/27–6/20	6/21–7/14	7/15–8/7	8/8–9/1	9/2–9/25	1/1 9/26–10/20	1/2–1/25 10/21–11/13	1/26–2/19 11/14–12/9	2/20–3/14 12/10–12/31	3/15–4/7
1985	2/3–6/6	6/7–7/6	7/7–8/2	8/3–8/28	8/29–9/22	9/23–10/16	10/17–11/9	11/10–12/3	12/4–12/27	12/28–12/31	1/1–1/4	1/5–2/2

Table E. Venus Placements 1920–2000 (cont.).

Year	Aries	Taurus	Gemini	Cancer	Leo	Virgo	Libra	Scorpio	Sagittarius	Capricorn	Aquarius	Pisces
1986	3/10–4/2	4/3–4/26	4/27–5/21	5/22–6/15	6/16–7/11	7/12–8/7	8/8–9/7	9/8–12/31		1/1–1/20	1/21–2/13	2/14–3/9
1987	4/23–5/17	5/18–6/11	6/12–7/5	7/6–7/30	7/31–8/23	8/24–9/16	9/17–10/10	1/1–1/7 10/11–11/3	1/8–2/5 11/4–11/28	2/6–3/3 11/29–12/22	3/4–3/28 12/23–12/31	3/29–4/22
1988	2/10–3/6	3/7–4/3	4/4–5/17 5/28–8/6	5/18–5/27 8/7–9/7	9/8–10/4	10/5–10/29	10/30–11/23	11/24–12/17	12/18–12/31		1/1–1/15	1/16–2/9
1989	3/24–4/16	4/17–5/11	5/12–6/4	6/5–6/29	6/30–7/24	7/25–8/18	8/19–9/12	9/13–10/8	1/1–1/10 10/9–11/5	1/11–2/3 11/6–12/10	2/4–2/27 12/11–12/31	2/28–3/23
1990	5/5–5/30	5/31–6/25	6/26–7/20	7/21–8/13	8/14–9/7	9/8–10/1	10/2–10/25	10/26–11/18	11/19–12/12	1/17–3/3 12/13–12/31	1/1–1/16 3/4–4/6	4/7–5/4
1991	2/23–3/18	3/19–4/13	4/14–5/9	5/10–6/6	6/7–7/11 8/22–10/6	7/12–8/21 10/7–11/9	11/10–12/6	12/7–12/31		1/1–1/5	1/6–1/29	1/30–2/22

Table E. Venus Placements 1920–2000 (cont.).

Year	Aries	Taurus	Gemini	Cancer	Leo	Virgo	Libra	Scorpio	Sagittarius	Capricorn	Aquarius	Pisces
1992	4/8–5/1	5/2–5/26	5/27–6/19	6/20–7/13	7/14–8/7	8/8–8/31	9/1–9/25	9/26–10/19	1/1–1/25 10/20–11/13	1/26–2/18 11/14–12/8	2/19–3/13 12/9–12/31	3/14–4/7
1993	2/3–6/6	6/7–7/6	7/7–8/1	8/2–8/27	8/28–9/21	9/22–10/16	10/17–11/9	11/10–12/2	12/3–12/26	12/27–12/31	1/1–1/3	1/4–2/2
1994	3/9–4/1	4/2–4/26	4/27–5/21	5/22–6/15	6/16–7/11	7/12–8/7	8/8–9/7	9/8–12/31		1/1–1/19	1/20–2/12	2/13–3/8
1995	4/23–5/16	5/17–6/10	6/11–7/5	7/6–7/29	7/30–8/23	8/24–9/16	9/17–10/10	1/1–1/7 10/11–11/3	1/8–2/4 11/4–11/27	2/5–3/2 11/28–12/21	3/3–3/28 12/22–12/31	3/29–4/22
1996	2/10–3/6	3/7–4/3	4/4–8/7	8/8–9/7	9/8–10/4	10/5–10/29	10/30–11/23	11/24–12/17	12/18–12/31		1/1–1/15	1/16–2/9
1997	3/24–4/16	4/17–5/10	5/11–6/4	6/5–6/28	6/29–7/23	7/24–8/17	8/18–9/12	9/13–10/8	1/1–1/10 10/9–11/5	1/11–2/3 11/6–12/12	2/4–2/27 12/13–12/31	2/28–3/23

Table E. Venus Placements 1920–2000 (cont.).

Year	Aries	Taurus	Gemini	Cancer	Leo	Virgo	Libra	Scorpio	Sagittarius	Capricorn	Aquarius	Pisces
1998	5/4–5/29	5/30–6/24	6/25–7/19	7/20–8/13	8/14–9/6	9/7–9/30	10/1–10/24	10/25–11/17	11/18–12/11	1/10–3/4 12/12–12/31	1/1–1/9 3/5–4/6	4/7–5/3
1999	2/22–3/18	3/19–4/12	4/13–5/8	5/9–6/5	6/6–7/12 8/16–10/7	7/13–8/15 10/8–11/9	11/10–12/5	12/6–12/31		1/1–1/4	1/5–1/28	1/29–2/21
2000	4/7–5/1	5/2–5/25	5/26–6/18	6/19–7/13	7/14–8/6	8/7–8/31	9/1–9/24	9/25–10/19	1/1–1/24 10/20–11/13	1/25–2/18 11/14–12/8	2/19–3/13 12/9–12/31	3/14–4/6

Table F. Mars Placements 1920–2000.

Time	Sign	Time	Sign	Time	Sign	Time	Sign	Time	Sign
1920		1922		3/7–4/24	Capricorn	3/24–5/3	Aquarius	6/27–8/9	Taurus
1/1–1/31	Libra	1/1–2/18	Scorpio	4/25–6/24	Aquarius	5/4–6/15	Pisces	8/10–10/3	Gemini
2/1–4/23	Scorpio	2/19–9/13	Sagittarius	6/25–8/24	Pisces	6/16–8/1	Aries	10/4–12/20	Cancer
4/24–7/10	Libra	9/14–10/30	Capricorn	8/25–10/19	Aquarius	8/2–12/31	Taurus	12/21–12/31	Gemini
7/11–9/4	Scorpio	10/31–12/11	Aquarius	10/20–12/19	Pisces	1927		1929	
9/5–10/18	Sagittarius	12/12–12/31	Pisces	12/20–12/31	Aries	1/1–2/22	Taurus	1/1–3/10	Gemini
10/19–11/27	Capricorn	1923		1925		2/23–4/17	Gemini	3/11–5/13	Cancer
11/28–12/31	Aquarius	1/1–2/21	Pisces	1/1–2/5	Aries	4/18–6/6	Cancer	5/14–7/4	Leo
1921		1/22–3/4	Aries	2/6–3/24	Taurus	6/7–7/25	Leo	7/5–8/21	Virgo
1/1–1/5	Aquarius	3/5–4/16	Taurus	3/25–5/9	Gemini	7/26–9/10	Virgo	8/22–10/6	Libra
1/6–2/14	Pisces	4/17–5/30	Gemini	5/10–6/26	Cancer	9/11–10/26	Libra	10/7–11/18	Scorpio
2/14–3/25	Aries	5/31–7/16	Cancer	6/27–8/12	Leo	10/27–12/8	Scorpio	11/19–12/29	Sagittarius
3/26–5/6	Taurus	7/17–9/1	Leo	8/13–9/28	Virgo	12/9–12/31	Sagittarius	12/30–12/31	Capricorn
5/7–6/18	Gemini	9/2–10/18	Virgo	9/29–11/13	Libra	1928		1930	
6/19–8/3	Cancer	10/19–12/4	Libra	11/14–12/28	Scorpio	1/1–1/19	Sagittarius	1/1–2/6	Capricorn
8/4–9/19	Leo	12/5–12/31	Scorpio	12/29–12/31	Sagittarius	1/20–2/28	Capricorn	2/7–3/17	Aquarius
9/20–11/6	Virgo	1924		1926		2/29–4/7	Aquarius	3/18–4/24	Pisces
11/7–12/26	Libra	1/1–1/19	Scorpio	1/1–2/9	Sagittarius	4/8–5/16	Pisces	4/25–6/3	Aries
12/27–12/31	Scorpio	1/20–3/6	Sagittarius	2/10–3/23	Capricorn	5/17–6/26	Aries	6/4–7/14	Taurus

Table F. Mars Placements 1920–2000 (cont.).

Time	Sign	Time	Sign	Time	Sign	Time	Sign	Time	Sign
1930 (cont.)		6/23–8/4	Gemini	10/19–12/11	Virgo	1937		1939	
7/15–8/28	Gemini	8/5–9/20	Cancer	12/12–12/31	Libra	1/1–1/5	Libra	1/1–1/29	Scorpio
8/29–10/20	Cancer	9/21–11/13	Leo	1935		1/6–3/13	Scorpio	1/30–3/21	Sagittarius
10/21–12/31	Leo	11/14–12/31	Virgo	1/1–7/29	Libra	3/14–5/14	Sagittarius	3/22–5/24	Capricorn
1931		1933		7/30–9/16	Scorpio	5/15–8/8	Scorpio	5/25–7/21	Aquarius
1/1–2/16	Leo	1/1–7/6	Leo	9/17–10/28	Sagittarius	8/9–9/30	Sagittarius	7/22–9/24	Capricorn
2/17–3/30	Cancer	7/7–8/26	Libra	10/29–12/7	Capricorn	10/1–11/11	Capricorn	9/25–11/19	Aquarius
3/31–6/10	Leo	8/27–10/9	Scorpio	12/8–12/31	Aquarius	11/12–12/21	Aquarius	11/20–12/31	Pisces
6/11–8/1	Virgo	10/10–11/19	Sagittarius	1936		12/22–12/31	Pisces	1940	
8/2–9/17	Libra	11/20–12/28	Capricorn	1/1–1/14	Aquarius	1938		1/1–1/3	Pisces
9/18–10/30	Scorpio	12/29–12/31	Aquarius	1/15–2/22	Pisces	1/1–1/30	Pisces	1/4–2/17	Aries
10/31–12/10	Sagittarius	1934		2/23–4/1	Aries	1/31–3/12	Aries	2/18–4/1	Taurus
12/11–12/31	Capricorn	1/1–2/4	Aquarius	4/2–5/13	Taurus	3/13–4/23	Taurus	4/2–5/17	Gemini
1932		2/5–3/14	Pisces	5/14–6/25	Gemini	4/24–6/7	Gemini	5/18–7/3	Cancer
1/1–1/18	Capricorn	3/15–4/22	Aries	6/26–8/10	Cancer	6/8–7/22	Cancer	7/4–8/19	Leo
1/19–2/25	Aquarius	4/23–6/2	Taurus	8/11–9/26	Leo	7/23–9/7	Leo	8/20–10/5	Virgo
2/26–4/3	Pisces	6/3–7/15	Gemini	9/27–11/14	Virgo	9/8–10/25	Virgo	10/6–11/20	Libra
4/4–5/12	Aries	7/16–8/30	Cancer	11/15–12/31	Libra	10/26–12/11	Libra	11/21–12/31	Scorpio
5/13–6/22	Taurus	8/31–10/18	Leo			12/12–12/31	Scorpio		

Table F. Mars Placements 1920–2000 (cont.).

Time	Sign	Time	Sign	Time	Sign	Time	Sign	Time	Sign
1941		1/27–3/8	Capricorn	5/3–6/11	Aries	5/22–7/1	Taurus	6/11–7/23	Gemini
1/1–1/4	Scorpio	3/9–4/17	Aquarius	6/12–7/23	Taurus	7/2–8/13	Gemini	7/24–9/7	Cancer
1/5–2/17	Sagittarius	4/18–5/27	Pisces	7/24–9/7	Gemini	8/14–10/1	Cancer	9/8–10/27	Leo
2/18–4/2	Capricorn	5/28–7/7	Aries	9/8–11/11	Cancer	10/2–12/1	Leo	10/28–12/26	Virgo
4/3–5/16	Aquarius	7/8–8/23	Taurus	11/12–12/26	Leo	12/2–12/31	Virgo	12/27–12/31	Libra
5/17–7/2	Pisces	8/24–12/31	Gemini	12/27–12/31	Cancer	1948		1950	
7/3–12/31	Aries	1944		1946		1/1–2/12	Virgo	1/1–3/28	Libra
1942		1/1–3/28	Gemini	1/1–4/22	Cancer	2/13–5/18	Leo	3/29–6/11	Virgo
1/1–1/11	Aries	3/29–5/22	Cancer	4/23–6/20	Leo	5/19–7/17	Virgo	6/12–8/10	Libra
1/12–3/7	Taurus	5/23–7/12	Leo	6/21–8/9	Virgo	7/18–9/3	Libra	8/11–9/25	Scorpio
3/8–4/26	Gemini	7/13–8/29	Virgo	8/10–9/24	Libra	9/4–10/17	Scorpio	9/26–11/6	Sagittarius
4/27–6/14	Cancer	8/30–10/13	Libra	9/25–11/6	Scorpio	10/18–11/26	Sagittarius	11/7–12/15	Capricorn
6/15–8/1	Leo	10/14–11/25	Scorpio	11/7–12/17	Sagittarius	11/27–12/31	Capricorn	12/16–12/31	Aquarius
8/2–9/17	Virgo	11/26–12/31	Sagittarius	12/18–12/31	Capricorn	1949		1951	
9/18–11/1	Libra	1945		1947		1/1–1/4	Capricorn	1/1–1/22	Aquarius
11/2–12/15	Scorpio	1/1–1/5	Sagittarius	1/1–1/25	Capricorn	1/5–2/11	Aquariu	1/23–3/1	Pisces
12/16–12/31	Sagittarius	1/6–2/14	Capricorn	1/26–3/4	Aquarius	2/12–3/21	Pisces	3/2–4/10	Aries
1943		2/15–3/25	Aquarius	3/5–4/11	Pisces	3/22–4/30	Aries	4/11–5/21	Taurus
1/1–1/26	Sagittarius	3/26–5/2	Pisces	4/12–5/21	Aries	5/1–6/10	Taurus	5/22–7/3	Gemini

Table F. Mars Placements 1920–2000 (cont.).

Time	Sign	Time	Sign	Time	Sign	Time	Sign	Time	Sign
1951 (cont.)		9/15–11/1	Virg	10/14–11/29	Libra	1958		1960	
7/4–8/18	Cancer	11/2–12/20	Libra	11/30–12/31	Scorpio	1/1–2/3	Sagittarius	1/1–1/14	Sagittarius
8/19–10/5	Leo	12/21–12/31	Scorpio	1956		2/4–3/17	Capricorn	1/15–2/23	Capricorn
10/6–11/24	Virgo	1954		1/1–1/14	Scorpio	3/18–4/27	Aquarius	2/24–4/2	Aquarius
11/25–12/31	Libra	1/1–2/9	Scorpio	1/15–2/28	Sagittarius	4/28–6/7	Pisces	4/3–5/11	Pisce
1952		2/10–4/12	Sagittarius	2/29–4/14	Capricorn	6/8–7/21	Aries	5/12–6/20	Aries
1/1–1/20	Libra	4/13–7/3	Capricorn	4/15–6/3	Aquarius	7/22–9/21	Taurus	6/21–8/2	Taurus
1/21–8/27	Scorpio	7/4–8/24	Sagittarius	6/4–12/6	Pisces	9/22–10/29	Gemini	8/3–9/21	Gemini
8/28–10/12	Sagittarius	8/25–10/21	Capricorn	12/7–12/31	Aries	10/30–12/31	Taurus	9/22–12/31	Cancer
10/13–11/21	Capricorn	10/22–12/4	Aquarius	1957		1959		1961	
11/22–12/30	Aquarius	12/5–12/31	Pisces	1/1–1/28	Aries	1/1–2/10	Taurus	1/1–5/6	Cancer
12/31	Pisces	1955		1/29–3/17	Taurus	2/11–4/10	Gemini	5/7–6/28	Leo
1953		1/1–1/30		3/18–5/4	Gemini	4/11–6/1	Cancer	6/29–8/17	Virgo
1/1–2/8	Pisces	1/31–2/26	Pisces	5/5–6/21	Cancer	6/2–7/20	Leo	8/18–10/1	Libra
2/9–3/20	Aries	2/27–4/10	Aries	6/22–8/8	Leo	7/21–9/5	Virgo	10/2–11/13	Scorpio
3/21–5/1	Taurus	4/11–5/26	Taurus	8/9–9/24	Virgo	9/6–10/21	Libra	11/14–12/24	Sagittarius
5/2–6/14	Gemini	5/27–7/11	Gemini	9/25–11/8	Libra	10/22–12/3	Scorpio	12/25–12/31	Capricorn
6/15–7/29	Cancer	7/12–8/27	Cancer	11/9–12/23	Scorpio	12/4–12/31	Sagittarius		
7/30–9/14	Leo	8/28–10/13	Virgo	12/24–12/31	Sagittarius				

Table F. Mars Placements 1920–2000 (cont.).

Time	Sign	Time	Sign	Time	Sign	Time	Sign	Time	Sign
1962		2/21–3/29	Pisces	5/29–7/11	Gemini	6/22–8/5	Cancer	10/21–12/6	Libra
1/1–2/1	Capricorn	3/30–5/7	Aries	7/12–8/25	Cancer	8/6–9/21	Leo	12/7–12/31	Scorpio
2/2–3/12	Aquarius	5/8–6/17	Taurus	8/26–10/12	Leo	9/22–11/9	Virgo	1971	
3/13–4/18	Pisces	6/18–7/30	Gemini	10/13–12/4	Virgo	11/10–12/29	Libra	1/1–1/23	Scorpio
4/19–5/28	Aries	7/31–9/15	Cancer	12/5–12/31	Libra	12/30–12/31	Scorpio	1/24–3/12	Sagittarius
5/29–6/9	Taurus	9/16–11/6	Leo	1967		1969		3/13–5/3	Capricorn
6/10–8/22	Gemini	11/7–12/31	Virgo	1/1–2/12	Libra	1/1–2/25	Scorpio	5/4–11/6	Aquarius
8/23–10/11	Cancer	1965		2/13–3/31	Scorpio	2/26–9/21	Sagittarius	11/7–12/26	Pisces
10/12–12/31	Leo	1/1–6/29	Virgo	4/1–7/19	Libra	9/22–11/4	Capricorn	12/27–12/31	Aries
1963		6/30–8/20	Libra	7/20–9/10	Scorpio	11/5–12/15	Aquarius	1972	
1/1–6/3	Leo	8/21–10/4	Scorpio	9/11–10/23	Sagittarius	12/16–12/31	Pisces	1/1–2/10	Aries
6/4–7/27	Virgo	10/5–11/14	Sagittarius	10/24–12/1	Capricorn	1970		2/11–3/27	Taurus
7/28–9/12	Libra	11/15–12/23	Capricorn	12/2–12/31	Aquarius	1/1–1/24	Aquarius	3/28–5/12	Gemini
9/13–10/25	Scorpio	12/24–12/31	Aquarius	1968		1/25–3/7	Aries	5/13–6/28	Cancer
10/26–12/5	Sagittarius	1966		1/1–1/9	Aquarius	3/8–4/18	Taurus	6/29–8/15	Leo
12/6–12/31	Capricorn	1/1–1/30	Aquarius	1/10–2/17	Pisces	4/19–6/2	Gemini	8/16–9/30	Virgo
1964		1/31–3/9	Pisces	2/18–3/27	Aries	6/3–7/18	Cancer	10/1–11/15	Libra
1/1–1/13	Capricorn	3/10–4/17	Aries	3/28–5/8	Taurus	7/19–9/3	Leo	11/16–12/30	Scorpio
1/14–2/20	Aquarius	4/18–5/28	Taurus	5/9–6/21	Gemini	9/4–10/20	Virgo	12/31	Sagittarius

Table F. Mars Placements 1920–2000 (cont.).

Time	Sign	Time	Sign	Time	Sign	Time	Sign	Time	Sign
1973		1975		1977		1979		1981	
1/1–2/12	Sagittarius	1/1–1/21	Sagittarius	1/1	Sagittarius	1/1–1/20	Capricorn	1/1–2/6	Aquarius
2/13–3/26	Capricorn	1/22–3/3	Capricorn	1/2–2/9	Capricorn	1/21–2/27	Aquarius	2/7–3/17	Pisces
3/27–5/8	Aquarius	3/4–4/11	Aquarius	2/10–3/20	Aquarius	2/28–4/7	Pisces	3/18–4/25	Aries
5/9–6/20	Pisces	4/12–5/21	Pisces	3/21–4/27	Pisces	4/8–5/16	Aries	4/26–6/5	Taurus
6/21–8/12	Aries	5/22–7/1	Aries	4/28–6/6	Aries	5/17–6/26	Taurus	6/6–7/18	Gemini
8/13–10/29	Taurus	7/2–8/14	Taurus	6/7–7/17	Taurus	6/27–8/8	Gemini	7/19–9/2	Cancer
10/30–12/24	Aries	8/15–10/17	Gemini	7/18–9/1	Gemini	8/9–9/24	Cancer	9/3–10/21	Leo
12/25–12/31	Taurus	10/18–11/25	Cancer	9/2–10/26	Cancer	9/25–11/19	Leo	10/22–12/15	Virgo
1974		11/26–12/31	Gemini	10/27–12/31	Leo	11/20–12/31	Virgo	12/16–12/31	Libra
1/1–2/27	Taurus	1976		1978		1980		1982	
2/28–4/20	Gemini	1/1–3/18	Gemini	1/1–1/26	Leo	1/1–3/11	Virgo	1/1–8/3	Libra
4/21–6/9	Cancer	3/19–5/16	Cancer	1/27–4/10	Cancer	3/12–5/4	Leo	8/4–9/20	Scorpio
6/10–7/27	Leo	5/17–7/6	Leo	4/11–6/14	Leo	5/5–7/10	Virgo	9/21–10/31	Sagittarius
7/28–9/12	Virgo	7/7–8/24	Virgo	6/15–8/4	Virgo	7/11–8/29	Libra	11/1–12/10	Capricorn
9/13–10/28	Libra	8/25–10/8	Libra	8/5–9/19	Libra	8/30–10/12	Scorpio	12/11–12/31	Aquarius
10/29–12/10	Scorpio	10/9–11/20	Scorpio	9/20–11/2	Scorpio	10/13–11/22	Sagittarius	1983	
12/11–12/31	Sagittarius	11/21–12/31	Sagittarius	11/3–12/12	Sagittarius	11/23–12/30	Capricorn	1/1–1/17	Aquarius
				12/13–12/31	Capricorn	12/31	Aquarius	1/18–2/25	Pisces

Table F. Mars Placements 1920–2000 (cont.).

Time	Sign	Time	Sign	Time	Sign	Time	Sign	Time	Sign
1983 (cont.)		4/27–6/9	Gemini	8/23–10/8	Virgo	9/20–11/4	Virgo	10/17–11/29	Scorpio
2/26–4/5	Aries	6/10–7/25	Cancer	10/9–11/24	Libra	11/5–12/18	Libra	11/30–12/31	Sagittarius
4/6–5/16	Taurus	7/26–9/10	Leo	11/25–12/31	Scorpio	12/19–12/31	Scorpio	1992	
5/17–6/29	Gemini	9/11–10/27	Virgo	1988		1990		1/1–1/9	Sagittarius
6/30–8/13	Cancer	10/28–12/14	Libra	1/1–1/8	Scorpio	1/1–1/29	Sagittarius	1/10–2/18	Capricorn
8/14–9/29	Leo	12/15–12/31	Scorpio	1/9–2/22	Sagittarius	1/30–3/11	Capricorn	2/19–3/28	Aquarius
9/30–11/18	Virgo	1986		2/23–4/6	Capricorn	3/12–4/20	Aquarius	3/29–5/5	Pisces
11/19–12/31	Libra	1/1–2/2	Scorpio	4/7–5/22	Aquarius	4/21–5/31	Pisces	5/6–6/14	Aries
1984		2/3–3/28	Sagittarius	5/23–7/13	Pisces	6/1–7/12	Aries	6/15–7/26	Taurus
1/1–1/11	Libra	3/29–10/9	Capricorn	7/14–10/23	Aries	7/13–8/31	Taurus	7/27–9/12	Gemini
1/12–8/17	Scorpio	10/10–11/26	Aquarius	10/24–11/1	Pisces	9/1–12/14	Gemini	9/13–12/31	Cancer
8/18–10/5	Sagittarius	11/27–12/31	Pisces	11/2–12/31	Aries	12/15–12/31	Taurus	1993	
10/6–11/15	Capricorn	1987		1989		1991		1/1–4/27	Cancer
11/16–12/25	Aquarius	1/1–1/8	Pisces	1/1–1/19	Aries	1/1–1/21	Taurus	4/28–6/23	Leo
12/26–12/31	Pisces	1/9–2/20	Aries	1/20–3/11	Taurus	1/22–4/3	Gemini	6/24–8/12	Virgo
1985		2/21–4/5	Taurus	3/12–4/29	Gemini	4/4–5/26	Cancer	8/13–9/27	Libra
1/1–2/2	Pisces	4/6–5/21	Gemini	4/30–6/16	Cancer	5/27–7/15	Leoa	9/28–11/9	Scorpio
2/3–3/15	Aries	5/22–7/6	Cancer	6/17–8/3	Leo	7/16–9/1	Virgo	11/10–12/20	Sagittarius
3/16–4/26	Taurus	7/7–8/22	Leo	8/4–9/19	Virgo	9/2–10/16	Libra	12/21–12/31	Capricorn

Table F. Mars Placements 1920–2000 (cont.).

Time	Sign	Time	Sign	Time	Sign	Time	Sign	Time	Sign
1994		12/1–12/31	Capricorn	9/19–11/9	Sagittarius	7/6–9/2	Scorpio		
1/1–1/28	Capricorn	**1996**		11/10–12/18	Capricorn	9/3–10/17	Sagittarius		
1/29–3/7	Aquarius	1/1–1/8	Capricorn	12/19–12/31	Aquarius	10/18–11/26	Capricorn		
3/8–4/14	Pisces	1/9–2/15	Aquarius	**1998**		11/27–12/31	Aquarius		
4/15–5/23	Aries	2/16–3/24	Pisces	1/1–1/25	Aquarius	**2000**			
5/24–7/3	Taurus	3/25–5/2	Aries	1/26–3/4	Pisces	1/1–1/4	Aquarius		
7/4–8/16	Gemini	5/3–6/12	Taurus	3/5–4/13	Aries	1/5–2/12	Pisces		
8/17–10/4	Cancer	6/13–7/25	Gemini	4/14–5/24	Taurus	2/13–3/23	Aries		
10/5–12/12	Leo	7/26–9/9	Cancer	5/25–7/6	Gemini	3/24–5/3	Taurus		
12/13–12/31	Virgo	9/10–10/30	Leo	7/7–8/20	Cancer	5/4–6/16	Gemini		
1995		10/31–12/31	Virgo	8/21–10/7	Leo	6/17–8/1	Cancer		
1/1–1/22	Virgo	**1997**		10/8–11/27	Virgo	8/2–9/17	Leo		
1/23–5/25	Leo	1/1–1/3	Virgo	11/28–12/31	Libra	9/18–11/4	Virgo		
5/26–7/21	Virgo	1/4–3/8	Libra	**1999**					
7/22–9/7	Libra	3/9–6/19	Virgo	1/1–1/26	Libra				
9/8–10/20	Scorpio	6/20–8/14	Libra	1/27–5/5	Scorpio				
10/21–11/30	Sagittarius	8/15–9/28	Scorpio	5/6–7/5	Libra				

Glossary

Achilles' Heel. A person's weak point, which corresponds to the inferior function in Jungian psychology and to the Missing Element in astrology.

Age of Aquarius. Because of the rotation of Earth's axis, the zodiac appears to slowly move in the sky (by one degree every 72 years) so that it "advances" by one constellation at an average of every 2140 years. Astrology considers this constellation, where the Sun stands at the time of the spring equinox, to be the symbol of the respective world age. Humanity is now experiencing the change from the Age of Pisces to the Age of Aquarius.

Androgyne. Bisexual gestalt. Symbolic figure: (a) in alchemy for the highest attainable good; (b) in psychology for wholeness; (c) for the type of person in the Age of Aquarius.

Anima. Unconscious feminine aspect of a man, which imprints his searching-image and desires to lead him above all to wholeness. It can be seen in the horoscope as the feminine planets.

Animus. Unconscious masculine aspect of a woman, which imprints her searching-image and desires to lead her above all to wholeness. It can be seen in the horoscope as the masculine planets.

Archetypes. Primeval images of the soul that all human beings have in common.

Ascendant. The sign of the zodiac that rises in the eastern heavens at the time of birth.

Aspects. Significant distances between the planets. They are differentiated into

harmonious aspects:
♂ = conjunction (0° apart);
△ = trine (120° apart);
✳ = sextile (60° apart);

tension aspects:
♂ = opposition (180° apart);
□ = square (90° apart);
⊒ = sesquisquare (135° apart);
⊻ = quincunx (150° apart).

Autarky. The endeavor to be perfectly independent of everything and everyone.

Conjunction. Harmonious aspect.

Conscious Functions. Term from Jungian typology used to describe the four basic character types, which are understood as the four conscious functions that each person has as a predisposition—but in varying forms.

Descendant. The sign of the zodiac that sets in the western heavens at the time of birth.

Detriment. See *Ruler System.*

Distortion. No aspect configuration or planet by sign is innately "good" or "bad." The only decisive factor is the way in which the energy is lived. The problematic forms of expression (immoderate, hardened, diluted, immature, unhealthy, etc.) are described in this book as distortions.

Ego. The center of the conscious personality. Its spectrum corresponds with the freedom of will.

Element. Fire, earth, air, and water are the "raw materials" of Creation and therefore also of the human being according to ancient Greek teaching. In astrology, the elements are active in the twelve signs of the zodiac; three signs belong to each element respectively. In Jungian psychology, the elements are four conscious functions.

Exaltation. See *Ruler System.*

Fall. See *Ruler System.*

Feminine Planets. Moon (☽) and Venus (♀).

Inner Persons. Pictorial way of expressing partial personalities. In this book, they are the father, mother, son, and daughter as they correspond to Sun, Moon, Mars, and Venus, and are inherent to every person as inner images.

Inner Relationship. The relationship the Sun, Mars, Moon, and Venus as the mirror image of our outer relationships with men and women..

Masculine Planets. Sun (☉) and Mars (♂). However, the Sun is a luminary and not a planet. We use the term "planet" to make it easier to discuss, but students should know the Sun is not a planet.

Missing Element. The four elements do not exist to an equal degree in every human being. Above all, one of the four appears to be missing at the beginning. Discovering, developing, and valuing the missing element is one of the most important steps on the path to wholeness.

Opposition. Tension-filled aspect.

Planets of the Opposite Sex. In the horoscope of a woman: the Sun (☉) and Mars (♂), in the horoscope of a man: the Moon (☽) and Venus (♀).

Planets of the Same Sex. In the horoscope of a woman: the Moon (☽) and Venus (♀), in the horoscope of a man: the Sun (☉) and Mars (♂).

Projection. The phenomenon of unconsciously attributing one's own but unknown character traits to another human being so that the related quality, way of behaving, intention, or predisposition is experienced as belonging to the other person.

Quarternity. The group of four, which archetypically describes wholeness.

Quincunx. Tension-filled aspect.

Relationship Quartet. The four inner persons who (according to C. G. Jung) connect to form relationships: (1) the woman, and (2) her masculine side (animus); (3) the man, and (4) his feminine side (anima).

Ruler System. Each sign of the zodiac and every astrological house is ruled by at least one planet. The planet is the ruler there, which means that it is very strongly placed. On the other hand, it is in detriment in the opposite sign/house, which means a weakening. Furthermore, for every planet there is another sign in which it is exalted (strongly placed), and it in turn stands in its fall (weakened) in the opposite sign/house.

Searching-Image. The image of the opposite sex inherent to every human being. It can be read from the Planets of the Opposite Sex.

Searching-Image Conflict. The friction that occurs when we form a bond with a human being who embodies our missing element, which commonly doesn't correspond to our searching-image, since the searching-image planets usually aren't in the sign (Sign Position) to which the missing element belongs.

Searching-Image Planets. In the horoscope of a woman: the Sun (☉) and Mars (♂), in the horoscope of a man: the Moon (☽) and Venus (♀).

Self. The entire personality of a human being, which includes the conscious and unconscious mind. The Ego, as the conscious center of the personality, relates to the Self like a part to the whole. It therefore always remains subordinate to it and will never completely comprehend it.

Self-Image. In this book, this term represents the way in which a person brings himself or herself into a relationship. It can be read from the Planets of the Same Sex with the help of astrology.

Self-Image Planets. In the horoscope of a woman: the Moon (☽) and Venus (♀), in the horoscope of a man: the Sun (☉) and Mars (♂).

Sesquisquare. Tension-filled aspect.

Sextile. Harmonious aspect.

Shadow. Everything for which a person has a predisposition, yet without being aware of it. This therefore includes both the potential aspect as well as the dark sides, which are frequently suppressed or projected.

Sign Position. The zodiac is an orbit through which the eight planets and the two luminaries move. It is divided into twelve equal sections (of 30° each), the signs of the zodiac, which have been named after twelve constellations. They serve as a reference in order to state the position of a specific planet.

Soul Guide. Pictorial expression for the anima and animus as the power that desires to lead the person to wholeness.

Suppression. Contents of the unconscious mind that want to become conscious or were already half-conscious or conscious but experienced by the ego to be threatening or undesired for other reasons. Because of this, they are kept out of the conscious mind and therefore remain unconscious. Or they are forgotten, which means they are made unconscious.

Symbiosis. The merging of two or more people into a unity in which one of the two loses his or her individuality.

Temperament. The classical teaching of the four temperaments that corresponds to the four elements is the characterology of ancient Greece.

Trine. Harmonious aspect.

Wholeness. The life goal in which the human being has developed his or her entire potential (all four elements).

Bibliography

ASTROLOGY

Adler, Oskar. *Das Testament der Astrologie* (4 Vols.). Munich: Hugendubel, 1991–1993.

Akron. *Das Astrologie-Handbuch*. Munich: Hugendubel, 1995.

Banzhaf, Hajo. *Der Mensch in Seinen Elementen*. Munich: Goldmann, 1994.

Banzhaf, Hajo and Anna Haebler. *Keywords for Astrology*. York Beach, ME: Samuel Weiser, 1996.

Goodman, Linda. *Sun Signs*. New York: Bantam, 1985.

Greene, Liz. *Relating: An Astrological Guide to Living with Others on a Small Planet*. York Beach, ME: Samuel Weiser, 1978.

Greene, Liz and Howard Sasportas. *Development of the Personality*. York Beach, ME: Samuel Weiser, 1987.

Hürlimann, Gertrud I. *Astrologie*. Zurich: Astroterra 1988.

Klein, Nicolaus. *Glück und Selbstverwirklichung im Horoskop*. Munich: Hugendubel, 1994.

Klein, Nicolaus and Rüdiger Dahlke. *The Senkrechte Weltbild*. Munich: Hugendubel, 1986.

Marks, Tracy. *The Astrology of Self-Discovery*. Sebastapol, CA: CRCS, 1989.

Riemann, Fritz. *Lebenshilfe Astrologie*. Munich: Pfeiffer, 1976.

Taeger, Hans-Hinrich. *Internationales Horoskope Lexikon* (3 vols.). Freiburg, Germany: Bauer Verlag, 1991–1992.

Weiss, Claude. *Horoskopanalyse* (2 vols.). Zurich: Astroterra, 1984–1986.

PSYCHOLOGY

Von Franz, Marie-Louise. *A Psychological Interpretation of the Golden Ass of Apuleius*. New York: Analytical Psychology Club of New York, 1970.

Von Franz, Marie-Louise and James Hillman. *Lectures on Jung's Typology*. Dallas: Spring, 1971.

Jung, C. G. *The Collected Works of C. G. Jung* (20 vols.) Bollingen Series XX. Princeton: Princeton University Press, 1953–1979.

Jung, Emma. *Animus and Anima*. Dallas: Spring/Analytical Psychology Club of New York, 1957, 1972, 1978.

Riemann, Fritz. *Grundformen der Angst* [*Basic Forms of Fear*]. Munich: Reinhardt, 1961/1982.

OTHER

Bach, Richard. *Illusions: The Adventures of a Religious Messiah.* New York: Delacort, 1977.
Bukowski, Charles. *Notes of a Dirty Old Man.* San Francisco: City Lights, 1973.

Index

A
Achilles' Heel, 13
air
    lack of, 15, 20, 32
alchemy in a relationship, 22
anima, xi, 25, 27, 37, 47, 53
    development of, 42
    elemental aspects of, 40
animus, xi, 25, 27, 37, 47, 53
    development of, 42
    elemental aspects of, 41
Aquarius
    feminine type, 116, 117
    masculine type, 166, 167
archetypes, 26
Aries
    feminine type, 76, 77
    masculine type, 126, 127
aspects, 178, 183, 179
    Moon-Mars, 195
    Moon-Venus, 194
    Sun-Mars, 195
    Sun-Moon, 193
    Sun-Venus, 195
    upgrading and downgrading, 179
    Venus-Mars, 196
astrology, 44

B
Bach, Richard, 199
binding, 22
birth date, finding the number for, 213
Bukowski, Charles, 179, 181

C
Campbell, Joseph, 53
Cancer
    feminine type, 88, 89
    masculine type, 138, 139

Capricorn
    feminine type, 112, 113
    masculine type, 162, 163
characteristics
    fatherly, 56
    motherly, 56
Clinton, Bill, 33
Clinton, Hillary, 34
compensation, 184
conflict
    center of, 13
    searching-image, 31, 42
consciousness, structures of, 4

D
Dali, Salvador, 205
dissolving, 22
Djakonova, Elena Ivanova, 209
Dream Woman, xii, 28

E
earth
    lack of, 14, 19, 32
elements, 3, 4, 39
    air, 10
    distribution of, 200, 201
    earth, 8
    feminine, 6
    fire, 7
    four, 5, 6
    masculine, 6
    missing, 13, 17
    water, 11
emotional person, 11
eroticism, 191

F/G
femininity, aspects of, 41
fire

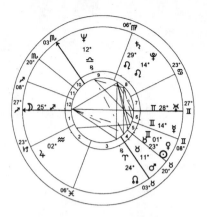

HAJO BANZHAF, born in
1949, studied languages in
France and philosophy at
the University of Münster,
followed by a twelve-year

Hajo Banzhaf. May 15, 1949, 00:02:00 CEDT. Gutersloh,
Germany, 008E23, 51N54, 22:02:00 GMT. Koch houses.

career in banking. He has been writing, lecturing, and working as an astrologer
since 1985. He is the editor of the Kailash book series at Heinrich Hugendubel
Publishing in Münich, Germany. He also gives tarot seminars on a regular
basis, publishes articles in well-known magazines, and has held lectures on
astrology and tarot for many years. Further information can be found at
http://www.maja.com/HajoBanzhaf.htm, or write to Samuel Weiser, Inc., and
we will forward mail to him. Lectures internationally.

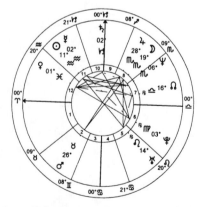

BRIGITTE THELER, born
in 1959, worked as a school
teacher before she attended
the School for Adults
(SFER) and completed her

Brigitte Theler. February 1, 1959, 09:43:00 CET. Zurich,
Switzerland, 08E32, 47N22. Koch houses.

training there in psychological astrology and psychosynthesis. She has worked
in her own practice for many years, is the editor of *Astrologie Heute* [*Astrology
Today*], and heads astrology seminars in Zurich and Münich.